Senator Max E. Benitz, Sr.

"Mr. Energy"

Eileen M. Benitz Wagner

with

Michele S. Gerber, Ph.D.

NorTex
Press

Based on the information I gathered during my research, to the best of my knowledge, I believe this book to be accurate.

First Edition

Copyright © 2014
By Eileen M. Benitz Wagner
Published By NorTex Press
An Imprint of Wild Horse Media Group
P.O. Box 331779
Fort Worth, Texas 76163
1-817-344-7036
www.WildHorseMedia.com
ALL RIGHTS RESERVED
1 2 3 4 5 6 7 8 9
ISBN-10: 1-940130-46-8
ISBN-13: 978-1-940130-46-0

Table of Contents

Preface

The information in this book is based on personal records, news articles, original letters, diaries, testimonies and state archival records. The years when Max Benitz lived in, and helped lead, Washington state, 1937 to 1990, were very formative ones. Debates that took place in those years about energy, taxes, nuclear power and nuclear waste, education, and diversified agriculture form the backdrop to many of the issues facing 21st century America. Benitz's firm beliefs in fiscal responsibility, small government, free markets, educational opportunities for all, and the need for a comprehensive national energy policy still resonate today.

Acknowledgments

In compiling the information presented in this book, I am indebted to Norma June Benitz Fortner and Nelita June Benitz Scheiffer, who provided ancestral family information and photos. Former Congressman Sid Morrison (R-Washington 4th District), former Washington State Representative Shirley Hankins (R-State District 8), former Washington State Senator George W. Scott (R-State District 46), Federal Energy Regulatory Commissioner Philip Moeller, former Washington Public Utility District Association lobbyist Jim Boldt, retired nuclear engineer Leo Kocher and former member of the Advisory Board on Radiation and Worker Health of the National Institute for Occupational Safety and Health Wanda Munn provided testimonials. Some of these individuals also read the early drafts of the book and provided their comments.

Joyce Hawkins, former executive secretary to Washington State Attorney General Ken Eikenberry, provided invaluable assistance in gathering records from the Washington State Archives in Olympia. Leo Kocher provided an inventory of the Max Benitz, Sr. wine grape collection. Vickie Era Pankretz, Senator Max Benitz, Sr.'s personal secretary for giving me a detailed list of his public life. John Stuhlmiller, Chief Executive Officer of the Washington Farm Bureau for providing his photo and Ramon Torres for proofreading. I also want to thank Dr. Edyth Willard for providing history of the Willard family.

Most of all, Max E. Benitz, Jr. provided comments on all parts of the book and added valuable information regarding irrigation in the Horse Heaven Hills near Prosser, Washington. His continuous dedication to details helped guide this work to publication.

Photographs & Illustrations

Introduction

Max Edward Benitz, Sr., (October 9, 1916 - August 29, 1990) was an American statesman, political leader, highly sought after speaker, farmer, cattle rancher, mechanic, and amateur winemaker. He held strong beliefs and was dedicated to preserving free enterprise, keeping government small and maintaining fiscal responsibility. He championed religious freedom, honesty and integrity for all. He served more than 30 years in elected public office.

Benitz, State Senator from Washington's District 8, was born in Wathena, Kansas, and graduated from Wathena High School in 1934. In 1937, when the Great Depression and mid-America's greatest drought (known as the Dust Bowl) made farming almost impossible, he left Kansas to seek opportunity in Washington state. After a series of agricultural and forestry jobs in the San Juan Islands off of Washington's coast, and milking cows in Ellensburg in central Washington to provide for the military during World War II, Benitz began farming on a share basis near Ellensburg. In 1946 he bought 80 acres of sagebrush land near Prosser, in southeastern Washington, correctly assessing the potential for irrigation. Over the next 45 years, he grew his farm to over 700 acres of diversified farming, including hops and wine grapes.

Active in political, agricultural, and community affairs, he was elected vice-president of the Washington State Farm Bureau in 1960 and soon became President. He resigned from that position in May 1968, to run for the Washington State House of Representatives. He was elected to the Board of Directors of the National Farm Bureau in 1963, and served two terms. He served as County Committeeman of the Farmers' Home Administration from 1952-57. In 1964, the Washington Chapter of the Future Farmers of America awarded Benitz its coveted honorary degree of State Farmer.

Benitz and his wife – the former Marie F. Wilson of Ellensburg – shared a deep concern for youth. They opened their hearts and home to twelve foster children over the years when local welfare services could not meet those needs. The Benitz family also included five children born to Max and Marie. The couple was married 50 years, and Benitz stated that they "worked as a team…having a good marriage is what makes everything else possible." In addition to their farm crops, they kept a large vegetable garden and donated to food banks throughout the lower Yakima Valley.[1]

In 1967, Washington Governor Dan Evans appointed Benitz as at-large member to a new state agency for vocational education, the Co-ordinating Council for Occupational Education (CCOE). This council had succeeded the State Board for Vocational Education in administering, or supervising the administration of vocational education, state-wide. Benitz served in this capacity, including three terms as Council Chairman, until the CCOE was replaced in 1975 by a new commission.

In 1968, Benitz ran as the successful Republican candidate for the 8th District seat in the Washington House of Representatives. He served three, two-year terms, and then ran successfully for the Washington State Senate in 1974. He served there until his death in 1990. During his years in the Washington State Legislature, Benitz was very active. He was the Primary Sponsor of 414 bills and the Secondary Sponsor of 1,210 bills.[2]

As State Representative, Benitz was a member of the Higher Education Committee, and serving as Chairman for two years. He was also a member of the House Committee on Revenue and Taxation, where he chaired a subcommittee on Forest Taxes, and he participated actively as a member of the Committee on Agriculture. Benitz' expertise in taxation grew over the years. He studied agricultural developments first hand in the Soviet Union and several European nations, and he participated in trade missions, both public and private, to Japan, Taiwan and Hong Kong. The CBS Evening News with Walter Cronkite featured his farming operation in a documentary comparing Soviet and U.S. food production methods, on October 30, 1963. In 1966, sponsored by the Association of Washington Industries, he participated in a statewide speaking tour.

In the State Senate, Benitz served on the Rules, Education, Energy & Utilities and Agriculture Committees. Washington State Senate, 1974 to August 1990. He became very involved with nuclear energy and traveled to areas of the world that produce nuclear power to learn about successful practices. He was an early champion of sensible nuclear waste and hazardous waste disposal.

Benitz's other community activities included membership on the Benton-Franklin County Fair Board from 1957 to 1960. During 1952, he chaired a Rural Telephone Committee that successfully negotiated pioneering agreements to bring telephone service into the then-new Roza Irrigation District. During the early 1950s, he was President of Whitstran Community Incorporated, a local non-profit organization in Whitstran, Washington (a small town four miles north of Prosser). The group raised funds, bought and renovated an old school into a community center that functioned for 40 years. Benitz also was President of the Benton County Farm Bureau in the early 1950s; President of Messiah Lutheran Church in Prosser in 1956; was elected to three terms on the Prosser School Board, 1957-60; was a County Committeeman for the Farmers Home Administration from 1952-57; member of the Benton-Franklin County Fair Board from 1957-60; served on the National Farm Bureau Board of Directors in 1963; and served many years as President of a local chapter of the National Rifle Association. During the early 1970s, he was a member of the Benton City Committee on Migrant Housing Problems.

Chapter One:

Early Years and Public Service to 1958

Early Family History

Max Edward Benitz was born October 9, 1916, as the fourth child of nine born to Nellie Willard and Alto Richard Benitz. The Benitz family roots can be traced back to Pomerania, a region in historical Prussia that has passed back and forth among Germany, Russia and Poland at various periods in modern history. Much of Pomerania now lies in Poland, along the southern edge of the Baltic Sea. Wilhelm Benitz, Max's grandfather, emigrated to America in 1871 and achieved citizenship in 1888. He settled south of Wathena, Kansas in the hills near the Missouri River, with his wife Sarah (Sinker). She had been born in Kansas Territory in 1859, two years before Kansas became a state. They had eight children, including Alto Benitz, before Wilhelm was killed in a runaway horse accident in 1892.

The Willard family is descended from Simon Willard, who is believed to have emigrated with his wife Mary from Kent, England in 1634 aboard one of the ships of Captain John Winthrop, founder of the Massachusetts Bay Colony. As Puritans, they emigrated partly to escape religious persecution and practice their faith. The Willards purchased property in the young colony, in what is today Concord, Massachusetts. Simon Willard was chosen representative to the General Court by the freemen of Concord in their first election. He was appointed to train the military company, served as chair of several town committees, helped audit local finances, surveyed land grants and boundaries, and served as commissioner of critical emergencies. The Willard home was burned in 1675 by Native Americans in a conflict known as King Philip's War. At some point the family moved to east Tennessee, settling in Blount County just south of Knoxville. Two great uncles of Max Benitz served in the American Civil War in the Third Tennessee Cavalry, part of the Union Army. They were captured by Confederate General Nathan Bedford Forrest, but survived the war and returned home to Marysville, TN. Max's father, Alto Richard Benitz, later served as Master Sergeant in the Coast Artillery in Astoria, Oregon at Ft. Columbia, 1902-1905.

Alto Richard Benitz while serving in the Coast Artillery in Astoria, Oregon at Fort Columbia, 1905.

Alto Richard Benitz
(Max's father)

Max's grandmother, born Elizabeth Bindord, was a Quaker whose family moved north from Tennessee to Indiana during the Civil War, but returned to east Tennessee after the war and helped found a Friends School to educate freed slaves. Elizabeth married Frank Willard and gave birth to Nellie Willard, Max's mother. The Willards then moved north and west to Doniphan, County Kansas, in the northeast corner of the state. Nellie met and married Alto Benitz and joined the Lutheran Church of his roots at a time before the Lutheran Services were conducted in English. She worked tirelessly on behalf of Christ Lutheran Church in Wathena, Kansas and started the movement there to have families sit together in church. (Previously, men had sat on one side, and women on the other side of the aisle.) She founded the first Cooperative

Extension Club (a non-formal extension program of the U.S. Department of Agriculture) in Doniphan County, and became a Republican Committeewoman. She campaigned for Bob Dole in northeast Kansas in his first bid for the U.S. Senate in 1969.

Max's family included some other prominent people. His distant cousin, Frances Willard, was the famous women's temperance leader. Her statue is the first of a woman to be placed in Statuary Hall in Washington, DC. One aunt, Elizabeth Anne Willard came from a background of crusaders and preached the gospel in England with her daughter. Another cousin, Shelby Smith, became Lieutenant Governor of Kansas and served under Governor Bob Dole. Yet another cousin Frank Willard became the well-known newspaper cartoonist creator for "Moon Mullins."

Alto and Nellie (Willard) Benitz settled on a farm five miles southwest of Wathena, Kansas, where they raised their eight children.[1] Life was not luxurious but needs were met. Their son Max would later recall that in the 1920s "times were economically very good…There was a demand for all the agricultural products, livestock, milk and cream… farmers were making money and my parents were doing quite well…. [We] children all had ambitions to go a long ways in life. But the economic crash that occurred in October 1929…changed all our lives." He remembered that his father said that the time: "We are in for big trouble."[3] The Great Depression set in and crops failed or could not be sold for enough profit to support a family. Max attended a one-room schoolhouse throughout his primary and secondary education. He began high school in 1930 when times were extremely lean. The family's wood-heated home burned down in January 1932, and they moved into a vacant two-room house with a garage that they converted to a bedroom. He and his brothers shared beds there, and he later recalled waking up some mornings with his face covered in snow. He also recalled that his father was "in poor health, but he was good at organizing and seeing that we kids got the work done."[4] Max learned the basics of farming by raising chickens, dairying, growing grapes, apples, strawberries and cattle with his father, and raising garden vegetables with his mother. These experiences helped shape his personality to be disciplined, strong and as careful with resources as possible.

Benitz worked as a substitute rural mail carrier during high school. He recalled "the worst years of the drought [in Kansas]…were 1932, '33,

1. One daughter, Maxine, drowned in early childhood.

and '34. In 1932, the crop had a very late start and some harvest. In '33 there was very little harvest, and in '34 practically nothing."[5] He said later that his parents and his uncle, who was a doctor, thought he should go to Kansas University and follow his medical trade. "I was very much interested and would have liked to have done just that," Benitz said. "My grades were good enough but there…was simply no money in which to pursue that kind of a profession. Both my parents and my uncle, the doctor, all admitted that he did not have the money either. So, it was back to work on the farm with the agricultural situation very depressed."[6] Max educated himself by reading everything he could find, allowing only for four hours of sleep each night his entire life.

Max Benitz had an agreement with his father that he would stay and help on the family farm until the age of 21. In 1937, when he turned 21, crop prices were better in Kansas but still inadequate. He sought a better life by moving to Washington State. He recalled that he rode a bus for three days, with "all the possessions I owned in the world in one bag… Had lots of extra money in my pocket – a total of $15. Of course, it was carefully spent, and it went a long ways at that time."[7] He met up with his uncle Roy Willard in Ellensburg, and obtained work milking cows for his uncle's neighbor. He lived in a bunkhouse on the farm, and recalled that he ate so much strong mutton and so many red beans that he disliked those foods for the rest of his life. At the end of the first winter he met up with his oldest brother Earl (Bud)and together they went to work splitting wood for a lime kiln in the San Juan Islands. *"Life was not easy,"* he recalled later. *"You worked all day every day for a paycheck. The boss owned the only grocery store on that side of the island and charged three to four times normal for his goods and allowed credit. If you charged, soon you 'owed your soul to the company store'."* He then moved back to Ellensburg and got a job as a farm hand. Soon he bought a team of horses and began to farm on a share basis. He supplied milk from his dairy cows for the United States Army Air Corps during World War II. For three years and four months he never missed one teat on any of the 65 to 90 cows he milked seven days a week. *"It didn't matter if you had the flu, or if the weather was below zero - you headed for the barn, because everyone had to do their part,"* he said later.[8]

In Ellensburg he met and married Marie Fern Wilson in 1940. They had two girls and a son, Norma June, Eileen and Alvin Ray, during their years in Ellensburg. Max Edward, Jr., and Ronald Richard were born

Max Benitz leaves Kansas for Washington State, 1937.

later when they had moved to rural Prosser.

Farming in Prosser

The city of Prosser in southeastern Washington State is named for Colonel William Prosser, a Civil War veteran who staked a homestead on the banks of the Yakima River in 1882 and began farming the dry land. Prosser is located about 50 miles downstream from the city of Yakima, where the river tracks a steep gradation from central Washington to arid eastern Washington, and then flows 28 miles further into the massive Columbia River. Prosser is the seat of Benton County, a place so dry and impoverished during the Great Depression that nearly half of the acreage was either abandoned or foreclosed. Life was lean and cash-poor, as farm commodity prices fell and credit was pinched. Abandoned land and drought combined to produce severe dust storms. Most of the farms that survived were small, subsistence-level operations that barely supported one family.

However, the farmers pinned their hopes on irrigation, which they believed could transform this rich, volcanic soil so it could grow anything. President Franklin D. Roosevelt had appropriated federal money to build the Grand Coulee Dam along the Columbia in northeastern Washington in 1933, and the gigantic project was already creating employment and sprouting hopes. In 1935, the President appropriated $5-million (later reduced to $4-million) from Emergency Relief Funds to begin construction of Roza Dam, to divert the Yakima River ten miles north of Yakima, and an irrigation distribution system that would flow down the Yakima Valley. The project, vastly smaller than Grand Coulee and the Columbia Basin Irrigation Project that it would make possible, had been surveyed and dreamed about since 1917. Lack of funding had prevented implementation. The Roza Irrigation District was established in September, 1935. The first blocks received water in 1942 and the last in 1951.

By 1946, Max and Marie Benitz had saved enough to make a down payment on 80 acres of sagebrush land north of Prosser. They pulled in two old trailers to make a home. In the far westerly portion of this land, a large canyon is named after the famous 19ᵗʰ century "Northwest Cattle King," Ben Snipes. Benitz, as a cattleman himself, knew this was a perfect place for spring and summer grazing. Many natural artesian springs and a clear water creek grace the canyons floor, and the high hills surrounding it are called the Horse Heaven Hills because of their lush feed grasses. He also bought 80 acres about three miles to the North. This land also backed up to Snipes Canyon. Every spring Max would drive his herd of about 125 cattle up the canyon to the North Ranch and farm. Then toward mid-summer, he would round up the herd and bring it back to the main ranch. As the farm prospered, Benitz bought more land until he eventually owned a 700-acre successful, diversified farming operation, growing potatoes, dry beans, apples, grapes and a mix of other crops over the years.

Benitz later recalled his move to the Prosser farm and the difficult early years there: "It didn't look like a very promising future but I had a lot of confidence in the soil, which turned out to be very good. [If you have] good climate, good soil, and if you take good care of it, it will produce well for you…There was a pioneer spirit. Everyone [neighbors] helped the other with almost any problem you had. Not to say that you didn't do your best to raise a better crop than your neighbor, but if he had a problem we were all right there to help."⁹ He also remembered that "When I began farming…there was really only one kind of schooling for folks in agriculture. It was called the school of hard knocks. We paid high prices for our mistakes. Most learned from trial and error. I came onto that scene in the very depth of the great depression. I had watched many neighbors lose everything they had worked a lifetime to gain. I learned economics the hard way."[10]

Local Public Service Begins

Benitz was talkative and gregarious, plunging into community affairs. One of his first leadership ventures came in 1951, when he volunteered to organize and chair a committee to bring telephones to the rural Benton County homes in the Roza Irrigation District. "Along with working seven days a week, long hours a day…we had 234 families in the community. Not a single one had a telephone."[11] He approached the county farm extension agent, and did most of the footwork himself. Local people were enthusiastic. Seventy people came to the first meeting of the new committee, and soon they had 181 signed applications, even

Max Benitz, Chairman of the committee for first telephones for rural Benton and Franklin counties, 1951.

though each applicant had to pay three years' advance rent of $108 to $118 – a large sum to small farming families in those days. Warming to public service and the interactions it brought, Max wrote that "we have found the solution of the phone problem. There are many other problems that as yet are not solved which will need cooperation, thought, work and money. Just to mention a few: What about the weed problem, loss of soil, fertility, health, disease, etc.? We can solve them if we will… the thing that pleased me was the satisfaction that comes from having been able to contribute a little to people who have a problem."[12]

In February1952, after working with the Benton County Farm Bureau since 1948, Benitz became Bureau President, and served two terms. As the young rural area began to grow, he felt it was very important to work closely with his neighbors to better understand their needs. Agriculture dominated the local economy, and was the engine that drove businesses in Prosser. Many local citizens opposed a low ceiling on pay for hired farm workers that had been imposed by President Harry Truman's Wage Stabilization Board. The Board had been established in September 1950, under authority of the Office of Defense Mobilization, three months after the United States entered the Korean War. It represented an attempt to control inflation in the booming war economy. In January 1951, the President froze wages and prices, an action aimed at large labor unions but one that made it hard for farmers to hire unskilled labor to work their lands and herds.[13] In 1952, federal regulations permitted farmers to pay only 95¢ per hour plus 10 percent. If they paid by the month the ceiling was $225 without board and room, plus 10 percent; or $195 plus house plus 10 percent; or $175 plus board and room plus 10 percent.

In Benton County, most farmers believed much work would go undone if these regulations were not revised upward. In November 1952, the county Farm Bureau formed a committee to seek relief from this federal Board's dictates. Benitz, as County Farm Bureau Chairman, worked closely with this committee, exercising and strengthening his views against federal control. He favored small government, with local control to the maximum extent possible.

In 1952, President Truman seized control of the large steel companies and placed them under federal jurisdiction, to prevent a strike for higher wages by the United Steel Workers.[14] The U.S. District Court, District of Columbia, and then the U.S. Supreme Court, ruled the President's action unconstitutional. The steel companies were returned to private ownership, the union struck in June and July that year, and the President re-constituted the Wage Stabilization Board with lesser powers that summer. It was an election year, and this issue of heavy federal control was hotly debated. The new Republican President Dwight Eisenhower dissolved the Board in February 1953, shortly after his election.[15]

However, the public service "bug" had clearly bitten Max Benitz. In 1954 he was elected president of Whitstran Community Incorporated, a local non-profit group dedicated to refurbishing the 1919, one-room Whitstran school building and making it into a Community Center.

The building was going to be torn down, but the community needed a gathering place. Benitz put the two needs together and devised a plan whereby the non-profit could lease the building from the School Board for a very low price and refurbish it, thereby avoiding demolition and new construction costs. For about $30,000, the project was completed. Benitz later said of the project: "It took a whole host of meetings... [but] the old community building still stands and has [had] a non-denominational Sunday School for over 40 years, still goes and is used for weddings, dances, by Boy Scouts and others. It has worked out quite well...It just proves that when you are honest with people, and have a good project and work it, you can do a lot of things in the community. By 1958, the 80-acre Benitz tract had been built up to 250 acres. His operation became highly diversified as he produced peaches, grapes, hay, cattle, hogs, sugar beets, corn and small grains. He also had a young apple orchard. He was a member of the asparagus association and the

Max E. Benitz, Sr. President of Whitstran Community Incorporated, at organizational meeting for the Whitstran Community building, 1954. Left to Right, Norton Grow, Mrs. Willard Blake, Max Benitz, Mrs. Norton Grow and A.P. Skeenland.

hay association. He also enjoyed working with young people in 4-H and Future Farmers of America. That same year, Benitz won second place in the Benton County Corn Growing contest, producing 151.6 bushels per acre. The purpose of the contest was to encourage local corn growing, as most corn consumed at that time in Benton County had been shipped in. He also won a statewide corn growing contest/production study

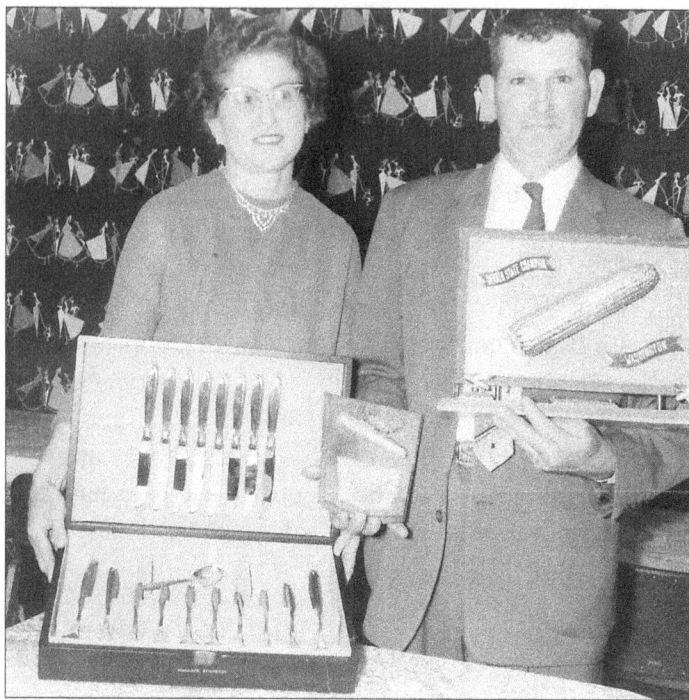

Marie and Max Benitz show Flatware Set and Gold-embossed Ear of Corn at banquet celebrating the Corn Awards, January 1959.

sponsored by the DeKalb Corp.[2], designed to encourage corn growing in areas outside the Midwest. He said it was "an honor to participate in this production study! This brought corn production to the Pacific Northwest."[17] The following month he received the Who's Who Award of the week sponsored by local businesses in Prosser.

In addition to farming, Max Benitz volunteered in a church-building campaign for Messiah Lutheran Church in Prosser during 1949-50 and served as church President in 1956; a leader in the Boy Scout Troop at Whitstran in the 1950s; a member of the Prosser School Board from 1957-60; a Farmers' Home Administration county committeeman from 1952-57, a member of the Benton–Franklin County Fair Board 1957-60; and chair of the committee that elected Pete Harrison as Benton County Sheriff in 1958.

2. DeKalb was a subsidiary of Monsanto Corp., headquartered in DeKalb, Illinois.

Statewide Public Service Begins

In 1960, Max Benitz was elected Vice President of the Washington State Farm Bureau. At the November meeting that year, he then was elected to serve out the remaining term of Heber Thompson, who resigned as President of the Bureau. At that time, there were 4,200 member families in the State Farm Bureau. At a membership drive in Moses Lake that December, he told a group it was his goal to have 10,000 Farm Bureau members within the next three years in Washington State. Busy with his irrigated farm, now grown to 410 acres, and with 850 head of hogs, Benitz worked at the same time with great enthusiasm for the Farm Bureau. He stated: "Its [the Farm Bureau's] philosophy coincides with my own-free enterprise and freedom from too much government. We must go slow in asking for government help when we should be doing more thinking for ourselves."[18]

During this tenure he also served on the national committee for the American Farm Bureau, and was a delegate to that organization's 42nd Annual Convention in Denver, Colorado, in December 1960. A news report of his speech stated that "Benitz, who has stated previously that his philosophy and that of the Farm Bureau coincides came home more convinced than ever that free enterprise is necessary with as little government interference as possible." He told the delegates: "Everything we ask the government to do for us must be paid for."[19]

Max Benitz becomes President, Washington State Farm Bureau, 1960.

Back home at a State Farm Bureau banquet the following month, he noted that only three and one/half percent of America's population provided 90 percent of the nation's food. At the time Benitz stated these figures, it was not generally known that the farm population was shrinking so fast. In 1945, just 15 years earlier, 16 percent of Americans had been engaged in agriculture.[20] The farm lobby was becoming smaller and smaller, but needed to preserve its strength "through unity and organization." Worried about government encroachment into the free enterprise of family farms, he stated: "The privileges we took for granted 25 years ago are what we are fighting for today to retain...[so that] our children will have the rights that we have enjoyed."[21]

Benitz outlined his plans for 1961 as State Farm Bureau President as expanding the Bureau and its legislative program, organizing a commodity program, forming of bargaining and marketing organizations, enlarging the safety program and expanding public relations work. Clearly, he recognized that public outreach and information, including utilizing the political process and political office, would be essential to achieving Bureau goals. In January, Benitz along with 130 farmers known as the "Grass Roots Delegation," visited the state capitol in Olympia to lobby Democrat Governor Albert Rossellini against a package of new taxes. The Grass Roots position was to "hold the line" against new taxation and stand for smaller government. Benitz presented the governor, sometimes jokingly called "Taxellini," with a copy of the Farm Bureau's 1961 policy.

Benitz Weathers Challenging Times in Farm Bureau Leadership

Almost as soon as Benitz became State Farm Bureau President, a series of challenging issues arose. For this staunch believer in the free market, it wasn't difficult for him to choose and fight for his position. In late 1960, Teamsters Union Local 760, with offices in several eastern and central Washington cities, struck against Washington apple producers because non-union firms were packing apples. The union organized a boycott and picketed 46 Safeway stores in Washington, advising consumers not to buy Washington apples. Max Benitz called the boycott a "rule or wreck tactic...a brazen attempt to apply an economic stranglehold on segments of the apple industry not in any way involved in the contract dispute between the union and Yakima Valley warehouse employees... if the boycott is successful, it could cause a financial hardship on many innocent growers, workers and others in the industry, not involved in any union dispute."[22] The State Farm Bureau supported Benitz, saying that it "recognizes and supports the collective bargaining rights of labor unions, but the attempted boycott of all Washington apples is a form of coercion, not collective bargaining."[23]

The dispute between the Teamsters and Washington apple packers was referred to National Labor Relations Board (NLRB), which ruled that consumer picketing in front of a "secondary" establishment (Safeway) was prohibited. The case was taken to the Court of Appeals for the District of Columbia, which set aside the NLRB order and held that the secondary establishment would have to show definite economic damages in order for the picketing to be prohibited. Eventually, the case progressed all the way to the U.S. Supreme Court, which reversed and vacated the Court of Appeals decisions and said that picketing of the stores to advise customers not to buy Washington

Benitz with Governor Rossellini, 1961.

apples was not allowed.[24]

In March 1961, Senate Bill [SB] 247 was under debate in the Washington State Legislature and similar bills were being debated in several states at the same time. The issue was "compulsory unionism," or the necessity of workers to join unions in order to keep their jobs. Unions argued that compulsory unionism was necessary to their survival, and that, in its absence, employers would use punitive and coercive means to abridge their employees' "rights of association" and prevent them from joining unions. The issue was so polarizing that it made its way the U.S. Supreme Court, but wasn't decided for many years. In 1961, the 173rd General Assembly of the United Presbyterian Church in the United States even declared a position – firmly against compulsory unionism.[25]

In Washington State, the Farm Bureau under Max Benitz took a definitive position against compulsory unionism. Benitz told the Prosser Chamber of Commerce that March: "We are not opposed to voluntary unionism, but we cannot live with compulsory unionism."[26] Even as he spoke, the Washington State Senate was about to approve a bill that would prohibit importing workers from out of state in order to break a strike. Such an action would definitely favor and strengthen unions. Again, Benitz and the Farm Bureau were opposed. "There is a tremendous principal involved here," he declared. "We may lose a lot of things on the farm, including perhaps our profits, but we do not intend to lose our right to choose."

The issues of price controls, unionism and marketing were prominent during this time period. The American Farm Bureau believed that these issues should be gradually taken away from the government and placed back into the farmers' hands. In December 1960, guest speaker Charles Marshall, president of Nebraska Farm Bureau, explained the American Farm Bureau Federation's policies and goals for attaining a more "free" agriculture to the Yakima Chamber of Commerce. He urged all citizens to pay closer attention to trends that eventually restrict personal liberties. "It's later than you think," he cautioned, warning that government "takes over so gradually most people let warning signs go unheeded." Benitz and the Washington State Farm Bureau were in perfect agreement.

Another bill that united Benitz and the Washington State Farm Bureau in opposition was the Emergency Feed Grains Program and Agricultural Act of 1961. The Act was a voluntary acreage reduction program, with payments-in-kind to farmers who cooperated. If a farmer reduced his planted acreage by 30 percent, he would receive subsidies from the government. Democrat President John Kennedy signed the Act on March 22, 1961, saying it would "curtail the surplus in feed grains which has reached almost unmanageable proportions."[27] Benitz described the Act as "ineffective," and told the State Farm Bureau convention meeting in Walla Walla that year that it would likely become a "scandal" after Congress reconvened.[28] He believed the government should stay out of the business of regulating farm production.

Second Year of Farm Bureau Leadership

In 1962, Benitz was reelected as President of Washington State Farm Bureau. In his first term, he had traveled 20,000 miles to urge opposition to increased real estate taxation. During his second term, Benitz and the Farm Bureau passed many resolutions. One asked for a minimum of national controls, another sought assistance to youth of 16 years and under seeking employment. Benitz opposed farm labor bills that would prevent employing juveniles to pick strawberries and perform other farm jobs, and in some cases require them to join unions. He urged farmers to write their congressmen expressing opposition to the measure.

In early 1962, a major scandal broke involving Billie Sol Estes, a Texas con man who made a fortune in cotton allotments, irrigation pumps, and ammonia tank mortgages. All of his profits came from manipulating government price controls, quotas and acreage allotments.

Estes purchased large numbers of cotton allotments — quotas that told each farmer how much he could or could not plant — by dealing with dispossessed farmers and convincing them to transfer their allotments to him. He leased the land and allotments back from the farmers, but once the first payments came due, the farmers would intentionally default and the land would revert to Estes. In effect, Estes had purchased the cotton allotments with the lease fees. However, because the original sale and mortgage were a pretext rather than a genuine sale, it was illegal to transfer the cotton allotments this way. Estes also paid "commissions" to farmers who agreed to take out mortgages to buy ammonia tanks used to store fertilizer. The tanks would then be leased back to Estes for the exact amount of the mortgage payments. Between 1959-1961, West Texas farmers mortgaged 33,500 tanks at a cost of more than $34-million. This number of tanks was far more than necessary for real farming needs, and not a single actual tank was ever found. The scheme was just a money-transfer. Eventually, Estes' schemes collapsed, and in 1963 he was tried and convicted on charges related to the fraudulent ammonia tank mortgages on both federal and state charges and was sentenced to 24 years in prison. His state conviction was later overturned and he was paroled in 1971. Eight years later, he was convicted of other fraud charges and served four more years.[29] As Benitz watched the Billie Sol Estes case unfold, he called it "a real example of what happens when government gets into agriculture...We have only seen the beginning [of manipulative schemes] in this case," he predicted.[30]

In June 1962, a national "Turkey Referendum" was held. Turkey growers who produced more than 3,600 pounds of turkeys per year were eligible to vote on a plan that would have amounted to a national turkey marketing order. They voted against the proposal overwhelmingly, not wanting to want to surrender their individual decision-making opportunities. Approval and implementation of the order would have provided the first nationwide order for any commodity and the first marketing order of its kind ever applied to animal agriculture. The American Farm Bureau Federation opposed the proposal, and was happy to call its defeat "a significant victory for the turkey industry and all of American agriculture...Turkey growers did suffer financially in 1961, due to excessive over-production resulting largely from talk of quotas and controls. A careful appraisal of the results of the turkey referendum should remove much of the glamour of nationwide market order proposals for other commodities and dampen the enthusiasm of those who suggest the national government"[31] should operate farming control programs. Max Benitz also celebrated the defeat of government interference in turkey farming. Due to the 3,600-pound rule, he said, "ninety percent of turkey growers" could not vote. He also worried that, had the referendum passed, the principle "would carry on to other phases on the meat business."[32]

The biggest challenge that year came from proposed legislation called the "Kennedy Farm Bill," formally the Cochran-Freeman Omnibus Farm Bill (SB 1643 and House Resolution [HR] 6400). In 1962, President Kennedy proposed a system of mandatory acreage and marketing controls in return for 90 percent of parity if two-thirds of participating farmers approved. His proposal came after corn and wheat prices fell to postwar lows while surpluses reached record highs in the year after his January, 1961 inauguration. The Feed Grains Program of 1961 had reduced the production of feed grains by only 11 percent, and prices were still depressed. While most farmers wanted federal aid, they were violently opposed to mandatory controls on amounts they could produce. Most state Farm Bureaus in the country, as well as the American Farm Bureau Federation, lobbied hard against the bill because they believed that any mandatory control would lead to controls on other commodities. They termed the bill a "rigid crop production control program."

As President of the Washington State Farm Bureau, Benitz strongly opposed the bill. "The Cochran-Freeman farm plan now before Congress is a bid to concentrate unprecedented powers to bring every section of agriculture under complete government control on a 'step by step' basis," he said.[33] He said that overall inflation, combined with government dumping of surplus crops on the market at inopportune times, had worsened the plight of farmers. However, government controls were not the answer. Benitz believed there was too much federal government involvement in agriculture. He was convinced that government regulation would be a hindrance to food production, not a help. He traveled from one farm state to another to rally farmers against the Cochran-Freeman Bill. In January 1962, he debated then-Secretary of Agriculture Orval Freeman at the Ninth Annual Pacific Northwest Farm Forum in Spokane. He called the Freeman Plan a "brazen attempt to destroy competition in agriculture...[and] a direct assault on the economic system that has made the agricultural industry of this nation the envy of the world."[34]

He recalled later that "I, as President [of the Farm Bureau] made speeches all over the United States. From the east coast, west coast we recruited a crew to help...eventually it [the Cochran-Freeman plan] would have ruing agriculture. You would have had bureaucracy similar to what you have in the U.S.S.R...You would have to get a permit to grow an acre of wheat. Oh, you could grow it but you couldn't sell it. It would be locked up until you had that [government] certificate... It had been a very long summer [of campaigning against the plan]."[35] He emphasized that government support payments to farmers "would become ceilings...the bill would also permit the Secretary of Agriculture to set arbitrary ceilings on the opportunities of individual farm family to raise their income and their efficiency."[36]

Benitz saw a need for new farm legislation to help farmers adjust the production of wheat and feed grains to market requirements. However, he advocated the national Farm Bureau's own cropland adjustment program that would help farmers adjust grain production on a voluntary basis by retiring cropland and expanding markets. "If the administration farm bill becomes law you simply will have no choice, [in how much you produce,]" he told farmers. "Allotments will be placed on all surplus crops and the allotment system will be extended and all the rest."[37] Farm price supports must be dropped gradually to return to a market price system, he insisted.

Speaking before the Pasco Chamber of Commerce, Benitz urged dropping farm price supports gradually and returning to the market-price system, without subsidies. He bluntly called the Cochran-Freeman Plan *"a step in the direction of complete socialization of agriculture,"* and urged farmers to read the bill closely. He traveled to Washington D. C. to testify before the House Agriculture Committee, about the bill, saying that *"we [Farm Bureaus] are* doing everything possible to see that farming problems are not settled by forcing us into socialized agriculture."[38]

The Washington State Farm Bureau's platform that year firmly opposed the Cochran-Freeman Bill, and was clear on the subject of government controls. The Bureau backed a farm program with a minimum of control and a maximum of freedom for farmers, opposed the extension and further promotion of federal quotas, diversion programs and marketing controls in the potato industry, and asked for improvement in grading wheat for export.

Dr. Warren Collins, American Farm Bureau economist, told farmers in a Prosser meeting in April 1962, that there would be "no place on the New Frontier for…a market system in agriculture, if the administration's proposed farm bill becomes law…It appears…that [backers of the Cochran-Freeman bill]…are interested in moving farmers here into a 'peasantry agriculture.'"[39]

T.C. Peterson director of program development for the American Farm Bureau, called the Cochran-Freeman Bill "a fiasco." Speaking at the Washington State Farm Bureau convention banquet in Walla Walla, he added that "the farm situation will not get straightened out until the farmer produces for the market instead of the government." He worried that the bill would give "absolute power" to the Secretary of Agriculture, who would be free to completely ignore the recommendations of a National Farmers' Advisory Board proposed in the bill. He also said the bill "reversed" the Constitutional roles of Congress and the Executive Branch of government because the Secretary of Agriculture could grant exemptions to any votes taken by Congress. Moreover, individual commodity programs could be pitted against one another, promoting "step by step adoption" of government control. Speaking at the same banquet, Max Benitz called the bill a "scandal."[40]

The Cochran-Freeman Bill was approved by the Senate. However, on June 21, the House of Representatives defeated the measure by ten votes. Virtually all Republicans voted against the measure. In the end the Food Administration and Agriculture Act of 1962, Public Law 87-703 (87th Congress), as adopted on September 27, 1962, was a somewhat watered down version of the original bill. It did grant significant decision-making power to the Secretary of Agriculture, and established wheat as the leading indicator of quotas to be set for other crops.[41]

Cuban Missile Crisis

In October 1962, the United States and the Soviet Union came as close as the two would ever come to nuclear war, when Soviet missiles were discovered in Cuba just 90 miles from Florida. The Cuban Missile Crisis unfolded in the public eye beginning on October 22, when President Kennedy told the nation he had ordered a "quarantine of all military equipment under shipment to Cuba," and said that the U.S. would "regard any nuclear missile launched from Cuba against any nation in the Western Hemisphere as an attack by the Soviet Union on the United States, requiring a full retaliatory response on the Soviet Union."[42] Two days later, Soviet Premier Nikita Khrushchev declared that the Soviet Union would not "instruct the captains of Soviet vessels bound for Cuba to observe the orders of the American naval vessels blockading that Island." The next day, October 25, tensions soared even higher as Kennedy stated: "National security must come first...we can't negotiate with a gun at our head... if they won't remove the missiles and restore status quo ante, we will have to do it ourselves." On the 26th and 27th, letters arrived from Khrushchev to Kennedy. The second letter mentioned a possible "deal" – a face-saving way out of the impasse for both sides. Unbeknownst to anyone on the American side but Kennedy and his brother, Attorney General Robert Kennedy, the Attorney General had held secret meetings with Soviet Ambassador to the U.S., Anatoly Dobrynin, beginning on October 23. No one in the American Cabinet or the Executive Committee of the National Security Council had been told, even as the secret meetings continued. As it turned out, the crisis was resolved on the 28th, when the U.S.S.R. agreed to remove its missiles from Cuba and the U.S. pledged not to invade Cuba. Secretly, the U.S. also agreed to remove some Jupiter missiles from Turkey.[43]

Benitz later stated that he "was totally convinced that we would have a world war out of that [the Cuban Missile Crisis] as the Russian ships approached Cuba and our military might challenged them."[44] However, as time went on, he was most concerned about the secrecy displayed by the Kennedy brothers during the crisis. President Kennedy had known about the missiles at least four full days before informing the public on October 22, yet he deliberately kept his pre-arranged schedule as Russian ships continued toward Cuba with more missiles during those four days. Robert Kennedy's secret meetings with Dobrynin, although successful, might not have succeeded, and in Benitz's view, threatened the democratic process of government at the highest levels. He became a strong supporter of the Freedom of Information Act that was signed by President Lyndon Johnson in 1966.[45]

Benitz Role and Perspective Expand in 1963

In 1963, the federal government conducted a "Wheat Referendum" – a vote of farmers across the nation who grew more than 15 acres of wheat, and any other farmers who grew more than two acres of wheat during the previous three years provided they agreed to comply with the outcome of the referendum. The program being voted on was basically a two-price system that incorporated both federal acreage allotments and land retirement. Essentially, it was a crucial test of the question of an expanded government role in agriculture, and was bitterly contested. The program would need a two/thirds majority to be approved. Max Benitz and the Washington State Farm Bureau strongly opposed the program. Benitz, as state Farm Bureau President once again, spoke widely, urging farmers to vote no. In a March 1, 1963 meeting with Kittitas Farm Bureau members, he said: "It boils down to the fact that government is making an all-out stand for socialized farming. Farmers and ranchers over the country, whether they know it or not, are presently involved in what may be their last fight for the right to produce under a 'free enterprise' system."[46] He remarked that once the program was passed, it would create a bigger bite into the taxpayer's pocket since all products using wheat would require manufacturers to use only certified wheat. To keep them from cheating, a government agency would have to "police" such regulations.

Swift Foods Company, one of the largest producers of pork and beef

Charles Shuman (left), President American Farm Bureau, Max Benitz's mother Nellie and Benitz, at Western States Farm Bureau Meeting, San Luis Obispo, California, July 1963.

in the United States, sponsored Benitz on a tour of 21 states that February, speaking against the government wheat program. Cattle and meat prices were slumping at the time, and Benitz believed that if the government prevailed in the upcoming wheat referendum, it would lead to compulsory controls for livestock, dairy and poultry products "down the 'supply management' road."[47]

True to his small government principles, he was convinced that no government agency was qualified to run the meat industry under mandatory controls for one day, much less one year. "The program is being sold on a one-year basis, but past history of the programs show that they have carried on and if the forthcoming program is passed, it will lead to no way out," he said.[48]

When the Wheat Referendum was finally put to a vote in May 1963, Benitz stayed awake all night listening to the radio awaiting the results. He considered it a crucial contest in his campaign to keep American agriculture a free market. Thirteen wheat referenda had been voted on since 1941, but the 1963 vote saw the highest turnout ever. More than 1,200,000 votes were cast, and the proposal was soundly rejected. Wheat farmers accepted just 50 percent parity payments in order to stave off government controls.[49] "Helping to defeat the wheat referendum in 1963 was the biggest accomplishment of my political career," Benitz would say in later life. "With all my work in politics and others it was one of my happiest days, evenings of my life when those results came in....It [passage of the referendum] would have been such a setback for agriculture that I had to devote all my time and energy to it. It was a difficult battle to win because everyone from President Kennedy on down was pushing it. But it was wrong for agriculture and, eventually, enough people could see that."[50] From that time forward, Benitz became a tireless campaigner and spokesman for free market agriculture. The "socialization of agriculture" in the United States was his biggest fear. He recalled later that the experience of campaigning against the Wheat Referendum influenced his decision, five years later, to enter politics.[51]

International Travel

In autumn 1963, Benitz embarked on a 22-day tour of the Union of Soviet Socialist Republics (U.S.S.R. – also known as the Soviet Union) and some of its satellite countries in Eastern Europe, as well as England and Germany, as part of a "People-to-People" exchange founded by former President Eisenhower. When Eisenhower left office in January 1961, he arranged to have the program privatized as a nongovernmental organization, dedicated to enhancing cross-cultural communication through tolerance and mutual understanding. It was nicknamed "United Statesmanship." Participants in People-to-People tours paid their own way, and Benitz told Farm Bureau members that he had "foregone fishing trips and other summer outings for two reasons: because of the expense of the trip, and because of the amount of work to be done in preparation for this kind of a 'jaunt across the pond.'"[52] Thirty agricultural participants from Washington state participated in this 1963 tour, which visited 11 countries. Benitz was becoming such a popular and passionate spokesman for free-market economics that the Washington State Farm Bureau wanted him out in public engaging in debate.

Before he left on the trip, Benitz reported to the state Farm Bureau that he was going "to make the most of the situation and learn everything possible in all the countries in which we will be traveling... we will be going to deep into Russia, and will have more freedom than many other groups preceding us in this type of tour."[53] The year 1963 had seen a decided thaw in U.S.-Soviet relations, after the near-disaster of the Cuban Missile Crisis in 1962. The top leaders of both countries drew back from threatening nuclear war, and signed the historic Atmospheric Test Ban Treaty, along with England, in August 1963. Kennedy called the Test Ban Treaty the "greatest accomplishment" of his Presidency, and spoke memorably in June, 1963 at American University's graduation, saying "we all inhabit this small planet. We all breathe the same air. We all cherish our children's futures. And we are all mortal…Peace is the necessary rational end of rational men."[54] Khrushchev called the speech the greatest by any American President since Roosevelt. Kennedy and Khrushchev established a "hot line" between their two offices in August, to avert accidental nuclear war.

However, Max Benitz wasn't convinced that the Soviet Union's goal of world domination had changed. He told his Farm Bureau supports just before his departure on the trip: "Regarding Russia, I honestly do not feel that the 'leopard has changed its spots'—not one little bit. Their methods are a little different now—offering peaceful coexistence and other gestures toward a friendly coexistence--chiefly because the Russians are having difficulty with the Red Chinese. But, this is just a squabble over "how" rather than "whether" they hope to bury us."[55]

Benitz was referring to one of the most famous phrases of the Cold War, uttered by Khrushchev while addressing Western ambassadors at a reception at the Polish embassy in Moscow in November, 1956. Khrushchev had actually said "whether you like it or not, history is on our side. We will dig you in." In his public speech after the same event, Khrushchev declared: "We must take a shovel and dig a deep grave, and bury colonialism as deep as we can."[56] Later, on August 24, 1963, he Khrushchev remarked in a speech in Yugoslavia: "I once said, 'We will bury you,' and I got into trouble with it. Of course we will not bury you with a shovel. Your own working class will bury you."[57] In referring to Khrushchev's remarks, once again fresh in the public's mind in 1963, Benitz was showing his disdain for communism and its failure to deliver on economic promises or virtually any promises.

Benitz warned his state Farm Bureau members that Agriculture Secretary Freeman had just returned from a visit to the Soviet Union and several European countries, and had come home recommending expanded trade with the U.S.S.R. He said that apparently Freeman believed that expanding trade with the Soviet Union would be a strategic way to exploit the tensions then building between that country and the

People's Republic of China. (By 1969, tensions would become so exacerbated that armed clashes took place along the Soviet-Chinese border
at Manchuria, and more than 500,000 troops were massed at this border.
The conflict was so serious that it absorbed fully one/third of all Soviet
military assets at that time.) Despite the seriousness of the Soviet-Chinese conflict, Benitz opposed Freeman's strategy of expanding trade
with the U.S.S.R.: "To me this is indeed a shocking move…It seems as
though we could sell a few bushels of wheat and possible other surplus
commodities to the U.S.S.R.—but what would we gain if we sold the
wheat and lost our freedom?"[58]

In the same column, titled "The President Reports" in the Washington State Farm Bureau newsletter, Benitz reminded his members that
federal acreage allotments were "a crutch…When we do have an opportunity to remove this 'crutch' as we do now, we should certainly take
advantage of it and to begin to stand on our own and cast aside farm
subsidies and unsuitable farm programs." Pointing out that Secretary
Freeman had scheduled a trip to the Pacific Northwest that October, and
would meet with local farmers in Walla Walla to hear their views on
October 10, Benitz pointed out that local views ought to be clear to the
Secretary: "To get the idea — he could read the result of recent referenda
if he chooses to do so."[59]

Finally the time came for Benitz's trip to the U.S.S.R, Poland, Hungary, Germany and England, to see socialism—and outright communism—first hand. Farming and food conditions in the Soviet Union
were indeed harsh at that time. Farms had been "collectivized" in the
Soviet Union under brutal Premier Josef Stalin, primarily in the 1930s.
Collectivization meant that landowners (farmers) were forced to give
up ownership of their lands and turn them over to the government. The
move was supposed to spur efficiency, and thus raise productivity. However, many farmers fiercely resisted it. Many leaders of local resistance
movements in Soviet towns and villages were executed, or sent to distant prison camps. As a result of the resistance and the loss of experienced farmers, productivity per acre fell dramatically. In 1959, Khrushchev announced a goal of overtaking the United States in production
of milk, meat, and butter. Local officials, with Khrushchev's encouragement, made unrealistic pledges of production. These goals were met by
schemes that forced farmers to slaughter their breeding herds and arti-
ficially increase recorded production. In 1962, food prices in the Soviet

Union were raised by 25-30 percent, particularly on meat and butter, causing revolts in some cities. Drought struck the Soviet Union in 1963. The grain harvest was down by 22 percent from 1958, and the shortages resulted in bread lines. Reluctant to purchase food in the West, but faced with the alternative of widespread hunger, Khrushchev exhausted the nation's hard currency reserves and expended part of its gold stockpile in purchasing grain and other foodstuffs. He thereby further impoverished the U.S.S.R.'s struggling economy.[60]

While surplus production, and hence the idea of government acreage restrictions and parity payments not to grow certain crops, were the problems in the United States, the exact opposite problems plagued he communist economies of the U.S.S.R, Poland, Hungary and much of the rest of eastern Europe. Forced to trade only with the Soviet Union, many eastern European nations had no choice but to accept shoddy goods produced in the Soviet Union, and live with regional food shortages. Political opposition and new ideas were simply not accepted. Polish demonstrations for reform in June 1956 had been summarily crushed by Polish military police who shot and beat many of the demonstrators. Repression was even worse in Hungary, where Soviet troops and tanks had marched into Budapest in November 1956, to quell demands for reform and more openness in many areas of life. Hundreds were killed.

Benitz was glad to be home! He wrote in a private diary entry composed on the way home: "This difficult trip...behind the Iron Curtain... makes you appreciate home, and the importance of the 'good old U.S.A'...When we landed at New York's Idlewild Airport a big cheer went up from many of the passengers." He was appalled at many of the conditions he had observed on the trip: "The things we saw made us sick at heart. The things other human beings are enduring in those countries are almost unbelievable to anyone who had enjoyed the great privilege of living in a free nation... When we saw what's happening to people in the communist controlled countries, we realized that we in American are the last ray of hope for freedom loving people everywhere."[61]

Benitz was also disturbed by trends he saw in England. He reported that newspapers in England had carried many stories about the shortcomings of the British Medicare system, which had been in effect since 1948. British Medicare was essentially a program of national health care administered by the government and offering care to all residents within a framework of limited choices. It was enacted under Prime Minister Clement Attlee's Labour Party government as people who hadn't been able to afford medical care in the past rushed to doctors, shortage emerged in hospitals beds and other types of care. He told his Farm Bureau readers: "Another observation that should be of concern to all of us is that it is not only in the Iron Curtain countries that people are losing their freedom and other individual rights. England, for the third time in her history, is on the verge of complete socialism...The British are paying highly for the socialized Medicare program both in terms of cost and terms of service...individual freedom is seriously threatened."[62] Benitz was also opposed to national ownership of railroads in Britain. The "big four" railways in England had been nationalized in 1948, again by Attlee, in the Transport Act. The British Transport Commission oversaw all operations, and decided fares and routes. A program of station closures began, aimed at improving efficiency, but railway revenue declined steadily. Finally in 1963, to stem large financial losses, a sweeping set of new, controversial closures began. This situation was covered extensively in the news during Benitz's foreign trip.

He then turned to one of his most characteristic themes and deepest beliefs. He told the Farm Bureau membership that if the U.S. followed the socialist path in allowing government price supports and controls in farming, that the "historically efficient" productivity of American farmers would drop. However, lower productivity wouldn't be the only outcome, as dangerous precedents would be set in government control. "History proves that government 'supply management schemes' will certainly lead to our downfall," he said. He urged individuals to get involved: "One of the most effective things a good citizen can do is to support the organization of his choice, and participate in its activities. If your choice happens to be Farm Bureau and its policies—the Farm Bureau needs you as I have never needed people before..."If you think, 'that can't happen to us' you had better take another look. It can and will happen here unless we maintain our strong support of our private competitive enterprise system and representative form of government... surely you have heard of the old saying: 'power tends to corrupt and absolute power corrupts absolutely.'"[63]

After the 1963 tour, Max Benitz was interviewed and filmed in October, by CBS Television about the proposed wheat sale to the U.S.S.R. He was told he was chosen for the interview because the People-to-People tour had been the last group to visit the Soviet Union before the proposed sale was announced, and because his diversified farm grew many of the same crops that were grown in the U.S.S.R. Benitz gave winesap apples from his farm to Robert Schakne, West Coast bureau manager for CBS, cameraman Fred Dietrich and the rest of the film crew. The interview aired on the *CBS Evening News* with Walter Cronkite on October 30, 1963.[64]

Benitz with crew of "CBS News with Walter Cronkite," October 1963.

Enormous American wheat sales to the Soviet Union, to alleviate its food shortages, were being discussed both during and after Benitz's trip. A large wheat sales deal was announced the day after he returned. While he did not oppose the agreement outright, he thought the Kennedy Administration acted too hastily in agreeing to the terms of the wheat sale. "We were in an excellent bargaining position" he declared: The U.S. has the only remaining surplus stock in the world large enough to supply the immediate needs of Russia and other European countries." Russia has come to us, not by choice but by necessity." The U.S. was in a "seller's market" as far as wheat is concerned, he said, and believed that nations friendly to the U.S. should have the first chance to buy wheat.[65]

After the 1963 trip to the Soviet Union and parts of Europe, Benitz more fully developed his "voice." He gave a series of slide shows and talks around the state describing the trip and his observations and worries about America's future. As he interacted with the audiences, he realized he was a good speaker – direct, plainspoken, friendly, and clear. Issues beyond farm policies entered his talks, as he linked local issues in the U.S. to issues of worldwide concern and significance. He gained valuable experience for his political campaigns that would begin in a few years.

He told audiences of an air of friendship prevailing in the Russian newspapers, because of the test-ban treaty and the wheat negotiations. However, he said the great masses of people seemed to be suspicious of their own people as well as tourists. "Streets were filled with people who appeared to be bored and worried and who did not talk or laugh."

In a talk to the Toppenish Washington Chamber of Commerce, Benitz related that two interpreters were assigned to guide the People-to-People group of which he was a member. There was always a conflict with the tourist guides who tried to keep the American tour group from taking pictures or questioning or noting subjects that were not on the carefully managed agenda. One guide called Tanya was particularly zealous and alert in her efforts to keep Benitz from seeing and filming forbidden subjects. However, Benitz managed to take many pictures, particularly of machinery that he described as "so poorly designed, it stood idle." On one occasion Benitz leaped from the Russian bus as quickly as it stopped and dashed over a mound, and off bounds, to get a picture of a huge junkyard filled with discarded agriculture machines. Among them were hay balers and swather combines. Benitz, something of a mechanic, examined wear points on the junked machines, and said they appeared practically new and unworn. He concluded, he said, that faulty design had not permitted use of the machines. At an exposition of farm machines in Moscow, Benitz photographed an eight-bottom plow with three-point hitch. It was hooked to a rubber-tired tractor, which, he said could never lift the 28-foot long plow span, let alone pull it in a field. Construction was so poor that only two five-eights-inch bolts held each plow bottom to the supporting beam. At Pittsdorff 1,000 miles south of Moscow, Benitz furtively photographed a spy plane. He said there were no private planes in the U.S.S.R. When the tour left the Soviet Union, Tanya's parting comment to Benitz was: "Thank heaven you're leaving. You're the most difficult group we've had."

Benitz was convinced that the root cause of the U.S.S.R.'s failure to provide adequate food and fiber was bureaucracy. The government dictated the wheat-seeding time, regardless of local field conditions, he said. In addition, "cultivations are often times limited by the amount of fuel. The people working on collective farms have no incentive to work and therefore production is low," he said. Cropping decisions took so long to come down from the centralized government that it was too late to carry out the ordered practice when it was needed. In one area that had had only a 10-inch annual rainfall the previous year, wheat and sugar beets were being seeded. Benitz knew that most American farmers would have let fields in that area lie fallow for a year, but that practices was not allowed by the government. He reported that all apples he saw were infected with apple scab disease, and observed hay balers in junk piles but not in operation and no hay bales. "Livestock in Russia is increasing but food production is not -- the end result, disease and starvation," he told the group. He added that "equality for women as preached by communism is where the women do the work. Men are supervisors in the fields or operate machinery while women are the workers." Primitive methods are in use, he said, and there was no incentive on state-owned farms to work hard. Results were "pitiful."[66]

In January 1964, he told the Adams County (Washington) Farm Bureau of everyday life as he observed it in Moscow. His party, while in Moscow, stayed at the Ukraine hotel; the city's finest and tallest. The lobby was always so cold while he was there that people stood in groups conversing while wearing their overcoats. There was no hot water above the tenth floor. People in Moscow gladly bought clabbered milk, from a passing wagon, he said, because it was the only milk available. It had not been pasteurized or homogenized. He filmed scenes of crowds of shoppers near the "world's largest department store," GUM – the State Department Store of the U.S.S.R. Located directly opposite the Mausoleum, on the eastern side of Red Square, GUM is an acronym of the *Glavnyi Universalnyi Magazin,* which means "main universal store"). After being closed by Stalin in 1928, GUM was reopened in 1953, and became one of the sites of the legendary Soviet queues, which could at times extend all the way across Red Square. Benitz reported that not a single motor vehicle was in sight, but so many people wanted to shop they overflowed the sidewalks. Throngs of uniformed soldiers were among the crowds, but tourists were given strictest orders not to take pictures of military personnel.

In Hungary, he was particularly impressed by a conversation he had with a woman who had worked with the underground following the unsuccessful 1956 revolution. "This woman now lives as a slave," he stated, "but knows what it is to be free. She expressed the opinion that she will never see the liberation of Hungary but hopes that the younger generation will." The woman told Benitz that Hungarians did not expect any change in their servitude for a period ranging from 50 to 200 years. "The hope of 97 million people in iron curtain countries rests with one people only, those of the United State of America," she said. He also photographed housing conditions that he termed "pitiful" in Budapest, Hungary's capitol.[67]

In Berlin Wall, Benitz took (forbidden) pictures of the Wall and the famous Checkpoint Charlie, from inside the bus while it was in motion. The Wall had been thrown up overnight by Khrushchev in August 1961, because East German residents were leaving that country in record numbers. On one day in June 1961 4,770 refugees left East Berlin, fleeing the stagnant economy and poor living conditions. If that level of exodus had continued, 1.74-million would have left in a year, out of a total population of just 17 million. Clearly, the communist economy of East Germany could not stand such losses. By August 1961, refugees reached 10,000 weekly, and topped 2,000 on many individual days. The bellicose Khrushchev had had to choose – build a wall and admit that socialism had to wall in its people, or not act and have total economic drain. He tried to devise economic incentives for East Germans, but realized the economy of West Germany was so strong and appealing that he could not compete.[68] Checkpoint Charlie was the best known border crossing between East and West in Berlin, and had become infamous in 1962 when an East German teenager named Peter Fechter was shot by East German guards while trying to escape. Fechter hung on a barbed wire fence at the crossing while he bled to death in full view of the world.[69] Max Benitz said the Berlin Wall was "very real to those living there," and that crossing back into West Germany from East Germany was extremely slow and tedious even for the cleared and carefully escorted People-to-People delegation. He stated that communism was the fastest growing system of government in the world, but "their growth is not through success, but rather through their objective, which is to infiltrate and take control such as they have done in Hungary, Red China and Cuba."

Shortly after Benitz returned from his trip to the U.S.S.R. and parts of Europe, and while he was giving speeches about the trip, President Kennedy was assassinated. While Benitz had strongly disagreed with many of the President's policies, he nevertheless termed the assassination a "horrible event," and he called each of his children to discuss it with them. Violence was never the answer, he told them.[70]

Continuing Free Enterprise Battles During 1964-1967

In 1964, Benitz was reelected to his third term as President of the Washington State Farm Bureau. One of the key national issues that year was legislative re-districting. As the U.S. population continued to shift dramatically into urban areas, some states had not changed their election districts to reflect where the majority of people actually lived. This situation meant that some farm areas had disproportionately high representation. A farming county with just a few thousand residents, in some cases, had a Congressional Representative, while a city with a much larger population also had just one Representative. Cases challenging this system began to come before the courts. In 1964, the Reynolds v. Sims case was brought before the Supreme Court, challenging the legislative districts in Alabama, which had not been re-drawn for many decades since the time when most people lived in farm counties. Farm Bureaus around the country rallied to keep the old system in place, because they felt the voice of rural America would be completely drowned out by city-dwellers. The issue was decided in favor of the "one-man, one-vote" rule however. Supreme Court Chief Justice Earl Warren wrote for the majority that "legislators represent people, not trees or acres. Legislators are elected by voters, not farms or cities or economic interests."[71]

Benitz was not happy with the Warren decision. He told the annual banquet of the Adams County Farm Bureau in November 1964, that the "one man one vote [ruling] will have far reaching effects on the farmer's voice in Congress...redistricting of state legislatures, as ordered by the Supreme Court, and new urban boundaries for the home districts of U.S. Congressmen will further diminish the farmer's vote in lawmaking bodies"[72] He pointed out, as he often did, that U.S. farmers constituted just three and one/half per cent of the total population but produced 90 per cent of the nation's food and fiber. He worried that farmers were being disregarded or made subservient in national life, due to their small population. He remarked that the Presidential election that had just concluded, in which Democrat Lyndon Johnson defeated Republican Senator Barry Goldwater, was "the first one in U.S. History in which the farm vote and issues were not an important element." [73]

Benitz again hit hard on his now well-known theme of limited government. He said that a "planned economy from birth to death, subsidies, price supports, marketing agreements and acreage allotments have not worked successfully in any country in the world. Argentina, once known as a world leader in beef production, has taken the road to socialism, and today the people of Argentina have two meatless days per week." He urged his listeners to make their voices known against an *"all-powerful"* federal government. "Historian [Arnold] Toynbee has pointed out," Benitz said, "that of 21 great civilizations, 19 perished from evaporation of belief from within."[74]

Max Benitz disagreed with nearly everything about the Johnson Administration, especially its domestic policies. Johnson advocated a huge expansion of federal welfare, education, health, medical and job training benefits, as well as civil rights legislation, known as the "Great Society" program. He declared a "War on Poverty." He implemented his programs with the help of a large majority of liberal Democrats elected in 1984 in the landslide in which Johnson had defeated Goldwater. Johnson also vastly expanded American involvement in the war in Vietnam. In 1980, Benitz would look back on Johnson's policies and say: "*We* entered that era known as the Great Society just as the Vietnam War was expanding… Johnson said 'we can have both guns and butter at the same time. We're also going to have a War on Poverty.' Thus old programs were expanded, and new ones were whisked through Congress with modest initial expenditure but with built-in increments. It was great stuff for re-election, and what happened? An entrenched bureaucracy arose to handle "unmet needs" and each agency became a lobbyist for further expenditures." Two things had happened in America as a result of these programs, he said – government by regulation and a loss of fiscal control. Initially during the Johnson Administration, he recalled, most citizens were "delighted as federal aid expanded…That meant that out of some great cornucopia in Washington would come much help and we would not need to worry about local taxes. States and cities…jostled to get their communities qualified for handouts, and many Congressmen ran on 'look what I got for you' platforms." However, he said, most of the federal money had not been spent wisely, and eventually brought infla-tion.[75] Benitz also stated that "there is little doubt in our minds that the Vietnam era did a lot to make the credibility gap [in foreign perceptions of U.S. leadership] much wider. We still have not totally recovered from that one."[76] He later called the Vietnam War "a very poor policy...the heart of the people was simply not in it. Military was not in it. It was a disaster."[77]

At the end of 1964, Benitz retired as chair of the Farm Bureau's Farm Safety Committee, but retained his position as President of the Bureau. At the time, concerns about agricultural pesticides were growing strong, largely as a result of the 1962 publication of Rachel Carson's best-selling book *Silent Spring*.[3] The book pointed out environmental and human health consequences of the use of pesticides, especially dichlorodiphen-yltrichloroethane (DDT). Pesticides were regulated by the U.S. Depart-ment of Agriculture, which some saw as a conflict of interest. (In 1970, pesticide regulation was transferred to the newly-created Environmental Protection Agency.) In 1964, the federal Insecticide, Fungicide and Ro-denticide Act (FIFRA) was strengthened for the second time. The 1964 amendments required that pesticide products have federal registration numbers and be labeled with "signal" words" such as "caution, danger and warning." In addition, the Secretary of Agriculture was authorized to suspend immediately the sale of pesticides believed to be harmful to human health.[78]

Benitz wasn't convinced that pesticides were harmful, and sided with Richard Maxwell, a Washington State University extension service spe-cialist who addressed the Farm Bureau's Farm and Home Safety Confer-ence in Yakima in November 1964. Maxwell told the group that agri-cultural chemicals were necessary to increasing yields, and safe if used properly. The bulk of pesticide mishaps were the result of carelessness, and often occurred when containers were not safeguarded from children or were punctured or kept for more than one season.[79] Benitz agreed, and would later voice a ringing defense of crop pesticides in a speech to the Western Washington Horticulture Association.[4] Using the example of corn, he noted that the normal production was 50 to 70 bushels an acre before the 1950s, but the yield in the late 1970s was 125 to 150 bush-els per acre even under adverse conditions. The difference was modern

3. Carson, Rachel, *Silent Spring*, Houghton Mifflin (Boston), 1962.
4. See Chapter 3.

pesticides and chemical fertilizers. Feeding the United States and the world was a high priority for him. He told his children, "The last war on this earth, will be about food." Benitz was very aware of the dangers of pesticides and the disposition of used containers and broken packages. Max and Marie's first foster child got into a broken bag of Parathion[5] and came very close to death. Max agreed that the proper use of chemicals, both fertilizer and pesticide, should become standard practice for farmers, but that it was imperative for farmers to follow chemical company regulations and provide important training for farm managers and workers.[80]

Benitz also favored the "Bracero Program," begun during World War II to bring seasonal farm workers to eastern Washington to harvest crops when the war imposed labor shortages in the region. Every year, Benitz would send travel funds to families in Mexico to come and take temporary agricultural work at his farm. By 1964, more than 4.5 million Mexican nationals were legally contracted for work in the United States, many in eastern Washington. Housing was provided by the host farmer. The family worked all season, moving from crop to crop. At season's end, the people would return to Mexico. By the 1960s, some families began to stay over and make permanent homes in eastern Washington. While some criticized the program as being exploitive, Benitz found it beneficial and treated the workers fairly.[81]

The Food and Agriculture Act of 1965[82] was another cause for concern for Max Benitz and the Washington State Farm Bureau that year. The Act was the first multi-year farm legislation, and provided for four-year price supports by the government for farmers who agreed to participate in existing acreage reduction programs. It applied to wheat, feed grains and cotton, and included a wheat certification provision. It also authorized a Class I milk base plan for 75 federal milk marketing orders. In 1968, the Act was amended to extend through 1970, and stood until President Nixon's Agriculture Act was passed in 1970.[83] Like his opposition to wheat certificates and government wheat control programs, Benitz opposed federal intervention in the milk industry. Extensive federal regulations were developed for various classes of milk and milk products, with federal price supports guaranteed for farms that complied with production limits. Regional compacts and dairy pools were

5. Parathion is an organophosphate insecticide sold under various trade names but manufactured by Miles Inc. of Kansas City, Missouri. It was banned by the Environmental Protection Agency in 1992.

developed, leading to extensive lobbying for unrealistically high price supports.[84] Benitz believed that market forces and the basic law of supply and demand should govern the dairy industry.

In his President's Report to the state Farm Bureau near the end of 1965, Benitz said that passage of that year's Food and Agriculture Act gave him "great cause for concern." It gave even larger powers to the Secretary of Agriculture, he stated, and made more farmers dependent on government compensatory payments for a "major share" of their farm income. Trends were heading in the wrong direction, he said, in terms of big government and "more people leaning on paternalistic government…We in the Farm Bureau are very conscious of a need to protect the free market system. This system is just one of the important parts of the free society we have known in this country for so many years and which we see slipping away from us a little at a time. We have a responsibility to do our part to safeguard the system that has made our standard of living, our individual freedom and dignity, the prize so many other people in the world can never hope to possess."[85]

Believing as strongly as he did in the free market system, Benitz said he was shocked and amazed that December to learn that the Johnson Administration intended to reduce the number of operating farmers to about one million, aiding the other two and a half million "marginal" farmers to find work elsewhere to supplement their incomes. He said the change back to market-based farming in the U.S. would have to be a gradual one, since the federal government had then been in agriculture for 30 years.[86]

He also warned against the tremendous power of union labor, and said that the Johnson Administration had deferred to this power. He hoped the present state legislature would repeal the excess train crew law, known as "featherbedding," which had been on the books since 1911. This law required train crews to include a fireman, even when technology had replaced antiquated, coal-fired train engines with locomotives that burned no fires. The term "featherbedding" became widespread, and was used to denote any job where unions and/or laws required excess personnel who did not contribute to productivity.[87] Railroad management had appealed to Benitz for state Farm Bureau support in repealing the train crew law in Olympia, because doing so would make railroads more competitive. The free market aspects of eliminating this law definitely resonated with Max Benitz.

Benitz was also concerned about food aid on an international level. Could the United States feed the world, he asked. He felt it would be much better to use U.S. agricultural expertise to teach productive farming techniques to other nations, rather than simply export food to them. He used the example of India, where the extraordinarily dry monsoon season of 1965 had produced drought and food shortages. India had been compelled to import nearly 12 million bushels of wheat, with nine million of those tons coming from the United States.[88] Still, food rationing was being instituted in India. "Did we really help them?" asked Benitz. "Before we embark on an all-out effort to feed the world let us learn something from our experience with India. We must realize that the only hope we have to help such countries is to give them the kind of aid that will get them on their own feet. The secret is in giving them the incentive to produce rather than only sending in shipments of food in a way that will wreck what markets they have for their own products. Providing incentive to produce is the key both here in our own country and abroad."[89]

Max Benitz during his tenure as Washington State Farm Bureau President.

In late 1965, Benitz listed his goals for the state Farm Bureau for 1966. He advocated a full time legislative representative in Olympia. The Bureau had had a part-time representative during the 1965 legislative session, and had seen the benefits in having stronger advocacy for farmers' issues. Distinctly, Benitz was becoming more interested in the political process and savvier in recognizing its influence. By now, he was registered lobbyist, and remained so for his remaining four years as

Max Benitz speaks in Calgary, Alberta, 1966.

state Farm Bureau President.[90] For the coming year 1966, he also recommended that the Farm Bureau help Washington apple growers and processers cooperate to maximize their market and influence. Along with Michigan, Washington was becoming a leader in apple production. Potato processing was also becoming big business in Washington state, and Benitz advocated that the Farm Bureau "take and active interest in bringing some order" to the wide variety in potato contracting practices. "We now have about a dozen different potato processors in the state, offering a dozen different contracts saying a dozen different things," he said.[91]

Throughout 1966-67, Benitz traveled extensively. He became well known throughout Washington for his slide presentation and commentary of is visits to the Far East and the U.S.S.R., at a time of intense curiosity about these regions where very few people had had a chance to travel. In 1966, the Association of Washington Industries sponsored Benitz to participate in a statewide tour, speaking about the Far East and the Soviet Union in major Washington communities. Clearly, he was warming to a quasi-political role, and relished speaking with groups about his beliefs.

That year, he also attended the Western Stockmen's 70th annual convention in Calgary, Alberta. His spoke on the topic of "Prices, Produc-

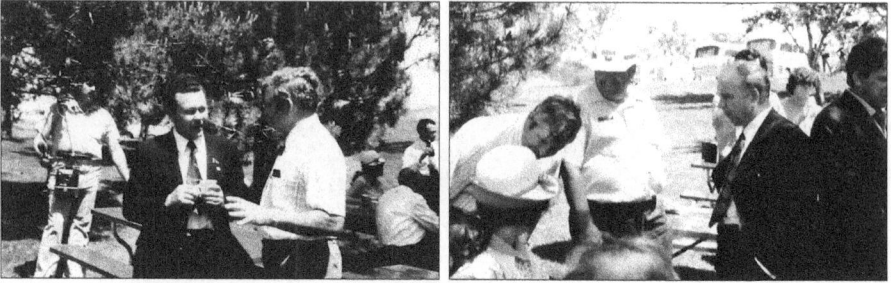

Max Benitz listens to the views of Canadian ranchers, Calgary, 1966.

tion and Politics," and shared his beliefs about the importance of free enterprise in agriculture and the need to keep the government out of the market system. As he did everywhere he went, Benitz also listened to the views and comments of the people with whom he was speaking.

In 1967, Republican Governor Dan Evans appointed Benitz as the one at-large representative to the Washington State Coordinating Council for Occupational and Vocational Education. This council received federal matching funds to go with state appropriations, and was responsible for oversight to ensure the best possible use of taxpayer dollars allocated for occupational and vocational training in the state's 22 community colleges and in some high school programs of the Farmers' Home Administration and Future Farmers of America. Benitz served in this capacity, including three terms as Council chairman, until the CCOE was replaced in 1975 by a new commission. He relished the responsibility, learning all he could about the strengths, shortcomings and needs in vocational education in Washington. Education would become one of his primary concerns in his later political career.[92]

During 1967, Benitz also spoke out in favor of the Agricultural Fair Practices Act of 1967, which was designed to help small farmers by allowing them to form cooperatives to efficiently move their products to market. The Act prohibited buyers from coercing or preventing any producers (farmers) from joining or belonging to voluntary cooperatives, refusing to deal with producers who formed cooperatives, discriminating in pricing or other terms of purchase against cooperatives, paying any producing to leave a cooperative, or making false reports about the management or finances of cooperatives. The Act was passed in April 1968.[93]

1968 Brings Major Foreign Travel and First Election

During late March and early April 1968, Max Benitz toured Japan, Hong Kong and Taiwan to attend meetings of the "Kokusai Noyukai," an association for international collaboration among farmers. The name literally means International Farm Friends Association, but he called it simply "the exchange program."[6] The program had been started in the Administration of President Eisenhower early in the 1950s, when Earl Warren, then-Governor of California, responded to a request from the Japanese government to train young farmers on California farms. The program sponsored young Japanese farmers, bringing them to the United States as "trainees" to learn successful farming techniques. The trainees were given free housing and a small monthly stipend. Their stipends increased gradually as they gained experience and became productive on the farms where they worked. The program had nearly faltered soon after it was started, but the California Farm Bureau and California Extension Service had helped to keep it viable. Now, it was nearly self-supporting, although the Japanese government contributed a small amount. The "Kokusai Noyukai" program also brought young Brazilian farm trainees to the U.S. by this time.

Benitz was interested because the exchange had extended into Washington state in 1967. Some of the trainees from California had attended the Washington State Farm Bureau Convention in Tacoma that year. Benitz also went on the trip to discuss agricultural trade with Japanese officials. He traveled with a group of young farm trainees returning to Japan after their year in the U.S. Other officials from the Farm Bureaus in Washington and Iowa, and from the California Extension Service also accompanied Benitz on the trip.

Max Benitz clearly enjoyed the trip. He was a "people person" and thrived on interaction. In his trip report, he commented on many aspects of Japanese life that he observed while traveling around before the formal meetings began. He said the Japanese had made tremendous strides in recovering from the destruction of World War II, and believed they would become important world traders and exporters in the near future. He believed that Japan would soon need far less U.S. foreign aid. He remarked on formalities and politeness in Japan, saying "you

6. Since 1984, the program has been known as the Worldwide Farmers Exchange, and has sponsored more than 10,000 young farmers from more than 70 countries.

have never in your entire life seen the amount of formality that they go through to make sure that you are having a good time. They are gracious people." At six feet tall, he laughed at the fact that he couldn't fit into the bathtubs at his hotel in Tokyo, even though it was one of the newest and most modern ones in the city.[94]

Benitz was very impressed at the work ethic and courtesy among the Japanese, and he observed the same thing in Taiwan and Hong Kong. "Employees are genuinely sincere with their courtesy in trying to do you a favor or a job for you. They seem to be very interested in their work, from the largest factory down to the very smallest business," he said. He commented that part of the reason could be that unions and companies worked closely together. He described "company unions" as unions formed only from employees of individual companies. He related that "the company explains very carefully that if the company does well, the union does; and if the company doesn't prosper, the union won't be in existence very long." Student apprenticeships in companies also fostered company loyalty. He described the Sony Corporation as a good example. "Visiting their [Sony] factory, we found young, female high school students who are given aptitude tests to see if they can do this particular kind of work. If the tests turn out good, they are given half a day employment at the Sony Corporation and they spend the other half a day in school. Their grades must remain as high as they were when they entered the employee of Sony. This corporation has built a large number of good apartments that they rent to the girls and their employee's at a very reasonable cost. Needless to say, these girls have a tremendous loyalty to the Corporation...We should take a lesson."[95]

As Benitz traveled around Japan visiting farms, he saw real benefit in the Kokusai Noyukai program. Trainees who had come to the U.S. in previous years were changing agriculture for the better in Japan, he said. Water buffalo were gone, and farms had become mechanized, especially with small tractors. Plots were generally small, he said, usually about two hectare or five acres. Japanese farmers did "not waste any space," he said. They were raising more wheat than ever before, but rice was still the main crop.

Benitz described examples of improved farming in citrus and vegetable production, due, in part, to farming chemicals adopted from the United States. In another case, he saw an "impressive" Holstein dairy herd raised by a former trainee from stock purchased in the U.S. Milk had been very expensive in Japan, but the price was coming down due to more successful breeding of Holstein heifers. *"One of the most inspiring farms we saw was a poultry operation"* owned by a former Kokusai Noyukai trainee. The man had learned poultry operations in California and then returned to Japan where he borrowed money and started his own broiler and laying operations. The man's father, who had loaned him part of his money, did not think the new methods would work, but they did. "When the neighbors saw his profit, they began to copy him. Now eggs in Tokyo are about half the price they were ten years ago and the Japanese farmer is making money." Benitz had to laugh, however, when he noted the wages the former trainee was paying. "He had twelve employees and counted his wife a half employee. (It looked like she was about four employees.) He said he paid top wages; the women get 35 cents an hour, and the men got 65 cents to 70 cents an hour."

Benitz noted that several Japanese poultry farmers had formed a co-op to buy American grain by the boatload. Buying in bulk kept their prices down, and provided a good export market for U.S. grain. "So really," he said, "the Japanese people have gained, the farmer has gained, and we in the United States have gained as a place for our exports. Their eggs are of high quality and their feed is good."[96]

During his travels around Tokyo before the farm exchange meetings began, Benitz had a chance to meet President Suharto[7] of Indonesia, who had come to Japan to discuss trade. Suharto was part of a coup that had taken power from left-leaning dictator Sukarno in 1965. Sukarno was kept as a figurehead until 1968, when Suharto assumed full leadership. Although he ruled for too long – 30 years – and became essentially a dictator himself, Suharto was full of promise in 1968. He seemed like a reformer. Max Benitz was impressed that Indonesia has rejected the communist Sukarno and was turning back to capitalism.

Finally it was time for the official Kokusai Noyakai meetings to begin. South Korea had been so impressed with the program that it wanted to participate. U.S. leaders welcomed this participation but when the subject was brought up at the meeting in Tokyo, Japanese delegates did not seem to be positive about it. Historical rivalries between Japan and Korea, as well as bitter memories from the Japanese occupation of Korea during World War II, and during other periods in the past, interfered. Scars were fresh. However, the Japanese eventually accepted South Korean participation. *"Perhaps before a year goes by, we will be able to bring*

7. Like many Indonesians, Suharto used only one name.

some South Korea farmers to the United States as trainees," Benitz hoped. *"It certainly is something to look forward to."*[97]

Once again, Max Benitz saw the bigger picture, and linked farm issues to larger national and international issues. "I think the program can be summed up...[by saying that] as long as you can expand a trainee program such as this that really benefits the nations involved, there will never come a time in the future in which these nations will be throwing bullets and bombs at each other."

Trade talks continued at the meetings. Benitz linked Japanese trade and U.S.-Japanese relations to the Vietnam War, then raging into its fourth year. He was in Japan on March 31, 1968, when President Johnson announced that he would not run for President in the upcoming election. The news was stunning, as the President had vastly escalated the war and staked his foreign policy reputation on it. However, the Tet Offensive in January 1968 showed that North Vietnam was determined to keep fighting and even to take the conflict into the cities of South Vietnam. Student strikes and many other protests against American involvement in the war jumped sharply in early 1968.[98] Benitz noted that editorials in Japan immediately following Johnson's announcement stated that if peace talks failed in the Vietnam conflict and the communists in North Vietnam got stronger, Japan would have no choice but to build up its military to protect its trade. Terms of the Japanese surrender at the end of World War II forbid it to re-arm. Still, Benitz understood that Japan, as an island nation, needed to trade to survive and therefore needed to protect its shipping and trade routes. He warned that the United States needed to be realistic in viewing Japan's needs. "Japan is a country about the size of the state of California. It has about as many mountains as California or even more, which means that there is very little room for the people to live. Yet this area has almost half as many people as we have in the entire United States. They have no natural resources, no oil, no good steel to work with, no rubber, none of the natural things that make a nation great. These people understand fully that they have to trade, and have to manufacture good products...and put them on the market if they are going to survive. They state very plainly that they will...trade with other countries around the world" if U.S. trade negotiations fail.

In talking with Japanese farmers and manufacturers of farm machinery, Benitz saw opportunities for increased U.S. trade, and hoped the potential would materialize. The Japanese had plenty of pending orders, he said, to export farm equipment to Taiwan, Indonesia and other developing countries in the Far East. Japanese tractors were small, he said, because the farms were small. However, he observed that Japan was making a variety of pickup trucks and farm trucks. He especially admired a diesel truck being manufactured in Japan. "I suspect in the very near future we're going to see some of those real good diesel trucks of theirs for sale in this country at highly competitive prices compared to what we now have. One of the reasons they will remain competitive is because their engines will always be efficient; they have to be by necessity . . . all gasoline is imported. They bring the crude oil in huge tankers from the Middle East and then refine it there. This makes gasoline very expensive and consequently they simply have to produce a very efficient motor which would be an advantage to us for economical reasons."

Benitz noted that Japan's two biggest exports were textiles and manufactured garments, and that the U.S. was the biggest customer for these goods. Yet, he said, when the Farm Bureau representatives began discussing selling more agricultural products in Japan, *"we really got hit between the eyes."* The day previous to their discussions, the U.S. Senate had passed a bill limiting textile imports from abroad, and particularly from Japan. Benitz called the situation *"very uncomfortable...* How can you answer their embarrassing questions when they are our biggest customer for agricultural products?" The news of this vote was the second time politics had intervened directly into issues being discussed on the trip. The Japanese "like to do business with us," he said, "but they don't like to do it when they receive the kind of political shenanigan as was pulled in Washington, D.C. in trying to keep the textile imports down... It [the embarrassing situation] was real serious, but once it cooled down, we did talk about agricultural exports to Japan." Max Benitz was thinking....ideas were germinating. Perhaps he should run for political office and try to influence trade in ways that he found more positive.

While in Japan, he endeavored to promote the alfalfa pellet business in the Northwest. "I indicated that we have the land, the sunshine, the right climate and the water, and a wonderful proximity to the Pacific Coast to raise the best alfalfa pellets for export," he reported. The alfalfa pellets would provide the vitamin A and protein badly needed in poultry feed. More healthy chickens would mean that the Japanese standard of living could rise, and the Northwest would have a good market. The Farm Bureau, he said, could step in and help with arrangements, so that the Japanese could obtain large shipments when they needed them, but local farmers in the Northwest would not be left without any pellets for their own feed. "There is some real responsibility here for us that we should not turn over to some other organization," he said. Likewise, the Japanese would need more grain for their poultry feed, and would have to get it from the U.S., Australia or New Zealand. "A new law in Japan allows the farm cooperatives to get into the importing business," he reported. "Previously, there was very little competition. They have high respect for the Farm Bureau and they want to deal with us. The question is, are we going to be ready to deal when they are?"

Summing up his trip to Japan, Benitz said that "the two programs, Young Farmer Exchange and the Trade Program, complement each other. In Japan they have a high respect for Farm Bureau. Their citizens have received good treatment over here [the U.S.]. It is a golden opportunity for the western region of Farm Bureau to make some money for Farm Bureau members and obtain some real work," he said. However, Benitz and his fellow Farm Bureau members wondered why there wasn't more publicity for their programs from the U.S. State Department. Cynically, he concluded, "*the Farm* Bureau does not set well with the present administration in Washington, D.C....because it is the Farm Bureau that made it [these programs] work...until there is a change in Administration, in all probability, we will receive very little publicity on it if any at all."

Benitz spent his last day in Japan in Osaka, helping an old friend from Washington State, Wayne Gentry, setting up exhibits and agricultural displays for an International Trade Fair. Gentry was then director of the Office of Foreign Trade within Washington State's Department of Commerce and Economic Development.[99]

From Osaka, he flew to Taipei, the capitol of Taiwan, an independent nation then formally known as the Republic of China. Taiwan and Hong Kong, another small island which was then still a British protectorate living under a 99-year lease from the People's Republic of China (PRC or communist China or "Red China"[8]), were the last non-communist areas of China. Benitz immediately started observing, asking questions and reporting on his findings. Most of the people in Taipei, he said, were refugees from Red China, and were strongly anti-communist. He reported that they were concerned that America's President would negotiate "*pre-*

8. The term Red China will be used in the narrative, because that was the term most used by Benitz. Red refers to the color of the communist flag.

maturely" with Red China, and compromise their independent status.

Taiwan was still very poor. While Benitz was there, Taipei newspapers reported that the average yearly wage in the small Republic of China had just exceeded $200 per year. He saw water buffalo plowing the rice fields. The economy, while strengthening, had *"a long way to go,"* he said. He was grateful that he had not had "the kind of start in life that many millions have on that island, and the opportunity for much improvement is not real bright." However, he stated, "they too are in the market for a lot of our agriculture products; they too, will manufacture and try to do the best they can." Taiwan, he pointed out, received quite a bit of U.S. foreign aid in the form of agricultural commodities, but also purchased goods for some of its needs.

In Taiwan, Benitz experienced an air raid drill he never forgot. As he described it, authorities pulled a "master switch" on the city of Taipei and "it was absolute darkness for 45 minutes. The lights went out, the elevators stopped, everything went quiet. They really live their national defense there."[100]

For the third time on this memorable trip, national events in the United States reached across the world so that he could see their effects. Civil rights leader Martin Luther King, Jr., was assassinated on April 4, while Benitz was in Taiwan. Riots in many U.S. cities followed the crime. Benitz described meeting some Australian cattlemen in Taipei who were en route to the United States to make some trade deals, but they canceled the remainder of their trip due to the riots. "I think very few of us realize how we are watched around the world. The eyes of the world are upon the United States. Responsibility is thrust upon us whether we like it or not."

Benitz then traveled to Hong Kong, to the small Kowloon Peninsula – the urbanized area of Hong Kong on its north side. Hong Kong at that time was British protectorate living under a 99-year lease from Red China. The lease was due to expire in 1997, and Benitz wondered what would happen.[9] He termed Hong Kong "the most interesting place I have ever visited." As in Taiwan, in Hong Kong he saw thousands of refugees from Red China, and he saw poverty. Refugees, he said, "live in places in which you would not believe any human being could live. The British government has built apartments six to ten stories high to try to take care of the people... a tremendous amount of people [have crowded in] there. They run to do a job for you, they do it in double time for their

9. In 1997, Hong Kong did become part of the People's Republic of China.

regular employer, tourist, or whoever it happens to be." Most of Hong Kong was fed by food from Red China. The income from these food sales was important to Red China, which made him think the PRC's government might renew its lease to Britain for Hong Kong in 1997. Despite the poverty in Hong Kong, he did note "a tremendous amount of activity going and many new buildings going up."

Ever curious, Benitz took a side trip to the Red Chinese border, about 30 miles outside of Hong Kong. He was able to get about one/quarter mile from the fenced border, and could look down and see the guards, guard gates and weapons. "It was a beautiful day, but it made me shudder when I stood there and took a real peak behind the Bamboo Curtain." Although Benitz could not know it at the time, Red China was struggling mightily. An enormous famine, now known as Mao's Famine or the Great Catastrophe, had killed millions between 1958-1962. Later government estimates reported that about 15 million people died, but independent historians have placed the number between 36-45 million people. Benitz would have been interested to know that today most who have studied the famine conclude that Mao's "Great Leap Forward" policies, especially rapid farm collectivization, were the prime cause.[101] In addition, he could not know of the repressive horrors of the Chinese Cultural Revolution, which lasted from 1966 through 1976. Liberals and even moderates were purged from the Chinese communist party and often killed or at least exiled to farm and labor camps where many died of malnutrition and exhaustion. In early 1968, during Benitz's visit to nearby Hong Kong, Red China was enduring some of the worst and most violent paroxysms of the Cultural Revolution, making the world behind what he termed the "Bamboo Curtain" more hellish than even he could imagine.[102]

From Hong Kong, Benitz flew to San Francisco to attend a meeting of the Cal-Farm Life and Casualty Company. As soon as he returned, he began giving speeches about his trip and his observations to local groups in the Tri Cities[10] and Prosser area. In June, he told the Pasco Chamber of Commerce of the huge potential for Washington agricultural products in Japan. "They're improving their diet [the Japanese] and want more meat…if we don't fill their orders in that tremendous market, someone else will," he stated. He also noted a large market opening for alfalfa pellets. He was proud that Washington had been the only state to have an exhibit at the International Trade Fair in Osaka. He contin-

10. The Tri-Cities of Washington State include Pasco, Kennewick and Richland.

uously pointed out the benefits of the free enterprise system, citing an "old-fashioned and unusable" Russian tractor he had seen at the fair in Osaka fair. "Their [Russia's] machinery is not developed because they have no incentive to compete," he observed. He also contrasted richly developed land in Hong Kong with barren land that he observed just across a river in Communist China.[103]

In May, Benitz resigned as President of the state Farm Bureau in order to declare his candidacy for State Representative from District 8B.[11-][104] He later said that he decided to run because he believed "someone with experience in agriculture needs to be there to speak up for agriculture."[105] Declaring his candidacy before the Prosser Chamber of Commerce that spring, he stated "I would like to be a part, even if only a very small part, of an effort to get our country back to what it was originally intended to be...we must have a return to the family as the basic element of a stable society. And we must have a return to law and order...and we need more local concern, more local control." He said he was "convinced that the future of Central Washington is based on agriculture, selective industry and distribution. I hope and believe I am qualified to protect and enhance these industries."[106] Benitz ran for the position being vacated by Republican Walt Reese, who endorsed him in the contest.

Benitz's campaign began with a primary race that he later described as "difficult" and "the hardest race I was ever in." His opponent was scientist, Lyle Perrigo, whom Benitz later stated was "Dan Evans' hand-picked choice."[107] He went to Perrigo and said "let's be honorable about it [the primary race]." Benitz campaigned throughout the summer and fall of 1968 on the same principles he had stood for as state Farm Bureau President - small government, fiscal responsibility, and market economics. He promised he would "work for reductions in federal spending and a return to the states of tax monies now going to Washington, D.C. This will return government closer to the people and provide more local control...[In addition he would] work to established a firm 25% ceiling on all property tax assessments, to abolish the B&O [Business and Occupation] tax and to eliminate the need for special levies to finance schools."[108] Trade for his district and for all of Washington State, and vocational education, were important to him. He stated that he was "a strong proponent of the competitive enterprise system and...I am convinced that our system of government needs legislators who have had

11. District 8B essentially included Benton County but not including Kennewick and some south Richland areas. Later, District 8 was consolidated in 1972 to include those areas.

much experience in the three principal fields which make our economy work. Those fields are labor, management and capital. . .with [my] experiences in [these fields] I will work equally as hard for efficiency and economy in state government."[109]

In his campaign, Benitz enlisted the help of associates and friends he had made in the Farm Bureau and on the CCOE. He also had some unusual help from a pilot named Emery Tresham, who volunteered and flew over the district in a helicopter advertising Benitz's candidacy through a bullhorn. He related that Benitz had saved his life when Tresham's small plane crashed near Benitz's farm in 1953. "Max, who was nearby, chopped me out of the wreckage and supervised getting me to the hospital...Without him I would have been dead." When he heard that Benitz was running for office, he offered the fairly expensive gift of his helicopter and his time for free. "If I flew 100 hours for Max," Tresham said, "it wouldn't balance the account."[110]

Benitz aligned his campaign with those of Congressional Representative Catherine May, Governor Evans, and Presidential candidate Richard Nixon. May, a Republican from Yakima, was a member of the House Agriculture Committee, and one of the first women to serve in Congress. It was a good year for all four Republicans, as May, Evans, Nixon and Benitz were each elected to the positions they sought. Benitz defeated Democrat Glenn Gunn by a wide margin of more than 15 percentage points. He received nearly 80 percent of the Republican votes cast in Prosser. The entire campaign cost only $9,900.44![111]

Max Benitz campaign flier, 1968.

Max Benitz being sworn in for his first term as a State Representative, by Justice Orris Hamilton, January 1969.

Chapter Two:
Early Years in the State Legislature
1969-1971 Budget Crisis

As Max Benitz's first term in the State Legislature began in January 1969, Washington state was just beginning an economic recession. The Puget Sound (Seattle-Everett-Tacoma area) had experienced enormous growth in the 1960s, largely due to aerospace work at Seattle's large Boeing Company, fueled by the U.S.-Soviet "Space Race." Production of commercial airliners at Boeing was also big business, as the number of miles traveled by airline passengers in the U.S. jumped by nearly four-fold in the decade 1960-1970. In addition, guided missile frigates were being constructed at the Puget Sound Naval Station, and in 1965 the new U.S. "nuclear Navy" began sending nuclear powered submarines to the station to be maintained. The Port of Tacoma, home to huge shipping businesses, expanded considerably, building new terminals to accommodate the new practice of "containerizing" cargo. The booming regional economy was so robust that the president of Seattle-First National Bank, the region's largest bank, termed the era the "soaring 1960s."[112]

However, in 1969 Boeing's workforce began to decline from its 1968 high. The first new 747, the first wide-body airliner ever produced, made its first test flight in February 1969, and began passenger service in 1970. It was two and one-half times the size of the 707, Boeing's previous model that had been the most popular commercial airliner up to that time. The 747 had a characteristic humpback upper deck in the front, and was sometimes called the "Queen of the Skies." Although successful, the 747 could not sustain Boeing through deep cuts in government aerospace work. The national economy began slumping as the U.S. struggled to pay for the social programs of President Lyndon Johnson's "Great Society," and the debts from the Vietnam War. Growth in airline passenger travel slowed, and Boeing went 17 months during 1970-71 without a single order from a U.S. airline. In March 1971, the U.S. Senate rejected further development of Boeing's "supersonic transport" (SST), an aircraft with both passenger and military applications. By late 1971,

Boeing's workforce was down to less than a third that of 1968, and the company was fighting off bankruptcy. The economy was so poor that two real estate agents put up an iconic billboard near SeaTac Airport in 1971, asking: "Will the Last Person Leaving Seattle – Turn Out the Lights." Seattle's unemployment rate stood at 13 percent, more than double the national average at that time.[113] In an effort to boost visibility for Boeing, Benitz attended a ceremony at the company when the first 747 rolled off the assembly line. He kicked a tire and said, "change the color and I'll take one."

To help fix the state's budget, Washington's Republican Governor Dan Evans began the 1969 legislative session by asking for a state income

Benitz, fourth from left, poses with first Boeing 747 and other dignitaries.

tax. Washington State revenues have always been derived mainly from a state sales tax. In the Legislature that year, Republicans held a strong majority of 56-43 in the House, and Democrats controlled the Senate 27-22. The Legislature passed a joint resolution supporting Evans' income tax measure, but voters turned it down that November by more than two to one. The 1969 session closed without resolving the state's budget shortfall, so Evans called a special session in early 1970.[12] Benitz spoke out that winter against a state income tax and increased welfare benefits, telling the Prosser Chamber of Commerce that he went to Olympia intending to vote for a state income tax, but after he arrived he changed his mind. He was "convinced [that] if we have a state income tax with no limit, it will go up rapidly." He favored an increase in the state sales tax, if needed, rather than an income tax "since this [sales tax] would affect all people." He added that "no taxpayer is really safe as long as the show is carried out in Olympia…where there are more ideas on how to spend taxpayers' money." He also stated that overly generous welfare benefits would simply draw more interested recipients to Washington state, and 'somewhere we must get better control or we're going to have more people on public assistance than before."[114]

In the end, the 1970 legislative session increased the state sales tax by one/half cent and gave local governments the power to impose an additional one/half cent sales tax if they chose. Along with Representative George Clark (R – King County), Benitz sponsored this "local option tax." Given that fact that more taxes were passed, this tax and the small increase in sales tax pleased Benitz more than would have other solutions. "We gave the cities like Richland and Kennewick the power to use a one-half percent sales tax to fund essential local services," he told his constituents. "The cities (and counties) must make provisions so that if people don't like the new taxes, they can vote to repeal them."[115] The 1970 session also extended the state Business and Occupation (B&O) tax to banks.[116] Benitz, a member of the House Committee on Revenue and Taxation, was extremely wary of imposing more taxes, especially at the state level, as he believed that new taxes ought to be imposed at the local level so voters could directly express their views by voting them down if they chose. He told his constituents that he believed in "weighing the needs of the taxpayer for relief from rising taxes, without losing sight of long-range investments in sound government and economic growth needed to protect our future citizens."[117]

Benitz's dedication to small taxes, assessed at the local level, was recognized at a tongue-in-cheek ceremony at the closing session of the State Legislature in 1970 in Olympia. He was presented with a painting said to depict Governor Evans in a "seventh term" still seeking tax reform. At

12. In those years, the Washington State Legislature met only every other year. It did not begin meeting in regular session every year until 1984.

Max Benitz shows his Prosser constituents the stack of bills passed during his first session in the State Legislature.

the ceremony, Benitz was jokingly called the "freshman legislator who talked the most about tax reform and gave the governor the most trouble."[118]

Another issue Benitz supported in his first term in the legislature was a proposal to merge four large railroads, the Great Northern Railway, Northern Pacific Railway, Chicago, Burlington and Quincy and the Spokane Portland & Seattle. As state Farm Bureau President he had supported the measure, because he believed it would improve service and reduce freight rates for farmers. He said sales of Washington fruit in eastern states had declined proportionately in recent years because of railroad rate boosts. Although the merger decision was not in the purview of the Washington legislature, Benitz spoke in favor of it when he could. The decision was controversial because it was seen by some as creating a regional monopoly. The merger occurred in March, 1970, creating the Burlington Northern Railroad, the largest railroad in the

U.S. at that time.[119]

Always interested in education, Benitz was elected as vice-chairman of the Coordinating Council for Occupation Education (CCOE) during the 1970 session. That spring he was also appointed by House Speaker Tom Copeland (R-Walla Walla) to a Special Levy Study Commission to help decide the needs of basic education and how to pay for it in the state.[120] Later, Benitz would recall his first session as a state legislator as a "very trying time…Coming in as a brand new freshman, not knowing much about the legislative process."[121]

The Space Race

During Benitz's first year in the state Legislature, historic events continued to unfold. On July 21, 1969 America astronaut Neil Armstrong became the first human to land and step on the moon. Armstrong's moon landing was the culmination of the "Space Race," essentially part of the military competition of the Cold War between the U.S. and Union of Soviet Socialist Republics (U.S.S.R. or Soviet Union). President Dwight Eisenhower had pursued the race quietly, but vigorously, and with flair by Presidents Kennedy and Johnson. The Soviet launch of "Sputnik" on October 4, 1957, the first satellite to orbit the earth, did more than wound U.S. national pride and prestige. Its military potential worried American citizens and policy-makers. Although Sputnik did little more than emit radio beeps, the U.S. Senate Armed Services Committee almost immediately held hearings in a specially reactivated Preparedness Subcommittee. At those hearings, then-Senate Majority Leader Lyndon Johnson asserted that "control of space means control of the world…the Soviet Union has appraised control of space as a goal of such consequence that achievement of such control has been made a first aim of national policy." Americans were concerned that the Soviets could perfect Sputnik and follow-on technology so their satellites could rain missiles on the U.S., control the weather by causing droughts and floods, raise sea levels, divert the gulf stream and change tides and temperatures.[122] Communities formed voluntary watches in which residents patrolled building rooftops to spot and report orbiting Soviet vehicles.

Max Benitz supported the Space Race, and, although not a supporter of President Kennedy, he was intrigued by the visionary determination the young President articulated. Kennedy told an audience at Rice University in Houston, Texas in September 1962 that, in the new frontier of

Max Benitz at NASA, with Apollo 8 -- Lunar Test Article 9 (LTA-8), Houston, Texas, December, 1971.

space "there is new knowledge to be gained, and new rights to be won, and they must be won and used for the progress of all people. For space science, like nuclear science and all technology, has no conscience of its own. Whether it will become a force for good or ill depends on man, and only if the United States occupies a position of pre-eminence can we help decide whether this new ocean will be a sea of peace or a new terrifying theater of war... We choose to go to the moon in this decade and do the other things, not because they are easy, but because they are hard, because that goal will serve to organize and measure the best of our energies and skills."[123] Space technology and superiority were important to the United States, Benitz believed, but the Space Race was expensive. The costs worried this fiscal conservative. After Armstrong's successful moon landing in Apollo 11 in 1969 clearly established American dominance in the space contest, President Johnson sharply cut back the National Aeronautics and Space Administration (NASA) budget.[124]

When President Richard Nixon was elected in 1968, he was presented with ambitious plans by NASA managers to establish a manned moon base by 1980 and send a man to Mars by 1983. Nixon decided

*In March 1970, Benitz took time to visit his
birthplace of Wathena, Kansas, where he was photographed
with his first cousin, Shelby Smith, who became the
Republican Lieutenant Governor of Kansas five years later.*

Benitz with future Governor Shelby Smith in Wathena, Kansas, March 1970.

against these missions, and concentrated on the space shuttle program
instead.[125] Benitz, an early Nixon supporter, characteristically wanted
to see and learn about the space program for himself. Although decisions about NASA's future would not be made in the Washington State
Legislature, he believed elected officials at all levels had a duty to stay
informed on important national and international issues. Benitz visited
the NASA Center in Houston[13] in 1970, to study program costs and benefits to the nation. He was very positive about America's space program.

In March 1970, Benitz took time to visit his birthplace of Wathena,
Kansas, where he was photographed with his first cousin, Shelby Smith,
who became the Republican Lieutenant Governor of Kansas five years
later.

13. The NASA Houston facility was re-named the Johnson Space Center in 1973

Second and Third Terms In State House

Back in Washington state, Benitz announced his candidacy for re-election in July 1970. He campaigned based on his record of supporting agriculture, vocational education and lower taxes. It was his "firm belief," he said, that "state spending must be carefully watched to avoid deficits."[126] He was featured that year in an hour-long documentary on CBS Television about the Neighbors in Need Project, a partnership begun by five church denominations called the Ecumenical Metropolitan Ministry, that opened and supplied 34 food banks in the Seattle area and Yakima in 1970, in response to the severe layoffs by Boeing and other major employers.[14-127]

Aside from fiscal conservatism, advocacy for foreign trade and the free market system, and opposition to government price controls, Benitz campaigned against legalization of marijuana. He had led the fight against that measure in the State House during the previous session. In addition, he campaigned in favor of greater availability of federal student loans, and educational benefits for prisoners of war and Vietnam veterans. In a debate shortly before the election, he was accused of being against environmental protection. He defended his vote against a bill that would have made oil companies responsible for damages cause by oil spills because he said that bill went "too far" and would have driven refineries out of the state by leaving them open to penalties for "acts of God." He also defended his vote against a Seacoast management Bill because he said it violated private property rights because "it would have zoned all land within 1,000 feet of the high tide mark for public use."[128]

In the November election, Benitz defeated Democrat Walter (Joe) Shipman, who was Mayor Pro-tem of Richland Washington, by nearly ten percentage points.[129] When President Nixon visited the Tri-Cities on September 26, 1971, he congratulated Benitz on his 1970 victory. Benitz shared Nixon's beliefs in a strong national defense and a leadership role based on respect for America in the world.

During his three terms in the State House, Benitz served on the Higher Education Committee, and was Chairman for two years beginning in 1972. He was also a member of the House Committee on Revenue and Taxation, where he chaired a subcommittee on Forest Taxes, and

---

14. Neighbors in Need is today known as Northwest Harvest, a non-profit that today secures approximately 26 million pounds of food each year for distribution through a network of more than 350 partner food banks, meal programs and high-need schools.

Max Benitz discusses policies of the national Education Commission of the States (ECS) with President Richard Nixon, September 26, 1971, Richland WA. Benitz was an ECS member.

he participated actively as a member of the Committee on Agriculture. As an elected official, he often said that "the only person who deserves public office is the one who justifies it every day."[130] He also was named vice-chairman of the House Committee on Education and Libraries in late 1970, and was re-elected as vice-chairman of the CCOE in June 1971 and June 1972. In addition, he served repeatedly as Washington State's representative to the annual convention of the American Vocational Association, and represented the state's education program at the annual meeting of the Education Commission of the States. [131]

In 1971, Governor Evans again proposed personal and corporate income taxes. The Democrats had gained seats in both chambers, so that they now held a substantial majority in the Senate (29-20), and the Republicans held the House by only a slim majority (51-48). Unemployment levels were up substantially in the state, and a large number of welfare recipients marched on Olympia seeking additional benefits. The Legislature approved extending unemployment benefits but did not act to increase welfare benefits. Benitz favored both of those decisions. The Legislature also repealed the prohibition against state lotteries, but, true to his word, Governor Evans vetoed a bill that would have legalized punchboards and pull tabs. He favored only bingo and raffles.[132] Benitz disapproved of all forms of gambling.[133] The Legislature limited annual increases in local property taxes to six percent, and in a special session in 1972 passed a constitutional amendment that limited property tax levies to one percent of the property's value. Governor Evans opened

Benitz (left) with Erret Deck of the Washington State Department of Agriculture and Senator Dan Jolly of (D-Spokane) (right), with Governor Dan Evans (seated).

the special 1972 session with an economic recovery package he called "Jobs Now," that included a series of bond issues and a sales tax on gasoline. The gas tax was roundly rejected in the Legislature and the bond issues were referred to the voters in initiatives on the November, 1972 ballot.   Measures for Open Government (generally favored by Democrats more than Republicans), and a state Equal Rights Amendment were also placed on the ballot. The Legislature did pass a modest supplemental budget, and in November, voters passed five of the six bond issues that were part of the Governor's economic recovery package. The only bond issue turned down by the voters was one for financing public transportation. Max Benitz was pleased that the Open Government Initiative 276 passed by a three-to-one majority, and relived that the Equal Rights Amendment passed, albeit by a tiny majority (50.1 percent to 49.9 percent).[134]

In the 1972 elections, Democrats swept the nation, partly in reaction to public disgust over the growing Watergate[15] scandal and Nixon's failure to end the Vietnam War. Washington State was no exception. Democrats gained a 58-41 majority in the State House, and retained their majority in the State Senate (30-19), making it harder for Benitz and other Republicans to accomplish their goals. In the 8th District (now renamed and redistricted to include Kennewick and all of Richland), Benitz defeated former Democratic National Committeewoman Pat Cochrane of Richland, again winning handily by nearly ten percentage points.[135]

Taxes were again a dominant theme in the 1973 legislative session in Olympia, and an income tax was once again considered. Two-thirds of both legislative houses voted to send the issue to the voters as an initiative once again. It was defeated by a three to one margin in November, the sixth such defeat in 40 years.[136] Just before the defeat, he wrote that "the unrelenting drive to impose an income tax in the state of Washington goes on. The new income tax proposal on this November's ballot is the sixth try in less than 40 years to impose an income tax in this state. Most recently, the 1970 election saw the defeat by the people of one income tax proposal with a margin of more than two to one against it. This message is clear to me. The next proposal to the people must be the most responsible one we can come up with as well as being simple, clear, and concise. I do not believe the proposal on the ballot for this November's election meets those requirements."[137]

No new taxes were enacted by the Legislature in 1973, but it did pass large salary increases for public officials and tripled the pay of legislators. The pay increases were met by public outrage and almost immediately put to a public initiative. Benitz opposed the size of the increases. They were defeated overwhelmingly, and salaries were limited to a 5.5 percent rise over 1965 levels. The Governor once again called a special session in 1974, passing a supplemental budget by one vote. That session overrode an unprecedented number of the Governor's vetoes, and some conservative Republicans like Benitz were not happy with their Governor.[138] He later described his 1973-74 term in the State House as "very frustrating. It was very very hard to get anything done."[139]

Open Space legislation was a key issue in the early 1970s, and in 1970 the State Legislature had passed the Open Space Taxation Act, also

---

15. In June 1972, Republicans broke into the Democrat party offices in the Watergate business complex in Washington, D.C. The scandal over the effort to steal Democrat election strategies engulfed higher and higher level accomplices, and eventually led to the resignation of President Nixon in August 1974.

known as the "Current Use" law. Basically, the law aimed to protect farm and forest land from development or "over-development" by those who wanted to exploit its scenic beauty or proximity to urban areas by developing vacation homes or suburban sprawl tracts. Because tax assessments are based on "comparable sales, new developments would raise property values above amounts that farmers could, or traditionally did, pay. Without the law, farmers and foresters worried, they would not be able to afford to keep their land, because tax assessments would be based on price levels far surpassing prices justified by the income producing ability of the property for farm or forestry purposes.[140] Benitz championed the Open Space cause, which continued to be challenged, year after year, by Democrats in the State Legislature. Looking back at the 1973 legislative session, Benitz expressed his pleasure that "the people voted a limitation on property tax of 1% of 'true and fair value,' to be exceeded only by a vote of the electors. I am very pleased to have the...1% limitation [placed]. For the past 10 years I have worked to place that measure before the people. Many citizens then ask why their property taxes continue to go up. Chiefly, because of the definition of 'true and fair value.' The Department of Revenue in Olympia, seems to have a never-ending campaign to force the assessor to raise the true and fair value figures higher each succeeding year...If agriculture is to produce food and fiber for our many customers, we must have the ability to tax that land for agricultural production."[141]

Due to his involvement in these key issues, Benitz became one of Washington's best-known public speakers on the subjects of international trade, state budget and taxation policy, agriculture and vocational education, during his years as a State Representative. He also continued to operate and grow his farm.

Washington's economy continued to be troubled throughout 1969-1974, Benitz's years as a State Representative. In 1973, a drought brought "brown-outs" to Benitz's district, as well as other eastern Washington areas dependent on hydroelectric dams for much of their power. Irrigated farming was particularly hard hit. Then the "real energy crisis" hit. Late in the year, the Organization of Petroleum Exporting Countries (OPEC) embargoed crude oil to the United States, and then raised prices, due to this nation's support of Israel in the October 1973 war against the Arab states of Egypt and Syria. Consumer prices rose sharply, increasing 12 percent in Washington State in 1974 alone. As the number of farms

Max Benitz speaks at Larson Air Force Base in Grant County, Washington, 1968.

in the state fell, and farmers and ranchers were forced to increase their prices due to higher fuel and water costs, Seattle area housewives organized a boycott to protest the rising cost of beef. Butchers began to see horsemeat and buffalo roasts.[142] The Washington Public Power Supply System (WPPSS), a municipal corporation authorized by the Washington State Legislature, was planning to build five nuclear power plants in the state, the largest single nuclear project in the nation. Construction had just begun on the first plant, but it would be many years before it started producing power. This plant, and two of the others, lay in Benitz's district in Benton County. By 1973, the construction project was already behind schedule, and environmental groups filed lawsuits asking for Environmental Impacts Statements (EISs – required under the national Environmental Policy Act that became law in 1970) to be performed before construction continued. Preparing an EIS involves a long process, and was sure to delay construction and raise costs even further.[143] It was at this time that Max Benitz intensified his interest in the subject that would become the signature issue of his career – energy. It was clear to him that energy – prices, methods of production, shortages, and geopolitical and environmental impacts – would affect every aspect of life in his district, the state and the nation in the years to come.

He set out to learn all that he could.[16]

1974 Brings Senate Race and Soviet Visitors

In 1974, Governor Dan Evans appointed Benitz as Washington's official host for eight high ranking officials from the Soviet Union who visited the state to study newly developed land, irrigation systems and sugar beet culture. The group had been invited by the National Council of Governors. The delegation was headed by A.P. Lyashko, Chairman of the Council of Ministers, Ukrainian Soviet Socialist Republic. The group met first with President Nixon in the White House on May 28, and then toured in Oklahoma, Wyoming, Washington state and California. Benitz enjoyed showing the bountiful productivity of Washington farms to the Soviet delegation.[144] The visit convinced him, more than ever, that agriculture was indeed one of the "fronts" of the Cold War, and that central government control of agriculture, as practiced so vigorously in the Soviet system, was bound to fail wherever it was tried.

Benitz (left) with A.P. Lyashko, Chairman, Council of Ministers, Ukrainian Soviet Socialist Republic, Washington State, 1974.

Soviet agriculture was again experiencing grain and fodder shortages during the visit, as the Ninth Five-Year Plan drew to a close. The U.S.S.R. was forced to buy grain from western countries, and could supply only about one/third of the customary grain shipments to its eastern bloc "satellite" countries such as the German Democratic Republic (GDR or East Germany). This situation forced the eastern European Soviet satellite nations to fend more for themselves and to look to increased trade with western European

16. Max Benitz's views and efforts in energy issues will be discussed in Chapters 3 and 4.

countries. At the same time, their poor economies, and tight Soviet restrictions, left them unable to trade significantly with western nations.[145] In addition, the U.S. Congress was considering the Jackson-Vanik Amendment (named for Senator Henry "Scoop" Jackson [D-Washington] and Congressman Charles Vanik [D-Ohio]). The amendment was known as the "free emigration" provision. It prohibited the U.S. from

granting Most Favored Nation (MFN) trading status to, and imposed other trade restrictions on, countries that denied their citizens the right and opportunity to emigrate freely, or imposed undue taxes or document requirements on citizens trying to emigrate. It was essentially a protest against harsh Soviet policies restricting Jewish persons from leaving the U.S.S.R. for Israel. The Jackson-Vanik Amendment passed unanimously in both houses of Congress, and was signed into law by President Gerald Ford on January 3, 1974.[146] Max Benitz favored the Jackson-Vanik Amendment due to his strong belief in human rights, although

Max and his wife Marie, flash victorious smiles following his win in November 1974.

it wasn't often that he agreed with Senator Jackson, due to Jackson's many liberal stances.[147]

In the meanwhile, on February 1, 1974, Max Benitz had announced his candidacy for the Washington State Senate for the seat being vacated by Senator Damon Canfield of Sunnyside. He told a news conference that he wanted to run because being a Senator would allow him to "concentrate on doing an in-depth job on legislation." The reason was that Senators served four-year terms, unlike Representatives who served two-year terms and had to run for office "all the time." He wanted to fight for more and better vocational education, nuclear power and agriculture, including corporate agriculture. Unlike some others in eastern

Washington, Benitz believed that corporate farms would benefit local produces, not drive them out of business. Although a bill to limit corporate farming bill hadn't moved out of committee during the current legislative session, he didn't consider it "dead...we need food and we need to sell it abroad," he said.[148]

Max Benitz with Vice President Gerald R. Ford at Republican Party State Dinner, Seattle.

During the 1974 Legislative session, and his first Senatorial campaign, one bill that made him most proud, but did not pass that session, aimed to "provide clear-cut guidelines for cities to follow in the regulation of obscene outdoor motion pictures that are easily visible from public thoroughfares and family dwellings...I intend to pursue further the passage of this needed legislation."[149-17] During the campaign, he was "everywhere...plays, supermarkets, meetings," reported the district's largest newspaper, the *Tri-City Herald*.[18] He continued to welcome corporate farming, saying that "increased food production is a national concern, second only to inflation." He also advocated a higher state gas tax, with the funds to be used for highway improvements.[150] His campaign literature featured complimentary statements about his work by the Washington Association of Fire Chiefs, the Washington Council of Police Officers, the Washington State Grange, the Association of Washington Cities, the Washington Public Ports Association, the Washington Association for Children with Learning Disabilities, and the Washington Food Dealers Association, among others. In November 1974, he defeated Democrat Doris Johnson by approximately five percentage points, and became the first state senator from Benton County.[151] At his victory celebration, he

17. In 1977, Washington State voters approved Initiative 335, which prohibited "places where obscene films are publicly and regularly shown or obscene publications a principal stock in trade." Benitz was pleased.
18. Kennewick, WA.

Max Benitz with President Ford during Ford's visit to Washington State, for Annual Republican Party Fall Dinner.

said the biggest task facing Washington State was to increase food production. "We have to get more land under irrigation. We have to show good faith that we're willing to get [more] irrigation projects started in the Tri-Cities area...he said that would be his first goal as Senator."[152]

During Benitz's election campaign of 1974, President Richard Nixon resigned. His vice president, Spiro Agnew, had resigned in 1973, and Republican Representative Gerald Ford (R-Michigan) had become Vice President. Gerald Ford then became President on August 9, 1974. Benitz had met Ford while he was Vice President, and liked him and shared many of his views.

In a later speech, Benitz revealed his thoughts about the Watergate scandal that caused Nixon's resignation. The "Watergate era was one which will be a black mark in our history for a long, long time. The simple fact that the nation survived Watergate, and we as a part survived Watergate, is a great testimonial that the system we have works, and works quite well." However, he added with disdain that he thought the whole Watergate situation was "about as stupid a bit of strategy as I ever heard of in my life…as far as the Republican Party [is concerned]… Any political theorist who would believe we had to try to figure out what the (George) McGovern forces were doing in order to prevent his election to Presidency of the United States…would be about as smart as General Motors breaking into the Ford Motor Company at night to steal their Edsel[19] plans. It makes almost the same amount of sense."[153]

Late 1970s Farm and Education Issues

During most of Max Benitz's years in the Washington State Senate, 1975-1990, Republicans were in the minority. The party gained a slight majority in the middle of the 1981 session, but lost it again in the 1982 elections. Republicans also held a slight majority in the State Senate during 1988-89. Throughout most of his years in the Senate, Democrats also held a majority in the State House, with the exception of 1979, when the House was evenly divided, and 1981-82.[154] Therefore, it was difficult for Republicans to accomplish their agendas. However, Benitz managed to exert considerable influence in his committees. By the mid-1970s, he was deeply enmeshed in the energy issues that would come to define him almost as much as his representation of agriculture.[20]

The 1975 legislative session in Washington State was again dominated by tax issues and contention between the Governor and the Legislature. The session lasted well into June, and was followed by three brief extraordinary sessions in July, August and September. Thus it became the longest session up to that point since the statehood session of 1889-1890. Wrangling over funding for education was the primary reason for the longevity of the 1975 session, as local levies had failed in many areas of the state, but 6,000 teachers and 3,000 students rallied in Olympia demanding more money. By the end of the 1975 session, the education funding issue was still unresolved, and a special session was called for 1976. That session lasted 78 days, much longer than the stated goal of five weeks, and again was dominated by struggles over budget and taxes. Although it pleased no one, especially Benitz, a tax increase was inevitable to meet state expenses. The sales tax was increased one/tenth of one percent, and a six percent surcharge was passed on the B&O tax. The new taxes were expected to raise $36-million, but the Governor

19. Edsel was a Ford Motor Company model produced and sold during 1958-60. It was disastrously unpopular with buyers, and caused the Ford Company to lose millions of dollars. In this context, Benitz was using Edsel as a synonym for failure.
20. Max Benitz's role in energy issues and development will be discussed in Chapter 4.

Max Benitz aboard the USS Constellation, March 30, 1976, and USS Constellation depart Puget Sound to rejoin the Pacific Fleet, April 1976.

said the budget was still $18-million short. Benitz was not pleased with the trends he saw developing in state spending and government growth. Washington State's budget increased more than six-fold between 1965 and 1977, from $1.1-billion to 6.9-million. The number of state employees nearly doubled during the same period, from 30,000 to 50,000.[155] Shortly after the session ended, Governor Evans announced he would not run for a fourth term. Early in 1977, he became president of Evergreen State College.[156]

In the meanwhile, during the long 1975 session, Benitz sponsored, co-sponsored or supported several Senate Bills (SBs) consistent with his interests and views. Among these was a bill imposing fees to allow the state to inspect pesticide use to "eliminate problems created by the use or misuse of any one or all formulations of herbicides."[157] Benitz wanted to make sure pesticides were used properly so that their use could continue. Another multi-part bill specified many agricultural regulations, several of which aimed at giving "affected producers" a voice in various referenda.[158] Given his huge distaste for government dictation of production policy, he wanted to ensure that the concerns of on-the-ground local farmers were heard by government. He also helped shaped a new bill governing bonds for local irrigation districts, and bills imposing stronger penalties on persons violating hunting regulations, more heavily taxing gambling, regionalizing tuition and fees at the University of Washington Medical School so that students from Montana, Idaho and Alaska were exempted from non-resident rates, and establishing a state Department of Veterans Affairs for the first time.[159] Benitz was a strong supporter of veterans' causes and benefits. All of these bills were adopted as law.

Max Benitz visited the Puget Sound Naval Shipyard in March 1976 to learn about the huge facility and try to attract new missions to grow the state's economy. The occasion was completion of an overhaul, lasting more than a year, of the U.S.S. Constellation, a Kitty Hawk-class supercarrier.

During 1976, Benitz was also an active supporter of the local effort to place the Benton County Courthouse, built in Prosser in 1926, on the National Register of Historic Places. The beautiful brick rectangle with white columns surrounding the front doors joined the distinguished National Register on December 12, 1976.[160]

In June 1976, Max Benitz underwent open-heart, coronary bypass surgery in a Spokane Hospital. He recovered quickly and was on his hay-baler in his fields within one week, campaigning at the same time for his second term in the State Senate.[161] During the campaign, Chinese First Secretary (also known as Chairman) Mao-Ze-Dong died on September 9. His rule had been brutal, characterized by the imposition of "pure" communism with essentially no room for personal initiative or privacy. He has been attributed with the murder of 86 million Chinese. The worst years under Mao occurred during the Cultural Revolution[21]

21. The Cultural Revolution was a period of intense repression in China, ending with the death of Mao-Ze-Dong. Intellectuals, teachers and professionals were denounced and sent to work on farms, as an extreme form of communism was enforced.

from 1966-1976. Benitz abhorred Mao and all he stood for, and later noted that the Cultural Revolution had "set China back at least 2 decades."[162]

In 1977, Benitz was named as minority chairman of both the Senate Agriculture Committee and the Higher Education Committee for the upcoming legislative session. He was also a member of the Energy and Utilities Committee, and the Joint Ad Hoc Science and Technology Planning Committee. He would work closely with new Senator-elect Jeannette Hayner (R-Walla Walla), who was named minority chairman of the Judiciary Committee and would also serve on the Energy and Utilities Committee.

Characteristically, Benitz delved into each committee assignment to its fullest. As agriculture grew in eastern Washington and perishable fruits and vegetables were brought from the farms to processing houses, small towns such as Benton City, whose population was only about 1,500, experienced socio-economic effects that they could not handle alone. They had insufficient budgets to repair city streets and provide other services. Benitz led an effort to bring the main thoroughfare of Benton City into the State Highway System. The old bridge over the Yakima River was torn down and a new wider, stronger one replaced it. The roads were improved to handle the farm traffic.

The 45th Washington State Legislature met for one of the longest sessions in its history in 1977. Democrat Dixie Lee Ray, a marine biologist, had been elected as the first woman governor of Washington in 1976. The state was still experiencing the economic recession when she took office in January 1977, but the economy improved so much during the next several months that a budget surplus of nearly $75-million existed by mid-1978. "Increased state revenues have eased the financial crunch which had been projected," Benitz told his constituents in mid-June. He did not want "the spenders" in the State Legislature to get their hands on it.[163] Benitz supported Ray in many of her initiatives, especially in energy, education and fiscal conservatism. Upon taking office Ray tightened state purse strings, began an audit of state salaries and programs, and balanced the state budget.[164] In 1977, she established a trade office in Singapore, making Washington the first state to do so. Ray said that major activities of the office would be to relay information on new trade prospects back to the local business community, coordinate the state's participation in trade fairs and missions, analyze future trends in trade and increase shipping through Washington ports.[165] Benitz, long a proponent of increased foreign trade, especially for Washington's agricultural products, enthusiastically supported Ray in this new venture.

In 1977, the legislature also authorized a salmon enhancement program to increase the population of salmon, and that November state voters passed Initiative 345 eliminating sales tax on most food. Benitz supported both measures enthusiastically, and rejected the predictions of some state Democrats that Initiative 345 would cause a large budget shortfall. "The roof did not fall in [on the budget]," he joked.[166]

Another important taxation issue in 1977 was the variable gas tax, which was passed by the Legislature that year. It provided that motor fuel taxes would be raised or lowered in half-cent increments, based on consumption, between nine and 12 cents. Essentially, the issue was and eastern Washington versus western Washington issue, with eastern Washington Republicans and Democrats joining forces to pass it to make sure their areas received adequate highway funds and most of the funding did not go to the Puget Sound area. Benitz adamantly favored the variable gas tax, and campaigned hard against Initiative 348, which would have repealed it that year. He vowed that if the initiative passed, he would introduce new legislation to give local jurisdictions more options to finance local highway projects. Improving roads in his district was an important issue to Benitz. In November 1977, repeal of the variable gas tax was defeated by the narrowest of margins – 49.95 percent to 50.05 percent.[167]

Benitz was deeply enmeshed in energy issues. He sponsored an important bill during the Extraordinary Session of 1977 stipulating that the state and local governments would have important roles in selecting or siting energy facilities. He wanted to ensure that local environments, natural resources, industries and neighboring populations would be protected against strictly federal decisions. This bill, which became law in July 1977, would presage many important energy bills sponsored by Benitz in the future.[22-168]

Benitz sponsored, co-sponsored or supported additional important bills during the 1977 session. An emergency cloud seeding measure, to be carried out by the state Department of Natural Resources, was authorized.[169] Another key bill provided financing for a tree fruit research center at Washington State University, and another offered free burial

22. Energy issues will be discussed in Chapter 4.

and burial plots to state veterans.[170] Other key bills concerned agriculture, and included a very long measure ensuring good accounting, labeling, transparency and certification for seeds, horticulture district funds and weed control boards; emergency water withdrawal powers for the Department of Ecology; minimum wages for seasonal agricultural employees; and bonds for local irrigation districts. All of these bills became law.[171]

However, in looking back at the State Legislature's accomplishments for the 1977 session, Benitz told his constituents he was most pleased with the passage of two other new laws - The Juvenile Justice Act of 1977 and the Basic Education Act of 1977. "One piece of far-reaching legislation is the new Juvenile Justice Code...[which] goes into effect on July 1, 1978. All of the judges in the Benton-Franklin County Superior Court District supported passage...this [is a] very important field." The Juvenile Justice Act of 1977, governed the management of all juvenile offenders, and emphasized protecting society and holding juveniles accountable for their offenses. Parents were encouraged and required to participate in juvenile offender proceedings against their child. Youth between the ages of eight and eighteen could be charged with the same crimes as adults, if their offenses were serious. Juveniles who committed minor crimes, such as shoplifting, and did not have a record of serious offenses, could be offered diversion instead of being taken to court.[172]

Washington's "Basic Education Act" of 1977 provided the first full funding for basic education in state history. Education was important to Benitz, especially in ensuring that poorer school districts did not suffer. He favored the new measure because, he said, more state funding for education "would eliminate inequalities between districts." It would put "lids" on local levies "and begin a four-year phase-up of state funding for public schools...Making this commitment good will take all of the "new" money the state expects to get until 1982...the state has been experiencing an economic upswing, and it appears that we may continue to have a surplus rather than a shortfall. This would preclude for now, the need for any such tax increase to fulfill our commitment to funding basic education."[173] The new Basic Education Act was passed after Thurston County Superior Court Judge Robert Doran ruled in a landmark decision in January 1977, that it was the duty of the State Legislature to "determine the substantive contents of the basic program of education ... and to provide for...fully sufficient funding."[174] The Basic Education

Act set statewide goals for education, set course offerings for grades Kindergarten through 12, provided that the state would fully fund schools by the 1980-81 school year (including certified staff, buildings and supplies), mandated that the state would fund the handicapped education program and 100 percent of transportation costs, and delineated areas of accountability for certificated staff, including curriculum, discipline, safety, reports to parents and other matters. "This legislation is fairly broad and is expected to require some fine-tuning," Benitz told his constituents. "I am most interested in providing the changes necessary to make the legislation work properly.[175]

At the same time, Benitz stated that he opposed collective bargaining for higher education instructors because 'they are truly of a professional level, and should not be involved in the collective bargaining process." He believed that tuition increases in the state's college were "way overdue. I know the students are opposed but we must increase the amount students contribute to the overall cost of their education." And, as always, he remained dedicated to slowing or "possibly capping" state spending.[176]

Water Rights Issues

In January 1977, Initiative 59 was proposed to Washington state voters for consideration on the upcoming fall ballot. It asked whether "new appropriations of public water for non-public agricultural irrigation should be limited to farms of 2,000 acres or less." It was sometimes called the Family Farm Water Act, because farms larger than 2,000 acres would be limited to receive irrigation for only two 10-year periods. The issue struck right at the heart of Benitz's agricultural district and interests. Eastern Washington, particularly District 8, the driest in the state in annual rainfall, needed irrigation for crops to thrive. Since 1971, with the enactment of that year's Water Rights Act, the state Department of Ecology had made most decisions regarding water allocations and water rights. In principle, Benitz was opposed to any bureau of the government having such power. "This is simply government by bureaucracy and not be elected representatives," he said. "This is a very dangerous trend...As we all know so well there is a strong tendency during the last many years for the legislature to make increasingly greater restrictions on our ability to perform in a free enterprise society."[177]

In addition, he feared that powerful navigation and utility interests would sway state government to allocate more water from regional rivers to their own needs, leaving inadequate water supplies to be pumped out for irrigation. Large food processing companies, owning or looking at tracts of land in eastern Washington, would be driven away if adequate water supplies could not be guaranteed. Neighboring land in Oregon, where large water permits were issued in perpetuity, had seen the construction of four new food processing plants in the past four years, while Washington had seen none. True to Benitz's prediction, sugar beet processing giant U&I, Inc., announced that it would sell its 52,000-acre tract of land in his district in March, two months after Initiative 59 was proposed. "They [U&I Inc.] are tired of being a target, tired of fighting for the right to develop land," Benitz said. Perhaps now that U&I was selling, he continued, Initiative 59 might lose some of its appeal. "Initiative 59 has no target," he stated. "U&I's development in the Horse Heavens [Hills] was the target."[178]

Unfortunately for Benitz, voters approved Initiative 59 by a slim margin of 51 percent to 49 percent in November 1977. In Benton County, the vote was overwhelming against the initiative.[179] Benitz knew that legislation was needed. He worked to fund a state study in 1978, and then to amend the Washington Administrative Code in 1979, to reserve 1,320,000 acre-feet per year of water from the John-Day-McNary Pools (impoundments in the Columbia, Snake, Yakima, and Walla Walla Rivers) to provide a water supply for 330,000 acres of actual and potential farm land south and west of the Tri-Cities.[180]

In the meantime, during 1977-1978, the Yakima River Basin suffered one of the worst droughts on record and Governor Ray set up an Emergency Water Advisory Committee that asked everyone to conserve water and electricity. Benitz immediately began working with state agriculture officials, local farmers and other state legislators. The *Tri-City Herald* called him "the focal point for drought relief legislation" in 1977. Along with State Senator Sid Morrison (R-Zillah), Benitz sponsored legislation that would provide up to $45-million in a grant-loan program to eastern Washington irrigation districts.[181] He also proposed forming a Yakima Valley Conservancy District that would combine existing water control districts in the affected region, and would have the power to assess taxes to fund water storage, drainage, irrigation and recreational projects and other endeavors. It would provide water necessary to irrigate an additional 130,000 acres in the Yakima Valley and increase water storage by 600,000 acre feet. It would be managed an elected board of local officials who would control costs and maintain efficiency by keeping the resources within the control of those using and paying for them.

Benitz attended public meetings to discuss the issue in Yakima and Ellensburg with Morrison. The issue of local control was important to him, for the Yakima River as well as for the massive Columbia into which the Yakima flowed in his district. As Richard Harper of Washington State Department of Agriculture, put it, "a conservancy district could provide the mechanism to battle those who want the Columbia River to flow down the Santa Ana River (in Southern California.)" The consensus in the meetings was the multi-county district, covering Kittitas, Yakima and Benton counties would be the most logical because of their common watershed ties. Benitz promised that enabling legislation would be ready in time for introduction at the upcoming special session of the state legislature in 1978.

No special session of the State Legislature was called in 1978. However, when the next regular session began in January 1979, Benitz introduced two bills aimed at providing adequate and reliable water supplies to the Yakima Valley. One bill would amend the authority of public utility districts (PUDs) to allow them to "contract with irrigation, municipal and industrial water districts through existing authority in the Interlocal Cooperation Act," to provide water for irrigation, domestic and industrial purposes, he said. It would "encourage the full use of the PUD's water-related authority by encouraging them to maintain a necessary water supply, through contracts with existing districts, state and federal agencies, for the construction of reservoirs, enlarging existing reservoirs or off-stream regulating dams." The other bill would call for the creation of a Joint Water Board, whose members would be existing public water service providers. The board would allow the members to combine the financial resources to invest jointly the water-related facilities, such as reservoirs. Its focus would be to provide water to member districts, and, through larger storage facilities, maintain an adequate water supply for members. Benitz emphasized the need to plan ahead to avoid future droughts. "Although it appears that what we in the Valley faced two years ago may have just been a drought scare, I think we should learn from it. With these measures, we can be better assured that our water supply will be adequate to serve our crops, businesses and personal needs if a long drought does occur," he stated.[182]

The *Wenatchee World* (newspaper) called the bill a "major 'sleeper'"

Max Benitz's photos of the AAM's Tractorcade in Washington, DC, January 1978.

item...a controversial bill that might put PUDs, by a vote of the people, into the farm irrigation business...Proponents, led by Benitz, see this as a way of using the PUD's tax base (45 cents per thousand dollars assessed valuation) to provide "seed money" -- financing administrative steps preliminary to selling bonds to pay for irrigation and domestic water project construction...PUDs already are authorized to get into the domestic water and sewage business. This would add irrigation and drainage project by allowing formation of so-called water conservancy districts."[183] Benitz's bill creating a Yakima River Basin Water Enhancement Project (YRBWEP) was passed as SB 2504, the Agricultural Water Supplies Facilities Appropriation. However, the state Department of Ecology denied the appointment of board of directors for nearly eighteen years.[23]

Relief finally came for Yakima Valley farmers when state officials, including Benitz, worked with the U.S. Congress to authorize the YRB-WEP Feasibility Study in December 1979. The project was managed by the U.S. Bureau of Reclamation, and began implementation in 1980 by installing fish passage enhancements, including fish screens and fish

---

23. In 1996, Commissioner Max E. Benitz Jr. (R-Benton County) appointed the first board members and placed the law into operation.

ladders, at major water diversion and dams along the river.[184]

American Agriculture Movement

The American Agriculture Movement (AAM) was started in the fall of 1977, as a protest against the farm policies of the new President Jimmy Carter. The movement demanded that the federal government establish higher prices of various crops, claiming that farmers needed 100 percent parity (equality) between what they had to spend to grow crops versus revenues received from their crops. One of the slogans of the group was "Parity not Charity." Farmers in the movement demanded they make as much profit per acre, adjusted for inflation, as farmers did at the turn of the 20th century. Representatives of AAM met with President Carter on December 24, 1977. Not satisfied with his answers, they held a rally called the "Tractorcade" in January 1978, in which farmers drove their tractors into Washington, D.C., displaying signs that said "Hell No, We Won't Grow."[185]

Max Benitz was curious about the AAM, and wanted to see the impact it might have on Washington, D.C. However, he strongly disagreed with its philosophy. While the AAM wanted greater price supports, Benitz wanted a smaller government role in agriculture. Additionally, the AAM wanted to form chapters similar to those of the Farm Bureau, essentially competing with the Farm Bureau. Benitz believed that negotiation was better than confrontation, and did not like the AAM's call for farmers to force government action by reducing planting by 10 percent.

Still not satisfied with Carter's farm programs, AAM held another Tractorcade rally in Washington, D.C. in February 1979, but Max Benitz did not attend. By this time, he viewed the AAM as both radical and marginal.[186]

Trip To Communist China

In June 1978, Benitz announced that he had received clearance for entry into the People's Republic of China (PRC or Red China) in mid-summer. Benitz was excited, having taken a brief look at the border of the PRC when he was in Taiwan in 1968. He told his constituents that "I will be making this trip entirely with my own funds and not as a representative of anyone. Red China has almost one-fourth of the world's population, now estimated to be over 900 million people in a geographic area almost identical in size to the United States. It is thought by many noted historians that what happens in Red China may well influence the destiny of the world for many generations to come. The Chinese have raised the Bamboo Curtain just a bit and I am pleased to be allowed to take a look."[187]

He traveled with the Association of Washington Generals, a service organization founded in 1970 by John Cherberg, the longest-serving Lieutenant Governor in Washington's history. Cherberg, a Democrat, served under Democrat Governors Rossellini, Ray and Booth Gardner, and Republicans Evans and John Spellman, for a total of 32 years. Because the U.S. and the PRC did not "recognize" each other in formal, diplomatic terms, there could be no official sponsorship of the tour. However, it was clearly a trade mission, undertaken to investigate and promote potential business between Washington State and the PRC.[188] The tour group spent 15 days in Mainland China, visiting Peking (now known as Beijing), Canton, Shanghai and Kweilin. They entered China via Hong Kong and left via Hong Kong and Singapore.[189] In his personal, handwritten notes, Benitz remarked that there was "evidence of change – [people] more friendly each day…[China] needs friends…[It is] now moving to join the world….Over 70% [of people are in] agriculture – want to mechanize [but] how?" He also noted a lot of people with dysentery, many with broken legs, and said the tap water was "bad" and ice cubes were a "luxury." Young people, he said, looked at the Americans as if to say "Why not we too?" He predicted that the government will "need a new cause soon…speeches will not be enough" to keep people oppressed and obedient. As in all Communist countries he visited, Benitz observed that workers were "slow [to perform work] – no incentives" and the fruit was produced with an eye toward "quantity not quality." [190]

Reporting on the trip to his constituents in 1979, he disdained the "welfare state" and its results in Red China. "I looked at that kind of system last year in the People's Republic of China, he said, "and I can guarantee you that…there is equality of outcome. All are poor. Very, very poor….They are very disturbed but with the kind of social system they have, they have no incentive to produce and now they are trying to make a stab at capitalism…As our PRC guide said to us last summer, 'What can you do to help us? We are in dire straits, and we need not only technology, we need many other things if we are to emerge and become part of the world.'"[191]

Gene Wirth, a young agronomist who traveled to China with Benitz,

Benitz rides in push car near Great Wall of China, 1978.

Benitz at Great Wall of China, 1978.

Max Benitz surrounded by crowd of people, Communist China, 1978.

recalled him as a "wise, observant, knowledgeable friend." He said they found that most commerce "operated with abacus, dip pen and ink well. No calculators. No ballpoint or other flow pens. . . a lathe factory was manufacturing heavy lathes without the use of even a micrometer caliper. All 'precision' cuts were with old friction dividers and a metal ruler." He also commented on the tremendous overcrowding in China, and said that "the Chinese have never seen a place as empty as our state [Washington]. And conversely, we don't understand that our riches are often a result of our low population density." And, like Benitz, Wirth observed no "freedom of expression…rights to change jobs if dissatisfied…privacy…[or] freedom to worship…Communist principles degrade individual freedoms of choice and initiative."[192] However, the visit may have helped fulfill its mission of promoting trade, because late that year Boeing announced the sale of several of its 747 aircraft to various airlines in the PRC, and Coca-Cola made public its plans to open a production plant in Shanghai.[24]

The following year, the United States and the PRC officially recog-

---

24. Larger forces for change were already at work in China, primarily the rise to power of Vice-Premier Teng (Deng Xioaping) following the death of Mao-Ze-Dong in 1976. Deng favored "market socialism" and greatly expanded economic reforms and personal financial incentives during his next several years in power.

nized each other and established diplomatic relations as of January 1, 1979. At the end of that month, Vice Premier Teng (later known as Deng Xiaoping) arrived in the United States for a visit that included a trip to the Boeing plant in Everett, Washington. On February 4, Benitz was in the audience when Teng spoke to a luncheon crowd of 600 at the Washington Plaza Hotel ballroom. The *Everett Herald* wrote that Teng was 'the hottest celebrity Seattle had seen since the departure of King Tut, and the best draw until the coming of Neil Diamond.[25][193]

Four months later, President Jimmy Carter signed the Taiwan Relations Act, which stated that commercial, cultural and other relations between the U.S. and Taiwan would be conducted "without official Government representation and without diplomatic relations." Instead, dealings between the two could be carried out by American Institute in Taiwan, a nongovernmental entity incorporated under the laws of the District of Columbia, and the Coordination Council for North American Affairs, a nongovernment al organization in Taiwan. Carter said that the Taiwan Relations Act was "consistent with the understandings we reached in normalizing relations with the Government of the People's Republic of China. It reflects our recognition of that Government as the sole legal government of China."[194] Benitz was contemptuous of Carter's decision to cut official ties with Taiwan. "The Carter Administration absolutely gave away Taiwan as a pawn," he said. "There was no need to do that...The Carter Administration did not show the necessary leadership and gave away something I felt hurt us immensely in the eyes of the world."[195]

Fiscal Conservatism Grows Stronger, 1978-1980

Just after his trip to Red China, Benitz threw himself into his Senate re-election campaign, telling his constituents that he had worked on new laws dealing with not only "drought and water emergency problems... [but] legislation giving local governments a much more equitable share of the nuclear generating tax." As a fiscal conservative, he reminded them that he always worked to keep taxes low and rein in state spending. "I know it meant a lot to you also when a budget containing NO general fund increases emerged from the last session. Good working relationships between myself and some other Republican colleagues...made that a victory for the taxpayers." He predicted "demanding times ahead. The dilemma of how to pay for more costly public services out of sharply

25. Diamond was a popular singer at that time.

Max Benitz being sworn in for his second term in the State Senate, by State Supreme Court Justice William H. Williams, January 8, 1979.

curtailed tax receipts already faces California lawmakers in response to Proposition 13.[26] Similar measures are pending elsewhere. The message is plain. But the solution is not simple. Getting new accountability from the bureaucracy is complex and sometimes painful. I believe our current budget got a good start in these directions already and that fiscal restraint by budget writer can make it possible for us to avail revolutionary tax changes and still live within our means....I hope you will agree and lend me your support."[196]

During the campaign, he also told the Prosser Chamber of Commerce that he was on a "hit list" of organized labor and teachers' unions "designed to remove legislators with conservative labor voting records." The reforms he favored, but unions opposed, he said, included unemployment compensation limitations, as well as curbs on pensions for state employees, teachers and law enforcement, and full funding of Kindergarten-12 public education.[197] However, Benitz easily won re-election to the Washington State Senate, again defeating Doris Johnson, this time by a huge margin of nearly 20 percentage points.[198]

At the same time that Benitz won his election in 1978, the voters

26. Proposition 13 was an initiative passed by the voters of California in June 1978, sharply limiting property taxes to no more than one percent of the property's full cash value.

WARREN G. MAGNUSON, WASH., CHAIRMAN

JOHN C. STENNIS, MISS.
ROBERT C. BYRD, W. VA.
WILLIAM PROXMIRE, WIS.
DANIEL K. INOUYE, HAWAII
ERNEST F. HOLLINGS, S.C.
BIRCH BAYH, IND.
THOMAS F. EAGLETON, MO.
LAWTON CHILES, FLA.
J. BENNETT JOHNSTON, LA.
WALTER D. HUDDLESTON, KY.
QUENTIN N. BURDICK, N. DAK.
PATRICK J. LEAHY, VT.
JIM SASSER, TENN.
DENNIS DE CONCINI, ARIZ.
DALE BUMPERS, ARK.

MILTON R. YOUNG, N. DAK.
CLIFFORD P. CASE, N.J.
EDWARD W. BROOKE, MASS.
MARK O. HATFIELD, OREG.
TED STEVENS, ALASKA
CHARLES MCC. MATHIAS, JR., MD.
RICHARD S. SCHWEIKER, PA.
HENRY BELLMON, OKLA.
LOWELL P. WEICKER, JR., CONN.

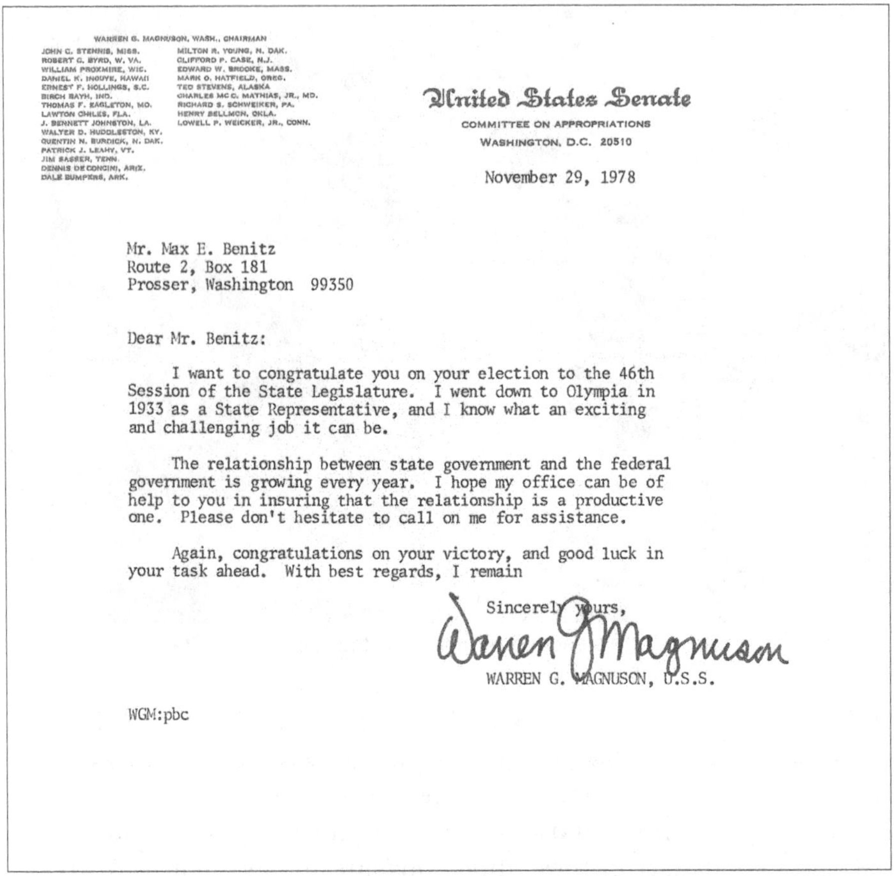

United States Senate
COMMITTEE ON APPROPRIATIONS
WASHINGTON, D.C. 20510

November 29, 1978

Mr. Max E. Benitz
Route 2, Box 181
Prosser, Washington 99350

Dear Mr. Benitz:

I want to congratulate you on your election to the 46th Session of the State Legislature. I went down to Olympia in 1933 as a State Representative, and I know what an exciting and challenging job it can be.

The relationship between state government and the federal government is growing every year. I hope my office can be of help to you in insuring that the relationship is a productive one. Please don't hesitate to call on me for assistance.

Again, congratulations on your victory, and good luck in your task ahead. With best regards, I remain

Sincerely yours,

Warren G. Magnuson

WARREN G. MAGNUSON, U.S.S.

WGM:pbc

Benitz congratulatory letter from Democrat Senator Warren Magnuson, 1978.

of Washington elected 49 Democrats and 49 Republicans to the State House, a huge gain for the Republicans. This fact delighted Benitz, although Democrats still controlled the State Senate by a wide margin. "In our state the 49-49 tie in the House is absolute proof [that voters do not like big spending in government]," he said afterwards. "Who in their wildest imagination would have dreamed that the Democrats in the House would drop from 62-49 in an election year such as we had last November."[199] Benitz said he attributed the Republican "sweep" to the fact that House Democrats had supported a $411-million tax increase during the last legislative session.[200]

His ability to work "across the aisle" with politicians who would champion state issues is shown by his congratulatory letter from Senator Warren Magnuson (D, Washington), then chairman of the powerful

Senate Appropriations Committee.

As the State Legislature convened in early 1979, Benitz took a strong stand against extending the state timber tax, which had expired in December 1978. The State Senate passed SB 2111 in February, extending the previous six and one/half percent tax and applying it retroactively to January 1, 1979. Benitz proposed reducing the tax to five percent, which he said would not decrease state revenues because other proposed legislation would make up the difference through increasing land values. "Extending the present timber tax will "kill the goose that laid the golden egg," he said. "Some legislators here are reluctant to put the 'brakes' on this thing. [But] we must consider helping the timber industry, which is the number one industry in our state…Half of the private industry is made up of small timber companies and…[the] present tax rate would drive many of the small firms out of business."[201] Despite Benitz's opposition, the timber tax bill was extended at the higher level.[202]

Another issue important to Benitz in the 1979 legislative session was reconsideration of a bridge across the Columbia River connecting North Richland with rural Franklin County at Taylor Flats Road (just north of Pasco). In March, he was instrumental in persuading the Senate Transportation Committee to recalculate the cost and write new legislation to build the bridge, which had been studied in various proposals over the previous 20 years. Benitz supported the bridge, and testified in favor of it at a public hearing in Olympia. He knew that funding the bridge was a long shot, but he said he was "cautiously optimistic." In April, he participated, with Senators Morrison and Hayner, Senator Al Henry (D - White Salmon), Chairman of the Senate Transportation Committee and representatives of the State Transportation Department in a meeting in Olympia that hammered out a compromise. Increased tolls would pave the way for access roads to a North Richland bridge, especially in Franklin County. In May, the full Senate authorized a $75-million bond issue in SB 3034, and Governor Ray signed the bill authorizing the bond measure.[203]

Once again, Benitz sponsored, co-sponsored or supported important agriculture bills during the 1979 legislative session. A long and complex bill detailing omnibus agriculture regulations was passed, as were registration requirements for a pesticide control board, inspection fees for commercial feed distributors, licensure mandates for pesticide applicators, appropriations for agricultural water supply facilities, assistance for irrigation districts in developing hydroelectric generation facilities, protection of agricultural activities from nuisance lawsuits and legal immunity for those donating food to nonprofit organizations.[204] All of these bills became law. As always, Benitz believed that if agriculture could be well regulated, with food and pesticide safety ensured, and public confidence in accounting and pricing maintained, that federal control could be minimized.

Benitz also sponsored or co-sponsored additional bills in areas of his core concerns – students, education, the elderly, the ill and infirm, and property rights. He promoted a bill ensuring that state student financial aid was open to students attending all forms of accredited post-high school institutions, including students in vocational schools and performing arts programs; and bills granting reduced rates for Public Utility District serves to low income senior citizens, specifying care standards in nursing homes, as ensuring fair and humane procedures in committing persons for mental health treatment. He also supported a bill specifying that mineral rights and other geothermal resources below ground belonged to the surface landowner, and another bill tightly regulating inheritance taxes.[205]

In April 1979, Benitz was elected vice-chairman of the Agriculture Committee of the Western Conference, Council of State Governments at its meeting in Sacramento, California. He reported that his committee would look at three major issues that had long been important to him. "We'll be primarily concerned with energy for agriculture, federal ownership of state lands and foreign ownership of farm lands," Benitz said. "These are areas in which the federal government is interfering more and more with state powers. Most of the western states resent that interference, so Washington [state] has lots of company."[206]

The Washington State budget was again controversial during the 1979 legislative session. Economic times were relatively good in the state, as a streamlined Boeing had recovered substantially from its slump earlier in the decade. Spending didn't have to be as tight as it had earlier in the decade. Still, fiscal conservatives like Benitz and George W. Scott (R-Seattle), minority leader of the Senate Ways and Means Committee, fought against the budget package proposed by the Senate's Democrat majority. It was $9-billion – a figure $329 million above Governor Ray's request -- and increased state spending by almost 36 percent over two years. During floor debate, Scott offered two amendments that would

JOHN D. SPELLMAN
P.O. Box 4248
Pioneer Square Station
Seattle, Washington 98104

December 2, 1980

Max E Benitz
Rte 2 Box 2521
Prosser, Washington 99350

Dear Max:

Lois and I both wish to extend our personal thanks for your support during my election campaign.

Your assistance helped bring about the tremendous victory that we all celebrated on election night.

My family and I have just returned from a short vacation. We are now looking forward to the challenges that lie ahead for all of us in Olympia.

During the next four years I hope you will continue to remain in touch with my office. Your support will always be needed and appreciated.

Thanks again for a job well done.

Sincerely,

John D. Spellman
Governor-Elect

JDS/s

Encl.

Thanks, Max, I look forward to working with you in a great New Year!

Governor Spellman's Letter of Appreciation to Benitz for help in 1980 election.

have saved $133-million. One of these amendments would have reduced all state agency appropriations by five percent, and the other would have lowered the percentage of pay increases for the Legislature. To the chagrin of Benitz and Scott, both amendments were defeated.[207] The debates were so stormy that the Legislature was called back in extraordinary and reconvened sessions seven times during 1979, a state record.[208] Another issue in the State Legislature that year was abortion, as a House measure

Max and Marie Benitz (right) with John and Lois Spellman, ca. 1980.

was introduced to remove state funding for abortions. After heated debate, the measure lost, and was not reported out for a general vote. In a speech afterwards, Benitz commented that he opposed all "single-issue politics....such as the anti-abortion crusaders, [and] many other crusading interests, who are interested in one issue only. There is considerable danger that we could end up without either party, and that [would be] the end of the two-party system. That would not be in the best interest of this nation."[209]

1980 Campaigns

In May 1980, Max Benitz was elected as Washington State Republican Party Chairman.[210] In this role, he campaigned for Republican candidate John Spellman for Governor. Spellman, a former King County Executive, defeated Democrat Jim McDermott by a wide margin, amidst a nation-wide Republican sweep that also elected Ronald Reagan as President. McDermott had defeated Governor Ray in the primary election. Benitz also met with Reagan's campaign staff and campaigned for the Republican candidate. He was delighted with the Presidential outcome. He had said during the campaign that, "On the national level our present administration is one which I just believe does not have the confidence of the people...[We Republicans will be]doing the utmost to get Jimmy

(Carter) out of the White House."[211]

During the 1980 campaigns, Benitz spoke at length against big government, big spending and the "welfare state." "The welfare state, he said, does not enlarge people's freedom...we can enlarge freedom... [only through] the free enterprise system. Much hard work and the extremely high production of our agriculture and industry are responsible for putting this nation at the top of the world, and it is only because of that that you can afford a welfare state for even a little while," he told an Abe Lincoln Day Republican dinner. "It is also clear that social welfare has grown to the point where it is the central function of all modern governments, welfare is the biggest of big business." He pointed out that public social welfare spending had more than doubled between 1960 and 1976. He squarely blamed the Democrats: "The Democrat party has been the party of big spenders, wasting much of the taxpayers money... Most people winning elections [today]...are turning away from wide-open spending by government and towards more conservative policies. In fact, most candidates, whether they call themselves a Democrat or a Republican, are simply trying to get to the right[27] of their opponents.... we have the best form of government in the world, because no one wants to have government dictate to them." Benitz's fiscal conservatism ran so strong and deep that he simply ignored blatant threats to his career made by lobbyists urging him to change his vote on important budget issues during the 1980 legislative session.[212]

Benitz was a big supporter of the "Reaganomics" policies of Republican Presidential candidate Ronald Reagan. "Reaganomics" basically espoused a return to the free enterprise system in the United States before the Great Depression, and advocated "supply-side" economics, which was the opposite of "demand-stimulus" economics or the welfare state that provided whatever the constituency demanded. Reaganomics advocated reducing the growth of government spending, the federal income tax and capital gains tax and government regulation, and controlling the money supply in order to reduce inflation. Benitz supported these principles even though they would mean reduced federal spending and thus greater burdens for, and demands on, state and local governments. Benitz was also delighted when Republican challenger Slade Gorton defeated long-standing Democrat Senator Warren Magnuson for one of the two U.S. Senate seats from Washington. Magnuson had

27. Right in this context references conservative government, while left would reference liberal policies.

served 36 years in the Senate, and was the senior-most Senator in the nation during his last two years in office.[213]

Benitz continued by worrying about the effect of inflation on the average person's life style and life savings. During the collective decade of the 1970s, inflation in the U.S. reached its 20th century peak, and topped 10 percent in some years.[214] Characteristically, Benitz related the complex issue straight at his audience in ways the members could understand, and he related it to the U.S. position as role model to the world. "People are disturbed about inflation [which] has started the decline of real disposable income of our citizens…They are demanding economies…If we can end this wild spree we've been on it will give us the opportunity to restore stability of the dollar which is so important to those of us involved in our own savings, annuities and pensions, but much greater than that, we, the United States, have an awesome responsibility in protecting not only the liberties we cherish, but also economic stability in the world."

The State Legislature was called into session only briefly in 1980, as it was not a regular session but an extension of the 1979 (46th) session. Nevertheless, it had to meet due to budget shortfalls. During the brief 1980 session, Benitz supported bills specifying mandatory minimum amounts of motor vehicle insurance, and providing funds to maintain delinquency prevention programs.[215] His work in energy issues was consuming increasing amounts of his time and attention.[28]

Mount St. Helens Eruption

On May 18, 1980, in the midst of the campaigns, Mount St. Helens, a volcano in southwest Washington state, erupted, raining ash as far away as Benitz's district in eastern Washington, producing a cloud that darkened the entire state for more than a day and disrupting air traffic throughout the Northwest. The air was so dark that streetlights came on in Spokane, Washington, nearly 300 miles from the blast and even further north and east than Benitz's district. The mountain, previously 9,600 feet above sea level, lost 1,300 feet off the summit. The eruption spewed out a glowing cloud of superheated gas and rock debris moving at nearly supersonic speeds. Everything within eight miles of the blast was wiped out almost instantly. The shockwave rolled over the forest for another 19 miles, leveling century-old trees and aligning their downed trunks to the north. Beyond this "tree down zone" much of the forest

28. Energy issues will be discussed in Chapter 4.

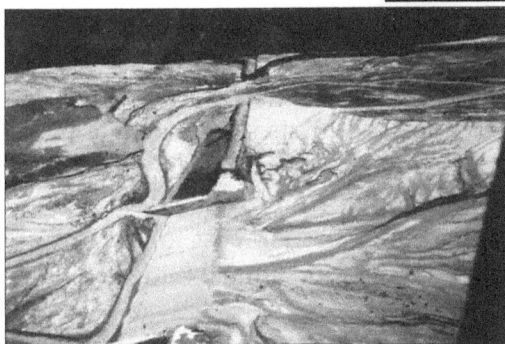

Photos of Mt. St. Helens area taken by Max Benitz shortly after the 1980 eruption.

that remained standing was seared and died. The area devastated by the direct blast force covered an area of nearly 230 square miles. Shortly after the first blast, a second, vertical explosion occurred, sending a mushroom cloud of ash and gases more than 12 miles into the air. Ash continued to erupt for more than nine hours. Ultimately, an estimated 540 million tons of ash drifted up to 2,200 square miles, settling over seven states.[216]

In terms of economic impact, the Mount St. Helens eruption was the most destructive in U.S. history. At least 57 people died, more than 200 homes were destroyed, and more than 185 miles of roads and 15 miles of railways were damaged. Losses to timber, civil works and agriculture were estimated to be about $1.1-billion.

The ash patterns were quirky. The ash, which became sticky when wet, spread mostly north and east, but did not fan out in a gradual pattern. Pullman, Washington area, about 300 miles almost due east of the eruption, was blanketed with about eight tons per acre of ash, and southwestern Montana, roughly 400 miles away, was left with approximately 350 pounds of ash per acre. However, Ritzville, Washington, a small farming community in Adams County just north of Benitz's district, was particularly hard hit. A current of warm, dust-laden air from the west collided with cold air from the east and dumped an average of five inches of ash on the town, but some streets had drifts two to four feet deep. Within hours of the storm, 2,500 stranded motorists sought refuge in Ritzville. Schools, churches and even restaurants were turned into shelters. During the worst of the storm, cars could run only about half an hour in the Ritzville area before stalling. The cleanup cost for Adams County was estimated at $2-million, while the total annual budget was only twice that amount.

Naturally, Max Benitz worried about his constituents, particularly the farmers. About 10 percent of the crops suffered damage in roughly a triangular swath stretching 200 miles to the east. Some alfalfa and wheat fields in eastern Washington were flattened by the weight of ash. Rains fell four days after the blast, and the ash on the ground formed a thick, cement-like stew that many feared would kill young shoots of grain.[217] Benitz's district began just about 195 miles east of the eruption. He served on a Reforestation Committee that rushed to Mount St. Helens by helicopter to take assess the damage, becoming one of the first to visit. However, the damage in the 8th District turned out to be less than feared. The U.S. Congress approved $950 million in emergency funds to the Army Corps of Engineers, the Federal Emergency Management

Agency and the Small Business Administration to help recovery efforts. Benitz told his family that the devastation was "awesome and unbelievable- but we also know the ash is what makes the finest soil in the Pacific Northwest. In a short time, Mother Nature had just replenished her fertile soil."[218]

Early 1980s State Budget Crisis

The 1981 Washington State legislative session was a stormy one. The Republicans took control of the State House for the first time in eight years, with a wide majority of 65-42. The Democrats controlled the Senate by one vote, 25-24, and Republican John Spellman was governor. Inflation was raging, and had stood at 13.5 percent in 1980. While most of the legislators had campaigned on pledges of no new taxes, the state faced a budget shortfall of more than $1-billion when the Legislature convened in January 1981. A minimum of $30-million had to be appropriated to maintain basic services until July 1. The state's economy was in a downturn, making the situation even tighter. In January, Moody's Investors Services,[29] a worldwide business that analyzes credit worthiness, lowered Washington State's credit rating for the second time in two months. As the State House and Senate wrangled over substantial proposed cuts in Medicaid and welfare, events took a dramatic turn on February 13. Democrat Senator Peter Von Reichbauer of Seattle announced that he was switching to the Republican Party, thereby switching control of the Senate to the Republicans. The new majority promptly passed a supplemental budget for the biennium, cutting social programs. A second supplemental budget was passed in April, with even deeper cuts. However, all members realized that new taxes would be required. They enacted a large raise in state college tuition, a slight increase in the gas tax, and several other small taxes. Benitz was still able to achieve passage of a bill appropriating funds for the North Richland toll bridge[30] and for emergency cloud seeding.[219] He also sponsored and passed four

29. Headquartered in New York, New York.
30. However, the North Richland bridge was never built. In a 1982 report, the State Department of Transportation detailed a resource allocation study that showed a higher need for a bridge across the Columbia River between Richland and Pasco along Route I-182. An important factor in lowering the allocation score of the North Richland Bridge proposal was the fact that major nuclear construction projects in North Richland had been cancelled, decreasing the congestion and transportation needs. See Neilsen, Robert, Shea, Daniel, and Yandon, Keith, "A Study of the Allocation of Transportation Resources Through the Evaluation of the Effectiveness of Transportation Services," Washington State Department of Transportation, Final Report WA-RD-43.1, May 1982 at http://www.wsdot.wa.gov/research/reports/fullreports/043.1.pdf The nuclear projects will be discussed in Chapter 4.

Thanks to your help, this moment was possible. Ronald Reagan

Max and Marie Benitz were delighted to be invited to attend the inauguration of President Reagan in Washington, DC, in January 1981, but did not attend.

bills assisting the fledgling Washington wine industry, a new project that interested him immensely.[31] The regular 1980 session adjourned with most members knowing a special session would need to called before the end of the year to find additional revenue.[220]

Benitz was watching the situation carefully, and stood firm in his fiscally conservative views. In mid-year, Governor Spellman declared a state "financial emergency" and proposed a cut of 10 percent across the board for all state agencies.[221] Many of the agencies began complaining publicly. To Benitz, their behavior was unconscionable on two counts. First, he believed that many of the agencies had become greedy and saw constant growth as an entitlement. "The reaction [of agencies], or overreaction, as it was in many circumstances, shows very clearly that State agencies have become ingrained with the idea that they will grow perpetually—that their budgets will be inviolate—that their budgets will always inflate whether or not that agency is making efficient use of the funds allocated and whether or not the taxpayers truly wish to pay for

31. Wine projects will be discussed in Chapter 5.

the "services" rendered." Second, he believed that state agencies, staffed by unelected bureaucrats, were usurping the role of the Legislature and trying to make policy. "I remind you aforehand that State agencies do no govern themselves, they do not perform for the benefit of their administrator, managers or employees - they operate at the bequest of the Legislature and the Governor... - not to rebel against their fiscal policies... They [agencies] are to serve the wishes of the peoples' elected representatives, they are not to serve themselves... It is very disturbing to see a State agency and State employees acting like special interest groups," he said.

It especially infuriated Benitz when state agency executives and boards appealed directly to the public through the press to preserve their budgets. "*We* hear from the school districts that they cannot, or will not educate at the reduced level. They say that they will take the state to court so as not to be required to make the cuts - even though in so doing they may be sentencing every other State program to cuts double the 10% already ordered...the school districts are out to protect themselves at all costs. This is not how government is supposed to operate...The Community College State Board...go[es] to the press with the claim that the 10% cut will 'decimate' the community colleges and the colleges may not survive...Even further off the deep end is Western Washington University [where the President] has made the claim, in the press, that the 10% budget cut could cause the closure of the University. This is a gross over-reaction to a very manageable situation and is a perfect example of the agency mentality I referred to earlier."

Benitz had specific ideas about expenses that could be cut from the state budget, to help make ends meet in 1981. As Chair of the Higher Education Committee, he suggested cutting the "ungraded courses" such as Adult Basic Education, courses for which no tuition was charged such as Senior Citizen classes, and rolling back the tuition waivers state employees and for persons taking General Education Degree (or high-school equivalency) classes. "I agree that these are all, in one way or another, beneficial programs but we are in a fiscal emergency and these are all, I repeat, all, expendable at this time, he advocated. "We must make room for the primary vocational and academic curricula." Benitz also proposed eliminating physical education and athletic programs, consolidating classes and eliminating night classes. "Again, I agree these are nice to have, but they are expendable at this time," he said. He also wanted to "clamp down on fee waivers. We must stop giving away education at community colleges. Some colleges have waiver levels as high as 15%. This is unacceptable."

To achieve long-term efficiency, Benitz stated, nothing was more important that eliminating competition and overlap among nearby colleges. The community colleges in the state system should specialize, so that not every school offered the same classes. Further, state vocational technical institutes and more vocational education classes should be fostered. "It is of great importance that the community colleges begin allocating a greater proportion of their resources to vocational programs. With the unemployment rate skyrocketing and far too many college graduates out of work, we must seriously look at what kind of training is offered at colleges. The most valuable training…that we can offer is the two-year (or four-year) vocational-technical training which…provides job training rather than education for the sake of education."

Returning always to the hard work ethic of his youth and his life, Benitz also advocated that colleges should be strict in enforcing minimum grade point average requirements and not let students repeat course more than twice. "*Any* students who cannot maintain a "C" average for two consecutive quarters should be released from college automatically. Why should the State pay for most of this student's education when the student isn't even putting in the necessary effort to get a "C" average?"[222]

In November, the Governor called another special session of the State Legislature to find additional revenue. Inflation was still at 10.3 percent, and Washington State's economy had continued to deteriorate, and the state was on the verge of defaulting on its obligations. Substantial spending cuts were passed on almost every aspect of state activities, including hiring and travel. Tight restrictions were placed on eligibility for social services, and a temporary sales tax increase from 4.5 percent to 5.4 percent was approved. Still, the gap between state income and spending was several hundred million dollars and no one was happy.[223]

By January 1982, it was evident that substantial new taxes would be needed, and Governor Spellman called a special 60-day session. He created another Tax Advisory Council in 1982, that again recommended personal and corporate income taxes, but the Legislature took no action on either issue.[224] Energy issues, including the very shaky bond ratings and imminent financial collapse at the huge WPPSS project, played heavily into the state's financial dilemmas.[32] The Democrat minority in the Legislature made it clear that participation in solving the state's budget crisis was dependent on extending unemployment benefits. At the end of the session, there was no substantive agreement on which programs to cut and/or which taxes to raise. A second special session was called, during which both houses of the legislature ran out of money for their own operations and had to pass special appropriations to finance their meetings. At the end of the special session in April, after intense wrangling and many compromises, state spending was cut by $142-million and taxes were raised by $272-million. Unemployment benefits were extended for 13 weeks.

However, by July the state was still short $177-million, and the third special session of 1982 was called. The Governor opened the session by stating that he would have to enforce across-the-board spending cuts of 8.2 percent. After a week of intense negotiating, spending was cut by another $100-million, a temporary three percent surcharge on taxes was enacted, and the first state lottery passed by the necessary 60 percent majority. As a safety valve, the Governor was given discretionary authority to impose further spending cuts up to $20-million if it became necessary.[225]

In June 1982, Benitz summed up his views of the 1982 legislative session for his constituents by saying: "The Legislature has made some important advancements… during the 1982 session…[but] There is no doubt in my mind that this was one of the toughest, most heated sessions ever…The toughest issue [of all] during the 1982 session was balancing the state's budget through a combination of spending cutbacks and revenue increases."

The problem, he said, was that "we faced a $1.7 billion deficit this biennium,[33] after 20 years of government overspending, coupled with the most recent economic slump." He squarely blamed the Democrats: "Despite repeated warnings from economists and most Republicans, the 1979 Democrat-controlled Legislature adopted a 1979-81 budget which spent every penny of the state's savings. [This] budget added 5,000 new government employees and increased state spending by 41 percent. Adding to the cash flow problem were previous property tax reductions

32. Energy and WPPSS issues will be discussed in Chapter 4.
33. Biennium refers to the two-year Washington State budget cycle. The Legislature that begins meeting in an odd-numbered year appropriates budget for that year and the following year (a "biennium").

and the voter-mandated elimination of the state inheritance tax. The sluggish economy and previous Democrat overspending left the state $800 million in the red[34]…Combined with federal budget cuts and the continued decline in tax revenues, we made budget adjustments totaling $2 billion, including a provision for some reserve funds."

The "paramount" step in "averting financial disaster" he reported, was reducing "the cost and the size of state government. About 60 percent of our financial solution resulted from new budget reductions." Benitz did not appreciate big government in any form, and wanted state employees to understand that growth was not a given. "We pared the budget of nonessential administrative functions wherever possible… We made performance, not just seniority, the new basis for salary increases and retention decisions for public employees, including managers…

Early retirement for state employees will help reduce government spending without massive layoffs. To save money, we have allowed state workers and teachers to retire with full pensions five years earlier than the current retirement age or after 25 years of service. We must make sure there is enough money in the pension funds to cover the early retirements, and we placed a cutoff date to control the increased costs to the pension system."

At the same time, he said, we "made minimal adjustments to education and to programs for the truly needy and the elderly…[We also] felt we needed to raise revenue to prevent the cuts from making our state unlivable. Without the revenue, we would have wound up cutting deeply into classroom dollars, instead of cutting one-half percent from education funding. We also would have been forced to cut 8 percent from human services funding instead of less than 1 percent. Reinstating the sales tax on food was the only measure capable of getting enough votes in both houses to break the deadlock and solve the problem…It will come off if the economy recovers and other revenues are sufficient. And the tax on food MUST end July 1, 1983."

Why wouldn't other revenue proposals have worked, he asked rhetorically? A flat rate personal income tax offered "too little revenue too late to solve the problem," he asserted. In addition, "imposing a corporate income tax in the middle of the budget cycle probably wouldn't have raised enough revenue. But more important, it would have exported jobs out of the state, as some employers would seek a state with a lower

---

34. In the "red" in this context means a negative budget figure.

cost of doing business. The administrative costs involved with collecting any income tax would have aggravated the state's budget problems as well."

Among the other key achievements Benitz listed for the recent legislative sessions were appropriating for new prison construction, passing "legislation requiring the Department of Labor and Industries to do everything possible to help disabled laborers return to work as quickly as possible. And we provided the funding needed to get the job of rehabilitation done right...[And passing] legislation making it easier for businesses to function and to create jobs of their own...Small business is a major source of jobs in Washington State and we passed two key measures to lower their cost of doing business by cutting government red tape." One of the new laws allowed businesses to fill out one master business license form, instead of applying to several different state agencies and paying separate permit fees and higher administrative costs. The other measure required state agencies to make it easier for small businesses to live with regulations by exempting small businesses from regulations that pertained mostly to larger firms.

He was pleased that "we put some teeth into the state's drunk driving laws. Hundreds of drunk drivers have steered around penalties by persuading judges to defer prosecution while the driver goes through alcohol school. We passed a new law, allowing only one deferred prosecution every five years. And, if officials find a serious drinking problem the drunk driver's license can be suspended until the driver goes through an evaluation or treatment program."[226] Benitz also strongly supported a new child abuse statute that toughened punishments for offenders, allowed children's statements to be admissible in court and made it easier to place children in temporary protective custody away from abusing parents.[227]

Always watchful for the interests of agriculture, Benitz reported "we acted promptly to give orchardists the upper hand in the fight against the apple maggot. We passed a law authorizing the Director of Agriculture to determine the severity of the maggot infestation. We've given the department the power to spray, and even to remove infested trees. The legislation allows the state to respond in a timely fashion of this potential threat to our orchards."[228] The Legislature also exempted aircraft used for crop dusting from the aircraft fuel excise tax, "which otherwise increases to 5 cents a gallon. The exemption applies to aircraft that aren't kept at fields benefiting from the excise tax funds." Knowing that international trade provided a major market for Washington State agricultural products, he informed voters that "we've cleared the way for the Port of Seattle to build a new shipping facility, including a freeze-chill storage plant to keep our produce fresh prior to shipment" overseas.

Highway construction was especially important to Benitz, as he helped secure funding to complete Interstates 82 and 182 through Benton County. State bonds were authorized, to be paid back when federal money became available in two to three years. Meanwhile, jobs would be created in the Tri-Cities and in some western Washington areas that also received highway funds. "We authorized port districts to provide for industrial developments through levies (creating up to 2,000 jobs)… Measures to expand port facilities on the coast and complete interstate highway projects will create thousands of new jobs…We changed the state's formula for distributing fuel tax money to counties, which means an extra $58,000 for Benton County, North Richland Bridge,"[35] he reported.[229] Highway 82, serving central Washington State, was constructed over much of the 1970s and 1980s in 23 different projects. However, as promised by Benitz, construction began in 1982 on the Yakima and Benton County portions between Union Gap and the Tri-Cities, and completed in 1986.[230] He also supported a 1982 bill that named State Route 504 as the Spirit Lake Memorial Highway to remember those killed in the 1980 Mount St. Helens eruption.[231]

---

35. Still, however, the North Richland bridge was never built.

Chapter Three:
Legislative Years, 1981-1990

Asian Trade Trip, 1981

In the meanwhile, Max Benitz was busy with another technique to solve Washington State's budget woes. He firmly believed that foreign trade – particularly agricultural trade with Asia – could boost state income. He was right. Between 1970 and 1980, exports from Washington State jumped more than six-fold, and imports rose more than seven-fold. In June 1981, he accompanied Governor Spellman on a trade mission to Japan, South Korea and Taiwan, along with three other state legislators and nine other state agency officials. "No question about it, if we play our cards right we in the state of Washington will be able to do a huge amount of business with these huge Japanese companies and many of the smaller ones in the very near future," he wrote. "If successful, I should add that we will be opening up a tremendous new trade territory both for our agricultural products and probably most important, the coming of Japanese plants...[to] Washington, and we should certainly both be winners if we continue to pursue it at the level it is now." The 1981 trip was his first return visit to Japan, South Korea and Taiwan since the spring of 1968, and he noted many changes that had occurred in the intervening 13 years.

On the flights to Japan he read *Wealth and Poverty*[36] an influential new book that offered a ringing defense of entrepreneurship. Its premise was that entrepreneurship is the engine driving free economies, but that entrepreneurship can easily be thwarted by over taxing and over regulation. However, the book wasn't just a policy prescription. It tackled head on the myth of the greedy entrepreneur. A real entrepreneur, the book argued, sacrificed his own resources to create something that benefits others. How else could he recoup his investment? The author saw entrepreneurship as benefiting society's moral health, as it was the least coercive form of social and civic benefit. The driving force behind it was not dictation or coercion, but individuals deciding to better them-

---

36. Gilder, George, *Wealth and Poverty*, Basic Books (New York), 1981.

selves by creating products people needed and therefore bettering others. The book fit and enlarged Benitz's own ideas about free enterprise. The book, he noted, was "a bit long…and rather deep reading but a very, very good book and one which certainly has its implications for us here in the United States."[232]

Japan

He commented early in his trip on the Japanese work ethic, a feature of the culture that had impressed him during his 1968 visit. "With no natural resources they are competing and there's evidence of it, but most of all the first general impression you get is that everyone seems to be wanting to help everyone else. All of the employees and everyone seem to be in a hurry and extremely interested in doing a good job and pleasing the customer, something I'm afraid we've lost a lot of in the United States." Benitz also noted that politeness, diplomacy and patience were needed in conducting business with the Japanese. "There's an old saying and we're reminded of it here many times…'If you cross my threshold twenty times then I know you want to do business with me.'…It's not a hit and run thing, you cannot just simply make one call on the Japanese."

Japanese agriculture was heavily subsidized at the time, due to national fears that, as an island nation, Japan could be cut off from food supplies if it became too dependent on imported farm products. Japan was less than 50 percent self-sufficient in food production at that time, and the percentage was dropping. Also, with Japan on a mad rush towards industrialization and rebuilding after World War II, life on the farm was considered less attractive and exciting than city life, and subsidies were needed to keep young farmers on the land. Rice was especially heavily subsidized, and thus was being over-produced. "They [the government] are trying their very best to get the farmers to produce less rice but the subsidy program brings them so much money that they refuse to cut production," Benitz reported early in the trip. "In fact, they are trying to get more soybeans grown and…the government has offered the farmers a subsidy of as much as $90 a bushel on soybeans to raise soybeans and not rice and yet rice is so lucrative to them that they continue to raise much more rice that they need."

The first official stop on the trip was a visit to the Portopia, a man-made island in the Osaka Bay at the port of Kobe. In 1981, Japan held a trade fair and exhibition to show Portopia to the world. In honor of

Governor Spellman's visit, the Japanese held Washington State Day at Portopia, where Japan then had the largest container handling port facility in the world. *"They have plans now to build an even larger island and to get the money they're having to go to Germany to borrow... It's becoming very evident that the world is depending on leading nations to trade, and the better shape we're in to trade the more competitive and the better our standard of living will be. We're not doing too well up to this point,"* Benitz noted. The exhibits at Portopia interested him for another reason as well. A group of Tri-Cities businessmen were trying to promote an event called "Energy Fair '83" in the Tri-Cities.[233] Benitz was trying to help them, and noted that *"there* are a couple of exhibits on the Island or Portopia that would work quite well, and the Japanese have expressed an interest in bringing those exhibits to Energy Fair '83 in the Tri-Cities."[37]

The last evening in Kobe, June 13, Governor Spellman hosted a banquet for the Kobe Portopia delegation and several Japanese political officials including the Governor of the Prefecture (equivalent to an American state). Benitz observed that "the Japanese are very, very rigid on protocol in seating and other arrangements have to be just right. I am seated next to the Governor in terms of protocol throughout all of these and...I'm particularly pleased that John Spellman is as down to earth as he is." He also observed that Japan was "most concerned about protectionism and the lack of free trade. Even though they themselves are guilty on some counts. The people in Japan know they have the most to lose as the protectionism head rears its ugly face again."[38]

On June 14, Max Benitz and John Spellman took a "bullet train" from Kobe to Tokyo, traveling at about 120 miles per hours. Benitz was impressed with the rail system, commenting that "they have so many of those trains, double track, going both way, they seem to be only 15 minutes apart. Again, the rail system in Japan seems to be first rate, not only for the bullet special but also for all the sidelines that take other passenger trains as well as their freight lines. It's really too bad we've allowed our railroad system to get into the shape it's in."

They spent three hectic days in Tokyo, holding high-level meetings. Benitz noted that Washington was "breaking of new ground by [being] the first state of the nation" to hold trade talks directly with a foreign government. They met with Mitsui and Mitsubishi, large Japanese im-

---

37. Energy Fair '83 did not take place
38. Protectionism refers to erecting fees, quotas and other trade barriers.

porting companies, along with the Agricultural Counselor of the American Embassy and the Vice Minister of Agriculture for Japan. Washington cherries were just being allowed into Japan, after the Japanese were satisfied that the fumigation systems met their standards. Apple imports were the real prize and were not allowed into Japan at that time due to fears of the coddling moth. If Washington farmers could open the Japanese market to their apples, the business would be lucrative. However, various discussions of this issue throughout the visit led Benitz to believe that the apple market would not be opened for a few more years. "They were frankly very cold on apple imports. Again they brought up the coddling moth... and indicated to us that we are not pursuing the coddling moth problem hard enough." Benitz thought privately that the issue was truly "more a political problem [that]...the protectionist policy continues to exist. That is, protectionist policy for the Japanese agriculture. But...the Japanese farmer must learn to compete but it will not happen for at least a year or two, perhaps a bit longer."

His solution was not to press too hard for trade that would allow fresh apples into Japan just yet, but to propose starting with processed apples, such as pie mixtures that could be sold to Japanese bakeries. "I'm totally convinced [that]... we should work on the processing, either with a Japanese company coming to the State of Washington or opening the market here in process. There's just no way they're going to let the apple from the United State come into Japan to compete with their fresh apples. Meeting with the Japan Export Trade Organization (Jetro – a public/private partnership dedicated to increasing Japan's foreign trade) convinced Benitz even further that beginning to open the apple trade with processed products would be the smartest tactic. With Jetro, he said, "we made the first big headway on the apples...they did say there would be room for a lot of frozen apple stock, pie stock we call it...[for Japanese bakeries to use] or at least put them out frozen [for consumers to buy]." Another idea was to begin trade by importing Washington State apples to Japan during Japan's off-season for the fruit.

The grain trade with Japan was much further advanced, as Benitz learned from discussions with the U.S. Feed Grains Council, and the Wheat Associates, in Japan. "I really think they have the grain export situation well in hand, wheat, corn and whatever...They're doing the job well. If we were that far along in other agricultural products ...we'd like to export we really wouldn't need to be over here," Benitz noted. In terms of forest products, he saw a huge market for Washington State. After attending a forest products luncheon at which Spellman spoke, he reported that major executives of large companies told him that "Japan would import more finished lumber and woodchips but they also need considerable number of raw logs." After meeting with large import-export company Sumitomo Shoji Kaisha,[39] Benitz stated that "*they are very interested in getting larger port facilities in the United States for trans-shipment of coal to Japan. It will be one of the very big things in the future. They are also interested in agricultural processing and so we had a very interesting discussion.*"

During his time in Tokyo, Benitz also visited a Japanese food store, and experience that captivated his ever-curious mind. The "food section" was in the basement of a large downtown department store. The store was crowded, he observed, and he described the prices as "*astronomical*," including California cherries with dried stems and "in poor shape" selling for $3.50 per pound, extremely expensive beef, and quart jars of canned apricots from France selling for about $15.00! "They did look good and were of good quality but how many people can afford that? Those are prestige items, we are told.… they expect to pay a very high price, but the quality must be good and must look good…I was more than impressed with the great variety of foods, and many kinds of fruits and vegetables that I could not even identify on sale and people buying them. Not in great amounts but in small amounts."

Benitz also noted a large amount of wine imported from California, Germany, Italy and France. Again it was very expensive, but customers were buying it. He described the wine as "only fair, no really good wine. I suspect there is a reason for that, Japan makes a considerable amount of wine and blends other wines from other countries with it. Nevertheless I believe there will be a big future in wine exports once we have that much from the state of Washington to Japan. I'm sure it will build its own image." Already excited and involved in building and promoting the wine industry in Washington State, Benitz also noted that everywhere he went in Japan, "when you mention a new wine industry you are simply clobbered with people wanting to know more about it and wanting to help in the export, and especially if you insist you have a quality wine."

On June 16, Governor Spellman signed a trade agreement in the Mitsui headquarters with the President of that company. Benitz described

39. Now Sumitomo Corp.

the new corporate headquarters as opulent, *"without* a doubt the most impressive board room I have ever seen… The table oval shaped perhaps 14 to 16 feet wide and probably 35 or 40 feet long, polished to a fare-the-well, not a flaw in it anyplace and a very beautiful piece of work." This agreement would become one of the hallmarks of Spellman's administration. By 1983, the states of Washington and Oregon led the nation in share of employment derived from foreign trade, and were the only states that ran a trade surplus with Japan.[234]

South Korea

The next morning, they flew to Seoul, South Korea, where they spent three days. At the time, South Korea was under martial law, being ruled by unelected military general Chun Doo-hwan, whom had taken power shortly after the assassination of elected President Park Chung-hee in October 1979. Chun was later elected President and served until 1988. However, when Benitz and Spellman visited he had just dissolved the National Assembly and was being condemned internationally as a dictator. Benitz immediately noticed the heavy police and military presence in Seoul. "I guess from the start of the drive from the airport in with a squadron of motorcycles, red lights, sirens running, all traffic held at bay, not paying attention to traffic lights but other traffic and, people scurrying for their lives, you have to come to the quick conclusion that this is a police state and when the police undertake to do something they have total authority and of course it comes in very quick order from the top down." Although Benitz and Spellman were *"very well received,"* the "top-down" nature of the government bothered them. *"It's very* apparent that if you happen to be in the ruling class, up close to the top, you're in pretty good shape, but I don't know how the man on the street fares… the Legislature only passes that which the President wants them to pass. He is virtually a dictator."

Benitz was most perturbed by new legislation in South Korea that established a large, government-controlled livestock cooperative. Chun then appointed his own brother to head the cooperative. "We met in the office of his brother, very plush and very first rate and very apparent to all that the power absolutely unprecedented." To Benitz, the cooperative came far too close to the collectivized farming model practiced in the Union of Soviet Socialist Republics (Soviet Union or U.S.S.R.) and the People's Republic of China (PRC or Red China). He also reported that private American import companies were "concerned what's going to happen to them in their business when they have to come through this new farm cooperative government sponsored kind of thing even to get their product. They see the handwriting on the wall...It would appear to me that nearly all, if not all, of the big businesses [in South Korea are] either dominated, owned sanctioned by the government"

Benitz was dismayed at the poverty of the average person that he observed. "When you get down on the street on the little man level there are literally hundreds of thousands of merchants, many of them with a shop no bigger than just barely a place to stand, selling whatever they have to sell. They are on the streets with the wagons and that kind of thing...I think that they are pretty close to where Japan was about 15 years ago...Of course here in Korea they're certainly miles ahead of the People's Republic of China, when I last visited it." However, he did appreciate the "frank" discussions he and Spellman had with Korean officials, and believed they had "opened doors." Fresh cherries had never been shipped to Korea, but he believed that condition would change soon. A Korean inspection team would be coming to Wenatchee and Yakima, Washington, and Hood River, Oregon, in just a few weeks to examine fruit fumigation methods on farms in those areas. "I'm quite sure that next year we will be able to ship some fresh cherries into Korea which will be a real break though," he predicted.

An unexpected highlight of his time in Korea was a chance to visit the Demilitarized Zone (DMZ) that separated South Korea from North Korea. He and Spellman had been told repeatedly by American officials that they had no chance of visiting the DMZ. Yet, after Spellman met with the South Korean President, they were allowed to go. Benitz, who had traveled as close to the border of Red China as he could in 1968, when that nation was closed to Americans, was excited by the opportunity. "Of course we jumped at the chance," he said. At five o'clock the next morning, June 20, they were picked up in military vehicles for the ride north to the DMZ. The highway was "pretty good," he reported, but was lined with "what's called 'tank traps,' they're huge concrete abutments over your head which would appear to be an overpass on the freeway, but not really not, they are mined and live, and the military soldier can on command touch a button and the demolition is instant. They cover the road to keep the tanks from getting through... it's still two nations at war, there's simply a truce. There's been no peace treaty and that's right where it is so they stay on the alert and they are in the act of war at all times." At the Imjim River, there was a "one lane very narrow bridge with one way traffic which shows the marks of the bombing heretofore… it's rough planks, it takes a long time to get across with a vehicle. That bridge is also live mined and on the touch of a button the bridge goes down in the river, so it really brings you to the realization of what it's all about."

In the center of the heavily fortified DMZ itself, there was a building that contained a table with a United Nations flag at one end and a North Korean flag at the other end. Soldiers from North and South Korea entered the building from opposite ends. Benitz and Spellman were told "to make absolutely no smile, point a finger, do absolutely nothing to them [North Korean guards], and our guards stand there twenty minutes at a time and then they are changed 24 hours a day on absolute alert with loaded guns." The military officer accompanying Benitz and Spellman said they could step across the room and have their photos taken in North Korea, which they did. Representatives from both sides met regularly at the special table, they were told, "but discuss little of importance, or they have fist fights between the opposing sides…and of course one of the goals of the North Koreans is to slip across the line wherever they can and plant land mines and kill the Americans as well as the Korean soldiers. It's a very bitter kind of thing and shows no sign of letting up. [North Koreans] were watching us with field glasses at all times."

Benitz and Spellman then were taken to another observation post where they could look down on the spot where a famous incident had occurred in August 1976. A work party of American and South Korean soldiers had gone into the DMZ to prune a poplar tree that partially obstructed their view of the North. Soldiers from North Korea appeared, a fight ensued, and two Americans were axed to death. North and South Korea came closer to war than they had at any point since the armistice was signed in 1953. President Ford condemned the killings as "murder."[235] Benitz photographed the tree and said that "I hope my pictures of the tree showed that…it was definitely on our side by at least 300 feet."[40]

Benitz also commented on a unique farming village of Tae Sung Dong, inside the DMZ and inhabited by South Koreans. When the ar-

---

40. A monument was erected on the site of the tree in 1987.

Max Benitz (left) at DMZ Korea with Gov. Spellman.

Max Benitz (left) at DMZ with Gov. Spellman (with binoculars).

Famous Poplar Tree at DMZ, Korea.

mistice was signed in 1953, each side was permitted to retain one village in the DMZ, where only inhabitants who had lived there before the war could reside. The North Korean village in the DMZ, Gijong-dong, had no real residents, but was frequented only by North Korean soldiers. Benitz noted the frequent harassment of the South Korean villagers, such as loud, patriotic North Korean music being blared at them along with shouted insults.[236] However, he said, "in their village are very proud of what they have so they continue to put up a bigger flag, and then the North Koreans put a bigger flag, and that continues. It certainly brings home to all of us that it is two nations very much at war as yet…you see the bitterness of this whole thing…Very, very interesting."

Taiwan

By the time Max Benitz flew to Taiwan, he admitted he was tired. He remarked about the huge amount of change and prosperity in Taipei since his last visit. "During the last visit here in 1968 you couldn't get up and down the streets for bicycles. They're all gone out to the countryside and it's now motorcycles, buses and automobiles. Fuel very expensive, about $3 a gallon." He also commented on the vigorous free market system he observed, as opposed to South Korea. "The nation as a whole is the most free enterprise thing I have ever seen, insisting that their unemployment is about 1.5% but the key difference is that it is an honor to be working here, irrespective of what you're doing, from the street sweeper to the finest job in technology… It is a total honor to be working and contributing to the gross national product, something we need a bit more of in our nation."

On the first morning in Taiwan, Benitz and Spellman attended a

Max Benitz greets Mou-shih Ding, Foreign Minister of Republic of China, Taiwan, 1981.

Benitz (left), Premier Sun and Governor Spellman in Taiwan, June 1981.

Benitz (second from left), Governor Spellman (third from left), Premier Sun (third from right) and others, Taiwan, June 1981, in China Post (Taiwan), with compliments of Ministry of Foreign Affairs, Republic of China.

ribbon cutting ceremony for a new technology institute, and Benitz re-marked that the Taiwanese would soon "achieve superiority" in technology. At the ceremony, he met Dr. Peter Shen, a scientist who had grown up in Taiwan but then worked for the Washington Public Power Supply System (WPPSS) in Richland, Washington, in Benitz's home district. Shen was working on a project in Taiwan to develop a high-pressure water jet capable of cutting rock and clay. Benitz was always interested in connections and technology that might be useful at WPPSS or the Hanford Site in Benton County. He and Spellman met with the American ambassador to Taiwan, and then with Premier Sun Yun-Shuan of the Republic of China (Taiwan). The Premier, Benitz related, "indicated the free trade [position] which we're interested in…[and] the Governor and I had a chance to pitch our Washington State wine to him in which he was very interested…All told, I think I've gained a lot and I hope that eventually the state of Washington does." [237]

Before they flew home, Governor Spellman issued a press release from Taiwan stating that the Republic of China (Taiwan) would continue to be one of Washington State's major partners in commerce, agriculture, science and technology transfer. He said that Washington State has for a long time played a leading role in manufacturing sophisticated, scientific and technological products. "This would provide a base for cooperation with local research and education institutions to manufacture similar products in this country [Taiwan]," he noted. He said that one-fourth of Washington's economy comes from foreign trade, and strongly criticized protectionism." [238]

1982 Election and Third Term in State Senate

Running for his third term in the State Senate in 1982, Benitz anticipated a strong challenge from Democrat Ed Alden, son of Tri-Cities labor leaders Harry and Christina Alden. Benitz campaigned on the basis of his record and his support of his traditional causes – agriculture; education; water projects; transportation projects and their jobs; low taxes; the rights of the elderly, minorities and students; and energy. "As your Senator," he told voters, "I must struggle to maintain the essential, necessary functions of government that you need and deserve – without recklessly adding to your tax burden." [239] He stated he could foresee "no circumstances" in which he would support a state income tax. He also said that the state's community colleges could not afford to continue their "open door" admissions policies, asserting that he supported "qual-

RE-ELECT

Experience . . . .

Benitz:

a 14 year record of
legislative achievement in:

* ENERGY

* TRANSPORTATION

* HIGHER EDUCATION

* STATE GOVERNMENT

* MINORITY AFFAIRS

* AGRICULTURE

Sen. Benitz confers with Senators Ted Haley and Jeannette Hayner, Majority Leader.

*when experience
was never more needed
in State government.*

**BENITZ' EFFORTS
CREATE NEW JOBS**

Bridges across the Columbia and Yakima rivers near Richland are nearing completion, the first links of I-182 in the area. As a member of the Transportation Committee, Senator Benitz played a key role in the passage of the Advanced Construction of Interstate. Bids will soon be let on 14 projects in Benton County alone creating 2000 new jobs and putting $162 million into the local economy.

Senator Benitz was instrumental in passing legislation that resulted in new markets for Washington's wine grapes and up to 1000 new jobs each year.

Sen. Benitz views construction of I-182.

WPPSS NOW ACCOUNTABLE

Public power ratepayers now have a greater voice in the management of WPPSS because of legislation supported by Senator Benitz which increases the accountability of WPPSS management and allows more participation by nuclear power experts.

BASICS FOR BASIC EDUCATION

Senator Benitz is working in support of keeping the priorities focused on the basics of education.

NO MORE FLOODS

Senator Benitz was successful in bringing together the necessary officials to solve the long standing problem of the Yakima River flooding in Benton City.

Sen. Benitz with Sen. Peter von Reichbauer.

**PEOPLE WHO RECOGNIZE THE
VALUE OF BENITZ' EXPERIENCE:**

. . . we thank you for your ability and your interest . . . Your work was truly admirable and I respect you for your task.
**Jim Boldt, Executive Director
Washington PUD Association**

On behalf of thousands of small businesses . . . (we) would like to thank you for your support. We are explaining to small business owners . . . your very positive efforts . . .
**Gary L. Smith, Executive Director
Independent Business Association**

. . . our state will be better off because of this Legislature's recognition that our economy must be improved. Your individual role was appreciated . . .
**Fred L. Esvelt, President
Columbia Basin College**

I personally want to thank you for your efforts on behalf of public ports . . . I deeply appreciate your support of the port activities in the state.
**Dean S. Hagerty
Washington Public Ports Association**

Max Benitz campaign flier, 1982.

ity education and not quantity."[240] He was elected by a slim margin.[241]

The Democrats again held majorities in both houses of the State Legislature, and immediately enacted a huge sales tax increase of two cents (amounting to approximately one billion dollars in additional revenue), and passed a budget 20 percent larger than the previous one. Early in the 1983 legislative session, the Democrats also increased the state Business and Occupation (B&O) tax by $500-million. This measure was vetoed by Governor Spellman, and then enacted again with a $400-million increase. The tax increases passed in the 1983 legislative session were the largest in state history up to that point. Democrats also repealed civil service reforms previously enacted by Republican majorities, but in this case the Governor's veto stood.

One of Benitz's first actions during the 1983 legislative session was to secure funds to replace the Grant Avenue Bridge over the Yakima River in Prosser.[242] The old steel and timber bridge was replaced with a concrete bridge in 1986.

Benitz also forwarded proposals for a Kennewick[41] interchange on Highway 12, which was constructed as I-182 was being completed in the

Grant Avenue Bridge, Prosser, WA. (photo courtesy of Dorian Dexter).

Kennewick-Pasco area.[42] He had secured funding for I-182 in his district in the previous legislative session.[243] He also once again sponsored bills to assist irrigation districts in developing hydroelectric generation facilities, regulate tree fruit assessments, limit property taxes, waive tuition fees and grant refunds to students who had to withdraw from higher education classes for medical reasons, remove community college trustees for malfeasance, support open public meetings, and provide interpreters in legal proceedings for non-English speaking persons. One of his signature bills that year was one to encourage and provide support for high technology education and training, an issue he felt was essential to state competitiveness in the future. All of these bills became law.[244]

At the end of the 1983 legislative session, Benitz told constituents that agriculture had "fared well" during the session. "We were able to defeat House Bill 199 and Senate Bill 4099 which challenged farm tax exemptions. We...killed the repeal of the $150 tax exemption for industrial insurance on part-time farm workers. But on the other hand, we voted in $600 million in new taxes. The farmers will have to pay their fair share of that, and that makes farming that much more difficult. "How-

41. One of the Tri-Cities, in Benitz's district in Benton County, Washington.
42. Before Interstate 182 was built, State Route 240 was known as US 12 in the Tri-Cities area.

ever, he counseled his farm constituents that "the only way we can win anything is to maintain our credibility...We keep agricultural issues as bi-partisan as we can...You had better avoid partisanship of you'll get yourself in real trouble."[245]

In June 1983, Benitz, was appointed to the Legislative Ethics Committee by Lieutenant Governor John Cherberg, and to the Joint Legislative Ethics Board by Republican Caucus Chairman John Jones.[246] He continued to serve on the Agriculture, Education, and Energy and Utilities Committees. Benitz spent a great deal of his time on energy issues in 1983.[43]

He remained a staunch promoter of exports and foreign trade, unrestricted by government. "The economic survival of agriculture in Washington depends on exports," he said. "We must ...not let unwise political decisions get us into the kind of trouble we are in now... Both parties are to blame for our predicament and the farmer takes the brunt of it. Gerry Ford embargoed soybeans and Jimmy Carter embargoed wheat, and both were wrong." Benitz also valued market research "to find out what our potential customers want, and agricultural research to find new crops which can be grown profitably under current conditions." His own research and inquisitiveness in Japan, he pointed out, had taught him that "Japanese consumers want corn on the cob from us...[even when they were told it] would be a lot more expensive that frozen kernel corn...Cost was not important. They want a quality product and are willing to pay for it," he said.[247] He favored co-sponsored a bill funding Washington State University (WSU) to conduct market research to determine the needs and preferences of Pacific Rim countries for Washington farm products, and the steps necessary for Washington growers to modify their crops or methods to meet those needs. House Democrats, particularly powerful Ways and Means Committee Chairman Dan Grimm, objected, saying that such research should be done by private firms. Exports, Benitz reiterated in June 1983, were the "key to the survival of Washington agriculture... it is a perfectly legitimate role for WSU to find out what consumers in the Pacific Rim countries want and how our products can be modified to meet their specific needs. That kind of research could uncover all kinds of opportunities for private industry to satisfy. Private companies do market research for their own benefit but what is needed is research accessible to all growers and

---

43. Energy issues will be discussed in Chapter 4.

processors, and that can best be accomplished by a public agency such as WSU," Benitz said.[248-44]

On September 1, 1983, Washington State was stunned by the death of Senator Henry "Scoop" Jackson. The powerful Democrat had been in Congress 42 years, and a Senator for 30 years. Although he was a Republican, Max Benitz had agreed with Jackson's very strong anti-communist, pro-national defense stances. Jackson secured many millions of dollars in funding over the years for the Hanford Nuclear Site, which lay in Benitz's district.[45] At Jackson's death, Governor Spellman appointed Republican Dan Evans to fill his Senate seat. Democrats in the State Legislature were outraged that a Republican had been appointed to fill a seat vacated by a Democrat. State law required that a primary be held immediately, and it was held just three weeks later. In the special general election held in November 1983, Dan Evans faced a vigorous challenge by Democrat Congressman Mike Lowry, but Evans was victorious.[249]

When the State Legislature re-convened in 1984, meeting for the first time in regular session in an even-numbered year, Benitz once again served on the Agriculture, Education, and Energy and Utilities Committees. For the first time, he was also picked to serve on the powerful Rules Committee, which, among other abilities, determined the bills that would reach the floor of the Senate for debate. "I am pleased to have been asked to serve on these committees," he stated, "because I believe these assignments will allow me to continue to best serve the people I representing. These are significant issues in our area," he said. "Because of my background, I have a very strong interest in agricultural issues, which bear heavily on the economy of the 8th District. Agricultural commodities, and their transportation to the marketplace, will play an increasingly important role in the economy of our state in the coming century." Benitz noted that education issues have been and will always be a major concern to residents of his district, and added that he is a member of the temporary Committee on Education Policy, Structure and Management, which was formulating far-ranging recommendations for the future of education in the state.[250]

In early February 1984, Benitz said he was concerned about flu-like symptoms and had a weak artery, which caused him to tire faster than usual. He continued to work long hours as the Senate convened through the weekend of February 4-5. He was admitted to a special heart unit at

44. However, the bill was not passed into law.
45. The Hanford Site will be discussed in Chapter 4.

St. Peter Hospital in Olympia, where tests determined that he had had a mild heart attack on February 2. He stayed in the hospital for approximately a week, and then rested at home, returning to work in the Senate in late February. [251]

Due to his illness, Benitz sponsored and co-sponsored fewer bills than usual in the 1984 legislative session. When he returned to work from his illness, he stated that he intended to devote most of his energies to stopping certain legislation, rather than passing bills.[46-252] He did sponsor and pass a lengthy bill specifying standards for milk and milk products, and a bill ensuring that eastern Washington was well represented on a regional conservation planning commission.[253] He also sponsored and passed two important bills assisting the Washington wine industry.[47] He worked hard to pass a bill that would allow areas of the Kennewick Hospital District to withdraw from the district, in order to increase the chances that at bond issue would pass for a new hospital. At the end of the 1984 session, Benitz was pleased that the Legislature had lowered the timber tax and the B&O tax on meat processors, and passed a $100-million bond issue for irrigation. The session ended with no new taxes and no overtime session.[254]

1984 Elections and Mid-1980s Politics

In 1984, Benitz campaigned for Governor John Spellman, but Republican Spellman was defeated by wealthy Democrat Booth Gardner, Pierce County executive. Benitz was most pleased by the re-election of Republican Ronald Reagan as President, and was invited to Reagan's 1985 inauguration.[48]

Both houses of the Washington State Legislature once again had Democrat majorities in the 1985 session. With a new Democrat Governor, and taxes again a key issue, Benitz was determined to work against big spending and government growth. In early March, he complained that "this is the slowest session of the Legislature I have ever seen here as a Representative or Senator…there is much uncertainty about the dollars available." House Ways and Means Committee Chairman Grimm proposed raising the state's B&O tax to a single rate at 1.8 percent, but granting tax deductions for business operating costs. Benitz opposed this tax hike, saying "small businesses may greatly benefit from the plan

---

46. Among the key bills that Benitz wanted to stop were those concerning radioactive waste and Hanford. These issues will be discussed in Chapter 4.

47. Wine issues will be discussed in Chapter 5.

48. However, he did not attend the inauguration.

The Committee for
the 50th American Presidential Inaugural
requests the honor of your presence
to attend and participate in the Inauguration of

Ronald Wilson Reagan

as President of the United States of America
and

George Herbert Walker Bush

as Vice President of the United States of America
on Sunday the twentieth of January
one thousand nine hundred and eighty five
in the City of Washington

Benitz's Invitation to President Reagan's 1985 Inauguration.

but large established firms like Boeing could have their tax liabilities increased by 25 to 30 percent." Boeing Vice President Dean Thornton stated that if the tax was passed, it would "*encourage*" companies like Boeing to move parts of their operations out of the state. Benitz also worried about the effects of the proposed tax on the beef packing industry. "*Unless substantive relief is provided, Washington State will lose,*" he predicted. Republican Senator Jeannette Hayner of Walla Walla introduced Senate Bills (SBs) 3422 and 3589, designed to save the beef packing industry $5.5-million per year by reducing its B&O tax rate from one/third of one percent to one/eighth of one percent. "*If signed into law,*" Benitz said, these reductions *"could save the state's meat processing industry."* Grimm said he would not support any bills that specifically reduced taxes for any one business, and the bills failed to pass out of the Senate Ways and Means Committee.[255]

In March, new revenue predictions from Washington's Economic and Revenue Forecasting Council showed a possible budget shortfall of $153-million for the 1985-87 biennium, with the state collecting about $9.493-billion instead of the hoped for $9.646-billion. However, Benitz believed the Governor's proposed budget was far too high. He was angry when Gardner reported on statewide television in April that a "revenue crisis" was imminent. Benitz called this statement a "Democrat smokescreen...Although Gardner is saying the sky is falling, his 1985-87 biennial budget is $1.2-billion higher than the 1983-85 biennial budget representing a 15 percent increase in state spending. In 1983, Democrats in control of the Legislature passed the largest tax increases in history. Those tax increases raised more than $1.7-billion. Republicans are convinced that the real 'crisis' is not due to a lack of revenue, but a lack of spending restraint."[256] Budget forecasters, he said, had underestimated the growth rate of employment in the state, and not given enough credit to the continued low rate of inflation (3.2 percent in 1983; 4.3 percent in 1984; and 3.6 percent in 1985). If they had incorporated these factors, he said, instead of planning for high inflation, the state would not face a shortfall.

Wrangling over taxes continued, as Gardner proposed other tax increases, including increasing the gasoline sales tax by seven cents to nearly 25 cents per gallon, making it the nation's highest. Towards the end of the regular legislative session in April, a frustrated Benitz spoke out publicly. "The Governor is attacking a phantom crisis with the hard earned wages of taxpayers...The Governor keeps referring to a revenue crisis while the most pessimistic estimates point to a 14 percent increase in tax revenue for the coming budget period... We just had the largest tax increase in state history two years ago...This [new] increase added to the historic $1.7 billion tax increase of 1983 stimulates government growth at the expense of taxpayers...We face a spending crisis, not a revenue crisis. This new round of tax increases will hurt every family in Washington. It will drive up the cost of all goods shipped by truck, from groceries to automobiles....An increase in the B&O tax on services will make everything from a haircut to tax return preparation more expensive."[257]

At nearly the same time, Benitz blasted SB 3189, which would allow state employees to make payments directly from their paychecks into union political action funds.[258] He called the bill a "gross misuse of the machinery of state government...[and] a transparent attempt by the union to dominate campaigns and elections in Washington State. They are seeking to use the state payroll system to balloon their already-huge campaign war chest...State employees are working to increase their salaries and benefits and now their unions are seeking to enhance their ability to elect legislators sympathetic to those increases," Benitz said. "Deductions for state employee association dues are already allowed. Part of which can be and are used for participation in political campaigns. State government must continue to observe the policy of separating its operations from the activities of political campaigns, or we will soon have a situation where state employees are being pressured to have payroll deductions funneled into the campaigns of the very elected officials under whom they serve."[259]

During the session, Benitz sponsored, co-sponsored or supported key bills that assisted and regulated aquatic farming, helped enhance salmon sustainability, preserved and strengthened irrigation district voting rights, and provided for public input into minimum flow determinations for streams, lakes and public water sources.[260] Ever mindful of education and the disabled and disadvantaged, he also sponsored or supported bills allowing higher education tuition and fees to be paid in installments, provided financial assistance to victims of sexual assault, made it easier for courts to issue restraining orders or injunctions in cases of child abuse, created a awards program for high-achieving high school student, mandated refueling assistance for disabled drivers at every service station in the state, and provided for Spanish and Japanese language instruction in selected school districts.[261] He also sponsored a bill requiring the state Department of Ecology to regulate the safe disposal of polychlorinated biphenyls (PCBs),[262] as well as another bill assisting Washington state wineries.

On April 25, with three days remaining in the regular legislative session, Benitz gave his constituents a "scorecard: It's now game time... The Game is Grimm Vs. McDermott or the House Vs. the Senate or $9.27 billion (House) Vs. $9.19 billion (Senate)...but it's not just money, it's where the cuts are, and who will get hurt the most." He was "disappointed" that education funding was not to increase, and not pleased at the large amount of funding given to social services. "Washington ranks seventh of the 50 states in the average amount of money granted to welfare recipients according to the Washington Research Council," he reported. "Washington Aid to Families with Dependent Children grants are 30 percent higher than the national average." He was also unhappy to see Washington State's unemployment rate at 10.6 percent for February. This rate was "the 8th highest in the nation, according to a report released by the U.S. Department of Labor. Unemployment is highest in Washington counties heavily dependent on the forest products industry." He was gratified to note that "Washington's $3.9 million Expo '86 Pavilion may be built on schedule for the Canadian World's Fair…the pavilion may help in Washington's business recruiting efforts because 40 other countries will be present including many from the Pacific Rim."[263]

Shortly after the regular session ended on April 28, Benitz gave his constituents a report he called the "Legislative Balance Sheet." It was "lopsided," he said, "but there are a few positive features…. No new taxes were enacted. One major victory was the evaporation of Governor Gardner's proposal to extend the sales tax to motor vehicle fuels and increase some business taxes…Also sidetracked was a budget-busting scheme for establishing a system of socialized medicine in this state." Always concerned that high state taxes would hinder Washington's business climate, he was glad that lawmakers "approved a plan to defer sales taxes for the new businesses that will operate in economically depressed area, and reduce the Business and Occupation tax for the struggling meat processing industry." However, on the "minus side" of the balance sheet, he said, "no significant action was taken to make badly needed changes in the state's education system. The Democratic majority also refused to adopt nine of ten important Republican-sponsored measures to crack down on child sexual abusers. They did see their way clear to approve allowing state employee unions to receive contributions directly from employee paychecks, thus fattening the union's political coffers. Taken altogether, Democratic lawmakers, who control both houses of the Legislature, as well as the Governor's office, have little to show for the 105 days of work."[264]

The 1985 regular session of the State Legislature adjourned without adopting a state budget. According to Benitz, this situation was "largely due to intra-party bickering between House and Senate Democrats." The following week, Governor Gardner said he would begin budget negotiations with "legislative leaders" but included no Republicans. Benitz drily told his constituents he was "surprised…because they [Republicans] represent some 46 percent of Washington's citizens."[265] The Legislature was called back into special session on June 10. "The highest priority," said Benitz, was "the adoption of a State General Fund Budget for the next biennium which starts July 1, 1985…If no General Fund Budget is passed by July 1, there will be no state paychecks or other funds expended until a budget is adopted." Governor Gardner renewed his call for an increase in state taxes, saying "everything is back on the table."[266] However, Benitz was adamant: "I believe that a tax increase at this time is absolutely unnecessary and will actually have a detrimental effect on the state's economy. While the rest of the country is well into a burgeoning economic recovery, Washington State is still struggling through a depression-like slump. One major reason for that slump is our state's unconscionably high taxes. Many jobs-producing industries would like very much to build their facilities in this state. But our punitive business tax system is forcing them to look elsewhere… Washington is not faced with a revenue crisis. We have a spending crisis. Necessary state services can continue, even in the face of declining state income, if the governor and majority-party budget writers will recognize the damage done by runaway state spending. *We don't need tax increases. We need responsible spending levels.*" He was outraged that, "against a backdrop of declining revenue forecasts and calls for state tax increases…the number of employees increased a remarkable 18.3 percent between 1982 and 1985. At the same time, the state's overall population increased less than five percent…The budget proposals that were being offered near the end of the legislative session prompted cries of outrage from state-agency officials…But the fact is that the budget proposals didn't call for cuts in services. What they proposed were cuts in planned increases. In truth, the budget plans offered called for increased state spending, to the tune of approximately 14 percent."[267]

At the end of the regular legislative session, Benitz was so disgusted with the drumbeat for more state taxes and spending that he issued a lengthy press release entitled "What's The Matter with Washington?" It served as one of the most compelling, distilled statements of his views. Marshaling statistics, he contrasted recent national prosperity with muted economic growth in Washington State. "Over the last three years, our nation has enjoyed one of the most vigorous economic recoveries in the last 25 years. Throughout the nation, unemployment has dropped, personal income has increased and interest rates have stabilized....So that's the matter with Washington State? Unemployment in Washington during February stood at 10.6% -- the 9th highest rate in the nation. The latest business climate ranking for Washington was 38th of the 48 contiguous states...our state's efforts to attract new businesses are still yielding only marginal results, and...projections for growth in personal income for Washingtonians have leveled off. Unfortunately, Washington is leading the nation in...taxes and government growth...In 1983, the Democrats approved...the largest percentage of tax increases in the nation... A recent study comparing the tax loads of 28 companies located in Washington with what those companies would have paid in 15 competing states showed that Washington's tax load was the highest for 16 of the 22 companies and among the three highest for 22 of the 28 companies. In addition, state spending has tripled in the past dozen years. And over the last decade, spending on social services has increased 311%; education 300%; general government 218%. While Washington's population increased only 1.5% from 1982 thru 1984, *the number of state employees increased 13%*, growing by more than 12,000 new state workers. Washington ranks 2nd in the nation for state debt per person. We're third in the nation for taxes on gasoline, 5th in the state and local sales tax, and 2nd in taxes on liquor. So what's the matter with Washington and our plans for economic development, new jobs and a brighter future? One significant answer: state government is one of Washington's only "growth" industries and higher taxes are one of its most consistent products."[268]

The special session of the State Legislature in June 1985, lasted only two days, and passed an operating budget with no tax increases. Benitz was pleased with this accomplishment, but dismayed over several new pieces of legislation that he believed would demand higher taxes in the future and/or further burden businesses and degrade Washington's overall business climate. "Another blow to the business climate in the state of Washington was struck when the majority party passed an unemployment compensation benefits extension for six weeks," he told his constituents. He was also displeased by increases in costs to employers of the state industrial insurance program, failure to implement a merit-based pay system for state employees that had been passed by the legislature in

1982, and the inability of legislators to agree on a state-wide water clean-up program. Statewide water cleanup legislation was derailed, he said, "when disagreements over the method of payment were not resolved... As written by Western Washington Democrat Senators, The Clean Water Act became a state bailout for Puget Sound without any meaningful aid for Eastern Washington. The compromise proposal approved in April by the Senate was truly a *statewide* water protection plan. The rewrite by Senate Democrats eliminates funding for restoring freshwater lakes and fighting pollution in groundwater. In addition, this proposal increased the amount of money Western Washington gets and ...[changed the Act] into the "Puget Sound Cleanup Act...Those of us who supported the original bill made it clear that we would not provide votes for any measure that placed another tax increase on the citizens of this state. The advantage of the original compromise was its equal treatment of Western and Eastern Washington water cleanup and its pay-as-you-go funding without the need for a tax increase."[269]

Always a champion of education, Benitz was pleased that the 1985 legislative session slightly increased the student/teacher ratio in Kinder-garten through 12th grade classes. As a member of the Temporary Committee on Education, he told constituents, "We recommended 52 chang-es in a six year plan, price tag $260 million. School funding, teacher training, and salaries are the focus of that money; also included is early childhood training and an enlargement of the Head Start Program." He worried that a recent ruling by the U.S. Department of Education re-quiring special programs for school-age alcohol and drug abusers "could spell financial disaster for school districts throughout the state....if such costly programs are required, we will all be forced to bear the brunt, either through higher taxes or through diverting substantial amount s of funding away from education programs and into alcohol and drug rehabilitation programs...a requirement that schools identify and treat the addicts goes well beyond the scope of our education system's mis-sion. Our schools are for teaching. They are not rehabilitation center for alcohol-or drug-dependents children. If schoolchildren are caught in the trap of substance abuse, other community services can be bought to bear on that problem. It is not the responsibility of our school system to change the focus of its mission from education to the treatment of addicts...I hope that Benton County schools, as well as schools through-out the state, will wait for a definitive court ruling on this issue before instituting such costly and disruptive programs."[270]

Benitz did favor a newly proposed anti-harassment bill that would protect people who were "maliciously harassed because of their sex, sexual orientation or age...The proposal would give victims some legal weapons." He was also gratified that the state budget adopted for the biennium beginning July 1, 1985, capped initiation of new social and welfare programs to those already in place as of March 1, and, to benefit agriculture, included "funding for enhanced export and domestic marketing in the agriculture development program... the IMPACT Center at WSU[49]...for noxious weed control materials and biological control agents and ...continued promotion of Washington wine."[271-50] He was also pleased that Governor Gardner "granted B&O tax relief to the beef processors, which will ensure that approximately 2,000 jobs will remain in the state of Washington. ..Until we have a better business climate in the state of Washington, we will always have a difficult time with the state budget."[272]

Max Benitz was a patriot who believed in a strong national defense. In a 1985 Memorial Day speech at American Legion Post 34 in his district, he reiterated his belief that American soil has remained free of military confrontations for more than 100 years because the U.S. retained a strong military force. "*Peace can* only be insured by a continuing commitment to defense and willingness to act when necessary to protect our country's interest and people," he stated. He honored military personnel as "the stalwarts of the American people. They have been willing to give of themselves and their families to uphold a greater good...Too many of our fighting forces have sacrificed their lives for the betterment of them but none of these people died in vain. In many cases one life was lost to avoid the loss of many more. We are proud of those now in our military and prouder in those who have recently given their lives for their country and world peace." Dedicating a flagpole that day, he presented a colorful description of the meaning of the American flag to him. Each color in the flag was a symbol. Again, free enterprise and freedom of opportunity dominated his thoughts. "The beauty of the red, white and blue reflects the opportunities, liberties and freedoms available to each of us. The white stripes represent the purity of our nation and the un-

---

49. The IMPACT Center, located in the School of Economic Sciences at WSU, exists to address economic, social, political, and technical problems that affect the competitiveness of Washington's agriculture and related sectors.

50. Note: Max Benitz's intense interest in, and support for, Washington wines will be discussed in Chapter 5.

charted open future that we have. We are able to determine our own destiny, without the interventions of any other force…The red of the flag's stripes indicate the blood that has been shed throughout the world to protect the American people and the sacrifices so many have made to insure a free nation and a free people. The white stars of the flag are reminders of the fresh new individual opportunities available to anyone willing to pursue them.… The blue background for our flag's stars represents to me the tranquility, strength and freedom that all American people are able to work and live under. …This meshing of the red, white and blue of our flag shows me the compatibility of purity, hard work and peace that we have in the United States."[273]

1986 Legislative Session and Election to Fourth Term

Throughout 1985 and especially 1986, Benitz spent also spent a great deal of his time on energy issues.[51]   Budget debates were not as dominant in the 1986 session because the biennium's budget had been mostly set in 1985. However, he reported to his constituents in spring 1986 that "pay increases for legislators, elected officials, school teachers, college faculty, state workers and State Patrol was three-quarters" of the budget increase that year.[274] In the 1986 legislative session, a statewide water cleanup bill was passed that Benitz felt was fair. It was funded from a new eight cents-per-pack tax on cigarettes. "Equitable distribution of funds will now go to Eastern Washington projects," he said. Importantly, tort reform also passed both houses of the legislature. Benitz described it as "a compromise effort which sets limits on damage awards in liability cases."[275] The state's Department of Ecology was given emergency authority to temporarily withdraw public waters, build water facilities, provide loans and grants, and take other actions necessary to combat an expected drought.

Benitz also sponsored, co-sponsored or otherwise helped to pass bills providing funding for a beef promotion and research program, funding to defend officers, agents and employees of irrigation districts, enforcement powers to collect crop liens, authorization for the use of deadly force by police and other peace officers, and tougher penalties for health care fraud.[276] Once again defending veterans, seniors and children, he supported bills granting reduced fees for camping and park passes to low-income seniors and veterans, strengthening and closing loopholes in laws against pornography and child sexual abuse, and more tightly

51. Energy issues will be discussed in Chapter 4.

Senator Max Benitz: Experience and Leadership working for us.

Senator Max Benitz has represented the Tri-Cities in Olympia with force and integrity. In the State Senate he has often been the lone voice calling for a reasoned approach to nuclear development.

Senator Benitz has seen the Tri-Cities through good times and bad. He's fought to counterbalance the liberal Western Washington policy makers that dominate the halls of power in Olympia.

Along with nuclear power and agriculture, the needs of senior citizens and of our state's colleges have been Max's top priorities.

"Nuclear power, which is based on scientific knowledge and great technical expertise, is being opposed by emotional attacks without any intellectual foundation."

"Seniors don't want a handout or condescension from government...I know because I am a senior. They want their independence and to not have to face an ever increasing tax burden."

With unique knowledge of our industries and economic realities, Benitz has been sought out by leaders across the political spectrum who trust his judgment.

Max Benitz Campaign Flier, 1986.

prohibiting conflicts of interest for members or employees of gambling commissions and the state lottery commission.[277]   He also sponsored three key bills easing restrictions for, and promoting, Washington's wine industry, and regulating radioactive operations in the state.[52]

As the 1986 session ended, Benitz announced that he would run for a fourth term in the Senate. He announcement ended long speculation that he would run for Benton County Commission instead, a position that paid more than twice as much as his position as State Senator. He admitted that the Commissioner job was "tantalizing," and that he done "a lot of soul-searching." However, he said, he hoped to become Chairman of the Energy and Utilities Committee in the Senate, a position where he believed he could accomplish important work for the state. His announcement in May 1986 also ended a round of "musical chairs"

---

52. Wine issues will be discussed in Chapter 5, and energy issues in Chapter 4.

speculation about other races, quashing rumors that other Benton County Republicans might seek his Senate seat. Once Benitz announced, they supported him, knowing that by this time he was virtually unbeatable.[278]

Benitz campaigned on the basis of his record and his traditional causes – agriculture, low taxes, defense of senior and the vulnerable, his experience and seniority, and, increasingly, energy issues. "I've been outspoken in my opposition to an income tax and other 'new ideas' to raise taxes," he told voters. "We need better service from the state, not more taxes." He also stated that "seniors don't want a handout or condescension from government…They want their independence and not to have to face an ever increasing tax burden." His campaign literature stated that he "has fought to counterbalance the liberal Western Washington policy makers that dominate the halls of power in Olympia."[279] He also made Republican party control of the State Senate an election issue, as the 8th District was one of nine with Republican incumbents up for election that year.[280]

Max Benitz was easily elected to his fourth term in the State Senate in 1986, defeating retired labor leader, Democrat Ed Alden by a nearly two-to-one margin.[281] The 1986 elections gave the Democrats a 25-24 majority in the State Senate, while they retained control of the House.[282]

As the 1987 session of the State Legislature opened on January 12, Benitz had lost his seat on the Agriculture Committee, but remained on the Rules, Education, and Energy and Utilities Committees.[283] In the first three weeks, Benitz told his constituents, "very little if any progress [was] made on the main issues, namely the budget and dollars needed to achieve orderly government."[284] Once again, Governor Gardner proposed tax increases, including a sales tax on services and an unemployment tax on small farmers. Benitz opposed both of these new taxes and they were defeated. Democrats in the House then proposed a rearrangement of the tax structure that would have lowered the overall sales tax rate from 6.5 percent to five percent, while extending sales tax to most services; boosted the B&O tax on all sales tax exempt services from 1.5 percent to 2.25 percent; raised the real estate tax from 1.07 percent to 2.75 percent; and increased the B&O tax exemption on interest income of businesses other than financial institutions. This new tax structure, said Benitz, would actually increase total state taxes by $400-million, and he flatly opposed the package.[285] Another proposal would have levied a five-cent increase in the tax on gasoline to fund additional road and

Max Benitz being sworn into 4th term, State Senate, 1986, by Washington Court of Appeals Judge James A. Andersen.

highway projects. "Fortunately," said Benitz, the proposal failed. If this increase had been approved and tacked onto our existing 18-cent tax, it would have made Washington's gas tax the highest in the nation."[286]

Early in the 1987 legislative session, Benton County Commissioner Bill Sebero, a Republican, resigned, once again prompting speculation that Benitz would run for his seat. Within a week, however, Benitz said that he had "seriously considered an invitation from county Republicans to take over the vacant seat, but decided against it. His primary reason was that he hoped control of the State Senate could be taken by Republicans in the next election, making it possible for him to help enact agendas that had long been important to him.[287]

In March, he told a Kennewick Town Hall meeting that tax and energy measures were making the 1987 legislative session "the toughest, hardest negotiating in the Senate" since he was elected to that office in 1974. He asserted that the Governor's proposed sales tax on services "is not going to fly."[288] On April 23, Benitz happily told his constituents: "I was pleased to vote for a bipartisan, no-new taxes budget which was approved today by the Senate."[289] At the conclusion of three extraordinary sessions, in addition to the regular session, the 1987 legislative year ended with the "no-new-taxes" budget that Benitz favored. The budget was, he said, "clearly in the best interests of taxpayers." He told his constituents that "the 1987 legislative session may best be remembered as the session that produced substantial improvements for K-12 and higher education without raising taxes, and in doing so proved that state government can provide quality services while living within its means." The Legislature again increased the required student/teacher ratio, and provided salary equalization funds for small, rural districts that increased minimum salaries for beginning teachers to $17,600. per year. "More individual attention will be given to students in the critical learning years of kindergarten through 3rd grade," he reported. As a consistent advocate of local control, Benitz was pleased that the legislature approved "Bringing Education Home" enhancement grants that allowed local citizens to decide which educational enhancement programs best fit the needs of their schools.

Benitz also reported a host of other important measures passed in the 1987 legislative session that again reflected his clear priorities and beliefs in favor of education, child abuse prevention, balanced water resource allocation, law enforcement, and benefits to senior citizens and agriculture, and against expanded welfare benefits. . . the legislature provided salary hikes for higher education faculty at state colleges, "in order to prevent quality faculty from leaving for better paying jobs in other states...this much-publicized 'brain drain.'" The Tri-Cities University Center benefited from a substantial construction appropriation that Benitz said looked "doubtful at the start of the session...[but] I worked hard to convince my fellow senators that the appropriation was a good investment." His seniority in the State Senate was paying dividends for his district. The "Master Plan for Higher Education" in Washington , developed by the Higher Education Coordinating Board,[53] was approved by the State Senate, calling for "tougher admission standards, improved funding for public colleges and universities, increased access to colleges and universities in urban areas, and a new testing system to assess quality of education." To assist vocational education, Benitz reported, "I authored a new law designed to protect students' tuition payments while helping private vocational schools stay in business...I introduced the idea of creating a Tuition Recovery Fund...Now, instead of having to obtain expensive surety bonds, vocational schools will contribute to

53. The Higher Education Coordinating Board was a 10-member citizen board chartered by the state to improve higher education. In 2012, it was abolished and merged into the state's Department of Education.

the recovery fund, and claims against schools will be settled by the fund rather than contributions to the fund can be lowered," he reported.

Several important bills dealing with water resources were passed, he reported. Another drought was expected in in 1988, and "spurred approval of a measure extending the Department of Ecology's authority to take emergency actions to combat [it]....Another measure would give the Legislature the final say on state water policy decisions...[not] the Department of Ecology. The bill authorizes a mediated study under which all effected parties, from agriculture and environmental groups to public utilities and fishery interests, would work together to develop water policy recommendations for consideration by the Legislature. Yet another bill calls for a water use efficiency study designed to...look at ways to increase water use efficiency, incentives for efficient water use, and possible changes in law to encourage efficiency. Study recommendations would be considered by the Legislature."

Child abuse prevention and public demand to deal with it "prompted lawmakers to make the issue one of their priorities for the session." The legislature approved funds for additional caseworkers and other improvements at Child Protective Services, the state agency responsible for family intervention in child abuse cases. CPS caseworkers would have to meet minimum training requirements in order to handle cases without supervision, and teachers and licensed day-care operators would be trained to detect and prevent child abuse and neglect...Trainees will learn to identify abused and neglected children, and will learn what steps to take to prevent further abuse. Benitz was pleased that the new program would "consider the safety of children its top priority. In recent years CPS caseworkers have received mixed signals over whether their primary objective is the safety of children or keeping families intact. The effect of this law is that CPS workers will be more likely to remove threatened children from homes where abuse is suspected."[290] Benitz also sponsored a bill making homicide by abuse of a child or disabled or dependent adult a Class A felony,[54] and helped to pass a House bill setting goals for youth employment in the Washington Conservation Corps. These goals included natural resource protection and developing the "state's youth resources through meaningful experiences.[291]

In terms of law enforcement, sponsored bills criminalizing custodial assault of an employee or volunteer at state correctional facilities, defining and restricting highway advertising signs, and worked to help

54. The most severe level of criminal offense.

pass a House bill tightly regulating fraternal benefit societies to prevent fraud.[292] He was also happy that the 1987 legislature voted to replace the State Patrol's "outdated fingerprint system with a new automated system featuring a central database, located in Olympia, that will be able to quickly exchange information with remote terminals in other areas of the state." Another new law allowed police officers to mark the license plates of persons caught driving without licenses, in order to more easily "nab those who violate license suspensions." He also supported new laws to "stop drug trafficking in the state." The laws imposed tougher penalties for selling or distributing drugs, to "eliminate more lenient sentences often given for initial convictions." In order to prevent evidence being thrown out of Washington's courtrooms because of vague wording in the state's search and seizure laws, the legislature "eliminated the conflict by changing the wording of our state constitution to read exactly like the U.S. Constitution."

The 1987-89 "no-new-taxes budget renews or expands a number of programs vital to seniors," he reported, including monies for an adult dental care program, pay raises for certain low-wage employees, including chore services and nursing home workers, long-term care services such as nursing homes, respite care programs, and a regional hospital pool "to offset charity care costs." He favored a measure that would request the federal government not to require the Bonneville Power Authority, a federal agency that provided power to several utilities, to pay off its loans on an accelerated scale. "Unfortunately, if the federal government takes this course economic hardships to Washington's poor and elderly and the possible loss of 23,000 to 70,000 jobs from closed down aluminum plants would likely result," said Benitz. "Also hard pressed agriculture could be devastated by higher rates."[293]

In what Benitz called a "landmark welfare reform measure," the legislature passed the Family Independence Program (FIP). "The plan," he said, "is designed to get people off public assistance by providing jobs, job training, work search skills and incentives to find employment...The cornerstone of FIP is eliminating the disincentives for welfare recipients to work. In the current welfare system, recipients often see no reason to find employment because the money they earn is subtracted from public assistance payments. FIP, however, makes, makes it possible for recipients to keep the money they earn as long as they do not exceed 135 percent of what they receive in welfare payments." Benitz called the FIP "one of the most important measures to pass the Legislature since it is a workable solution to the cycle of welfare dependence which traps so many families and drains the resources of the state."[294]

In terms of agricultures, Benitz sponsored bills licensing and setting fees for nursery dealers and slaughterhouses and other meat facilities, and granting tax exemptions to hops growers. He also helped to pass a House bill granting tax exemptions to seed conditioning activities.[295] Another agricultural concern of Max Benitz in 1987 was the growing backlash in the United States against the use of farm chemicals. He had always been a proponent of the informed, proper use of such chemicals, and was pleased to tell his constituents that the Environmental Protection Agency had formally repudiated a study by the National Resources Defense Council that indicted Alar,[55] an apple treatment chemical, as a carcinogen.[296] Consumer advocate Ralph Nader launched an anti-Alar campaign and convinced six national grocery store chains and nine major food processors to refuse to sell Alar-treated apples by early 1987.[297] Benitz took on the issue and titled a humorous bulletin to his constituents "12 Tons of Apples A Day Keeps the Doctor Away." He related a study of rats fed doses of Alar equivalent to a human eating 25,000 pounds of Alar-treated apples a day for life. These rats, he stated, "had less tumors than rats that had eaten no Alar... So on those occasions when one apple leads to another and before you know it you've polished off several tons, if medical difficulties arise, don't blame Alar."[298]

Energy issues dominated a great deal of Benitz's time and legislative efforts during the 1987 session, and he was able to pass a new law creating a Washington Wine Commission that became one of the signature accomplishments of his career.[56]

1988-1989 Education and Farm Issues

When the 1988 session of the State Legislature convened, Benitz again served on the Senate Education Committee, overseeing K-12 and vocational education.[299] He backed a comprehensive bill to stop the spread of the AIDS (Acquired Immune Deficiency Syndrome) virus. The AIDS Omnibus Bill required AIDS education for public school students once each year beginning in the fifth grade, AIDS education freshmen to state colleges, universities and vocational schools, AIDS testing

55. Alar was first a registered trademark of U.S. Rubber Co. of New York, New York, but at the time of this controversy it was a registered trademark of Uniroyal Chemical Co. of Middlebury, Connecticut.
56. Energy issues will be discussed in Chapter 4, and wine issues in Chapter 5.

for convicted prostitutes, sex offenders, and intravenous drug abusers, AIDS counseling for pregnant women, sexually transmitted disease patents and drug abuse treatment patients, authorized public health officials to detain AIDS carriers who ignored counseling and continued to engage in high-risk behavior that endangered others, protected persons with AIDS against unfair discrimination and provided confidentiality for those tested for AIDS, and established regional AIDS service networks across the state.[300] The bill passed in the same year that 35 other states passed 136 laws relating to AIDS education, confidentiality, testing, reporting and protection.[301]

He also sponsored successful bills allowing recipients of Washington Scholars Awards to attend private colleges and universities, setting licensing requirements for physical therapists to prevent fraud, and defining application requirements for concealed pistol permits.[302] In the interests of agriculture and rural constituents, he passed bills authorizing hydraulic projects to stabilize stream banks to protect farm lands, establishing a rural arterial trust account to fund replacement of bridges in rural areas, and requiring the state Department of Ecology to sell its interest in the Prosser well to accommodate irrigation needs.[303] He also sponsored a law adding key new definitions to portions of the Washington Wine Commission that had been created the previous year. However, energy issues were becoming so compelling in his district and indeed in the entire state that Max Benitz spent the majority of his time in 1988 on energy issues.[57]

Farm Chemicals and Pesticides

Early in 1989, Benitz also provided one of the most salient expressions of his beliefs about food production, food safety and farm chemicals in a speech to the Western Washington Horticulture Association meeting. It came at a time when farm chemicals increasingly had come under attack and public scrutiny. On January 2, *Time* magazine had emblazoned the words "Endangered Earth" on its cover. The featured article was titled: "Planet of the Year: What on Earth Are We Doing?" It said in part: "The use of pesticides has increased crop yields but polluted water supplies."[304] Celebrity figures such as comedian Whoopi Goldberg fasted to protest the use of "poisons" on food, and an "infomercial" fea-

---

57. Wine issues will be discussed in Chapter 5, and energy issues will be covered in Chapter 4.

turing movie superstar Meryl Streep termed apples sprayed with Alar a "mess." Streep also testified before Congress on the dangers of Alar.[305] In a letter to the *Seattle Times* in December 1988, a man asked: "What are we doing to ourselves? Never in the history of the world has a society worked so hard to manufacture its own death. And we export it too. DDT produced in the U.S. Still travels to the world. What are we gaining with all our chemicals? ...We have a raped environment, a bankrupt land."[306]

"THINGS ARE TOUGH OUT ON THE FARM," Benitz told his audience. Food safety, he acknowledged, was "on everyone's mind." He began by telling his audience that he was a "dirt farmer for over 40 years in Washington State...having lived by the seat of my pants in a day-to-day operation of agriculture production." Using statistics, he showed that the number of family farms in the U.S. was going down steeply. The number of farms in Washington in 1989 was less than half the number in 1945, and the acreage per farm had increased by approximately 40 percent. A much higher percentage of farms were corporate-owned, and were financed outside the region.[307] In 1940 when he started farming, Benitz recalled, "a farmer fed his family and 13 others. Today's farmer [feeds]... his family and 72 others...less than 2% of [Americans today are] agriculture producers, feeding not only this nation, but many parts of the world also." In addition, he said, "today our USA customer is buying the best food ever for smallest percent of a paycheck ever... Because of the U.S. farmer's productivity, Americans can buy higher quality food for less of their disposable income that even a few years ago (16.6% today vs. 23% in 1951)." Another major change in farming, he pointed out, was that the so-called "farm block," in Congress and State legislatures, formerly "huge and very effective," had "virtually disappeared. For example, of the 49 Washington State Senators, two of us (Senator Newhouse and myself), are the only ones with our fingers actually in the soil. There are four others who are either retired from Agriculture or have some direct connection, so all told, the number is six and that's a long way from the majority number of 25."

One of the principal reasons farmers were able to be so much more productive than in the past, Benitz emphasized, was the use of "crop protection chemicals [that] safeguard our food and fiber supply against devastating losses to insects, weeks and disease. They help to insure agricultural production that not only is of the highest quality, but production that is more than twice the levels of the 1930." He told the audience of wormy apples he had seen on Soviet farms during his 1963 tour, a condition present because the fruit had not been sprayed with pesticides. Then he tackled the farm chemical issue head-on. In some news stories, he said, "we as agriculture producers are made to appear that we are throwing chemicals around like they did not cost us any money... All of us here know full well that the chemicals we use cost us a bundle and we don't intend to use a drop more than is needed. Some of the examples of costs: Bayleton,[58] which is very effective in the raising of wine grapes costs upwards of $60 a pound." Aside from expense, he asserted, safety was "a preeminent factor in determining which candidate compounds... [are] commercialized. Only one in about 20,000 new compounds will finally become a commercial crop protection product...some very promising candidates are never tested or marketed because they don't meet safety criteria."

Benitz gave several interesting examples in which crop chemicals received a bad reputation because they were misused. In one case, some wealthy but inexperienced men bought a farm in the Columbia Basin (eastern Washington) and "very inappropriately spread Endrin[59] on some alfalfa hay to get at the mice... The neighbor's fancy Holstein milk cows broke the fence down and got into the hay. The odor from the Endrin attracted the cows and the hay was nice green hay and it was wintertime. Many of those cattle died an agonizing death. The next thing I know, there was a bill introduced in the Senate...to outlaw Endrin." He and two other Senators knowledgeable about farming eventually were able to quash the bill. However, he said, such events were "dangerous, because it becomes totally political...[and could] damage agriculture immensely." In another example, "*we* had an approved chemical, Measurol,[60] to spray [wine] grapes that did not kill the bird and it did not show up in the wine, but the bird did not like the taste of it. . . it was [also] very effective in keeping the birds from damaging the sweet cherries in the spring of the year, another very valuable crop. But a neighbor not very far away, inadvertently, and I'm sure by accident, put a double

58. Bayleton is a registered trademark of Bayer Crop Science Inc. of Research Triangle Park, North Carolina.
59. Endrin is no longer a registered trademark. It was formerly a trademarked product of Velsicol Chemical Company of Memphis, Tennessee.
60. Measurol was a registered trademark of Gowan Company of Yuma, Arizona.

dose on the cherries. In a sample taken later on, some of it showed up on the cherries and consequently we lost that chemical for the effective control of the birds in the wine grapes." In one of the clearest examples, he related, "some California watermelon fields were found to have been illegally treated with aldicarb (Temik).[61] It received coast-to-coast media coverage and decimated the market for watermelons. Because a couple of growers used a pesticide that wasn't registered for that crop, all other watermelon growers suffered."

Benitz then addressed the Alar issue. "Alar is a wonderful product," he said. "It is used chiefly on the red striped delicious and ...Alar improves the red color. It extends the shelf life and has other features, yet the Food and Drug Administration gave a report that Alar could cause cancer and has caused an immense amount of problems...One of the problems with Alar came from Ralph Nader. [As a consequence of his remarks]...one big retail food chain announced that they would not handle apples that had been sprayed with Alar, and after they refused to handle them many of the other large chain stores followed suit. It is not over with yet, but I am totally convinced that Alar will be cleared in time and will be back in use." At that time, he said, Taiwan was the only large market for striped red delicious apples sprayed with Alar. He emphasized that "WE DO NEED THE FOOD AND DRUG ADMINISTRATION, STATE DEPARTMENT OF AGRICULTURE, FEDERAL USDA, but darn it, they have a big responsibility to the public and the producer before giving a sensational story to the news media."

He briefly addressed organic farming, stating that some people had become so alarmed over crop chemicals that they had turned to this method. "Organic farming has considerable appeal to many...there is nothing wrong with 'organic' food. Except, that if it were our total production, our food supply would drop by a sizable percentage. The number starving would increase by a magnitude that would certainly be a world wide disaster."

Benitz bluntly warned his audience: "Growers cannot allow pesticides to be misused. The consequences and repercussions of misuse are severe... A single incident can go a long way toward creating or reinforcing misconceptions...If there is any information on an individual illegally using a pesticide, it should be immediately reported to the

61. Temik was first a registered trademark of Union Carbide Corporation of New York, New York; later a trademarked product of Bayer Crop Science Inc., of Research Triangle Park, North Carolina, and as of April 2011 is marketed as Meymik, a trademarked product.

proper authorities...If we want to keep pesticides available for use, we cannot afford to let misuse give anti-pesticide forces a soapbox. We must use pesticides as if a government regulator, an environmentalist, a farmworker representative, and a consumer advocate were watching our every move—because they are. In terms of public relations and public perceptions, he asked, "how do you un-ring a bell?"[308]

Hectic 1989 Legislative Year

In the elections of November 1988, Republicans had held their slim majority in the State Senate, but Democrats controlled the House and the Governorship. Max Benitz did not have to run that year, as Senatorial terms ran for four years, and only half of the Washington Senate seats stood for election every two years. He spent much of his time during the 1989 session consumed with energy issues, and some time on wine industry issues. In addition, as ranking Minority member of the Education Committee, he pushed hard to establish a branch campus of WSU in the Tri-Cities. He sponsored SB 6095 in March, providing for four branch campuses of WSU across the state, including one in the Tri-Cities.[309] Since the 1950s, the Tri-Cities had had a facility known sometimes as the Joint Center for Graduate Studies or simply the "Graduate Center." It offered an amalgam of courses, mostly concentrated in the sciences and engineering but also including business administration, taught largely by part-time instructors whose full-time work was at the nearby Hanford Site. Although courses at the Graduate Center were accredited, a student could not earn a degree there because the classes were offered by three different colleges and universities in Washington and Oregon. Importantly, Benitz's bill provided for the transfer of property, land, facilities, personnel and equipment to WSU from the other schools that participated in the Graduate Center. "This move," Benitz told his constituents, "is essential to solidify WSU's position as branch campus operator in the Tri-Cities, and lay a foundation for future branch campus expansion and improvements." WSU-Tri-Cities would offer upper division undergraduate courses, and graduate courses "designed to complement those offered by Columbia Basin College and other community colleges. Benitz believed deeply in the value of education, and called the bill a "giant step" toward securing a WSU branch campus in the Tri-Cities.[310] Although he was the principal sponsor, Benitz was also a savvy politician who sought the support of other Senators and Representatives whose districts would benefit from branch campuses of WSU and the

University of Washington. On May 10, 1989, SB 6095, sponsored by Senators Max Benitz, Jerry Saling, Al Bluechel, Emilio Cantu, Bill Smitherman, Lois Stratton, Marcus Gaspard, Tom Patterson, Al Bauer, Peter von Reichbauer, Jeannette Hayner and Linda Smith, was approved by the 51st Session of the Washington State legislature.[62] It became law on May 31, 1989, as one the signature achievements of Benitz's career.

It would be an understatement to say that Max Benitz was extremely busy throughout 1989. In addition to energy issues, wine industry issues and his key branch campus bill, he sponsored, co-sponsored or actively campaigned for successful bills in agriculture, fisheries and forest issues; vocational education; criminal justice; protection of children, other vulnerable populations and consumers; and public safety and public works projects. One bill enforced livestock liens to assure payment to stable keepers, veterinarians and others who cared for animals, another imposed mandatory fines for livestock theft, another placed limitations on civil liability for injuries resulting from equine activities, another promoted water conservation, and yet another granted emergency (but limited) emergency powers to the state Department of Ecology for drought relief.[311] Other bills provided for private contracting to promote the production of salmon smolt, assisted development of regional fisheries enhancement groups, regulated waste disposal and pollution discharge from upland[63] fin fish rearing facilities, and provided for research and policy development studies to enhance and protect the forests of Washington state.[312]

In terms of vocational education and the protection of vulnerable populations and consumers, Benitz's 1989 bills included one setting certification requirements for vocational education instructors, one revoking qualification certificates and terminating the employment of school employees for crimes against children, one setting rules of conduct for those providing assistance to immigrants (to "promote honesty and fair dealing"), one providing for equitable distribution of assets between spouses when one spouse was incompetent or institutionalized, one very long and complex bill tightly regulating commercial telephone solicitation, and another equally long and complicated bill carefully regulating the rate setting procedures of telecommunications companies.[313]

---

62. The WSU Tri-Cities Branch Campus Library was dedicated in September 1991, and will be discussed further in Chapter 5.

63. Upland facilities were those located outside state waters but whose activities resulted in the disposal of solid or liquid waste materials into state waters.

SENATE BILL NO. 6095

State of Washington   51st Legislature   1989 Regular Session

by Senators Benitz, Saling, Bluechel, Cantu, Smitherman, Stratton, Gaspard, Patterson, Bauer, von Reichbauer, Hayner and Smith

Read first time 3/23/89 and referred to Committee on Higher Education.

1   AN ACT Relating to branch campuses; amending RCW 28B.15.202,
2 28B.20.010, 28B.20.130, 28B.30.010, and 28B.30.150; creating new
3 sections; repealing RCW 28B.30.510; providing an effective date; and
4 declaring an emergency.

5 BE IT ENACTED BY THE LEGISLATURE OF THE STATE OF WASHINGTON:

6   NEW SECTION. Sec. 1. It is the intent of this act to fulfill
7 the recommendations contained in the Washington state master plan for
8 higher education, adopted by the higher education coordinating board,
9 regarding the establishment of branch campuses of the University of
10 Washington and Washington State University to serve the unmet higher
11 education needs in certain urban localities. It is the intent of the
12 legislature that additional upper-division and graduate educational
13 services be provided in Tacoma, Bothell-Woodinville, Spokane,
14 southwest Washington, and the Tri-cities through the creation of
15 branch campuses in these urban communities. The legislature intends
16 that these branch campuses should be governed and operated as
17 extensions of the University of Washington and Washington State
18 University, respectively. It is the intent of the legislature that
19 the higher education coordinating board shall monitor closely the
20 establishment of those campuses created by this act, and that the
21 University of Washington and Washington State University shall fully
22 cooperate with the higher education coordinating board in order that
23 the recommendations of the board, which resulted in the creation of
24 these campuses, be fulfilled.

25   NEW SECTION. Sec. 2. (1) The method of organization,
26 governance, and administration of branch campus programs established
27 in sections 5 and 7 of this act shall be proposed by the appropriate
28 institutional governing board and subject to approval by the higher

Max Benitz's handwritten vote tally approving the WSU Branch Campus.

Benitz recognized the new science of DNA[64] identification, and worked energetically for a authorizing the State Patrol and the University of Washington School of Medicine to work together to develop a DNA identification system to assist law enforcement. He also sponsored a bill ranking and specifying seriousness levels of felonies, tightly defining defrauding activities against public utilities, clarifying incorporation statures for nonprofit corporations, authorizing many statewide public works projects (including a road project in Kennewick), and providing for careful regulation of excursion an charter buses by the state Utilities and Transportation Commission.[314]

1989 Trip to Soviet Union

In September 1989, Benitz once again traveled to the Soviet Union, just prior to visiting France, Germany, Sweden and Switzerland to look at nuclear programs in those countries.[65] The Soviet portion of his trip lasted two weeks, and was focused on agriculture, as his Soviet trip in 1963 had been. His observations of life and the political climate in the U.S.S.R. were pithy. His dominant impression was that change was in the air. *"Nobody knows what's going to happen next,"* he emphasized in recounting the trip. That statement, he said, best summarizes my impressions of the tension filled country. Everywhere I went, I got the impression the people expect something big to happen soon, but nobody is quite sure what will happen and when." Evidence for his view came from several people, places and situations he visited. Most important, however, was "an increasing outspokenness on the part of Soviet citizens, and in their unmistakable dissatisfaction with the present situation. The Soviets have ample reason to want change. Two weeks in their country provided glimpses of an economy hamstrung by government mismanagement, of a thriving black market fueled by a severe lack of confidence in Soviet money, and of a near total lack of social and economic opportunity."

Benitz noted that one of the most "striking examples of the lack of confidence in Soviet government" was the "mad scramble" for American money. In the various cities he visited, including Moscow, Minsk, Odessa and Leningrad, Soviet citizens were out in the streets conducting a lively black market business in exchanging their own currency for U.S. dollars. Although the practice was officially against the law, "trading

64. Deoxyribonucleic acid
65. Nuclear issues will be discussed in Chapter 4.

for American money…it was practiced frequently and openly on every stop of our trip." The official exchange rate at that time was 1.6 rubles to one U.S. dollar, he saw people trading six to 12 rubles per dollar. Hotel porters asked for their tips to be in dollars, and in a Moscow bar a sign openly proclaimed that only "hard currency" (meaning American dollars) would be accepted. Police, he said, never bothered the money traders, except in one case in Leningrad where he witnessed officers confiscating the U.S. dollars of a trader on the street, pocketing the money, and then chasing away the trader. "Soviets want U.S. Money because they know it has value," he said. "They have no such confidence in their own currency."

In farming, he witnessed the near-collapse of the collective farm system. Small "backyard farms," were everywhere, he observed, selling produce at roadside stands. The practice both gave extra income to the small farmers, and helped to satisfy the food shortages that resulted from the poorly run state farms. Throughout the 1980s, Soviet agricultural production was so inadequate that the average person's diet was deficient in all five major food groups measured – meat, milk, grain, potatoes and vegetables. State production of grain plateaued at about 65 million tons in the 1960s, and remained fixed through the late 1980s, despite a population increase of about 80 million people. In January 1987, President Mikhail Gorbachev had told the National Communist Party meeting bluntly: "We are buying [the grain] because we cannot survive without it."[315] "Backyard farms are viewed as a necessary evil by the Soviet government," Benitz said. "They smack of capitalism but the Soviet people would go hungry without them. Although backyard farms represent less than one-quarter of one percent of Soviet farmland, they produce more than 50 percent of the USSR's poultry products and are similarly important for supplying vegetables and fruit." On the state-run farms, he observed poor practices and slow, unmotivated workers. Visiting a state-run diary, he saw "cows which have no grain in their diet because all grain is needed for humans; and a staggering 800 employees for an operation that milks 2,800 cows… Cows fed lots of grass silage, some corn silage, very little dry hay. The silage came out of the largest number of huge concrete block silos I had ever seen…they have not been used for 10 years. Why? Workers said they were waiting for someone to develop a good liner to reduce spoilage, but those silos would take far too much labor to load and unload. I doubt they'll ever be used for

Upper right photo depicts poor quality in 1963 U.S.S.R. while bottom photo is from Helsinki, Finland in 1998 and shows the first quality produce from a free enterprise system.

silage again." On another large farm, he saw "literally millions of dollars' worth of equipment parked at its headquarters. We were not told how big the farm was, but I do not believe that much equipment could be used efficiently on any farm, no matter how big." Benitz did not get to see potato harvesting as had been planned, but he did see a truckload of spilled potatoes on a road. The potatoes, he said, "were very small —most would have gone through out eliminator chain and back on the ground [in the U.S.]. Spuds very important in U.S.S.R. for food and vodka. Government is cutting vodka supply to citizens, which is causing a considerable uproar." Millions of acres of vineyards in the southern Soviet Union had been destroyed in recent years, Benitz was told by their guide, to reduce the "drunk" problem. The result was simply a proliferation of home distilling that produced poor quality, highly alcoholic and sometimes poisonous brews. People were making their own alcoholic drinks out of lemons, oranges, or "anything" they could find, he said.

Another huge change that Benitz observed, as compared to his 1963 visit was open criticism of the government, and open practice of traditions (particularly religious traditions) formerly harshly repressed by the government. "Evidence of the police state is no longer prevalent... During our visit to the Soviet dairy, a worker praised the efforts of new

Benitz's photos of concrete silors and oversize harvesters at state-run Soviet farm, 1989.

political leader Boris Yeltsin[66] and openly upbraided hardline party bu-reaucrats, bluntly stating the current system does not and will not work."

On a Moscow street we came across a Canadian religious group holding a full revival meeting, and filming it with no interference from authorities...When I visited the U.S.S.R. years ago, Soviet guides freely ridiculed anything religious... On this trip, the guides simply said that churches and statues... symbolized the religion of the time."

Benitz visited many of the major tourist attractions in the largest Russian cities, including the Museum of Czars, Red Square, parts of the Kremlin, and the Cathedral of St. Basil in Moscow, which he termed "stunning...amazingly beautiful." At Lenin's Tomb, Benitz quipped "he looks the same."

He visited the state-run GUM (*Glavnyi Universalnyi Magazin,* or "main universal store") department store, the largest in the country and one of the largest stores in the world. "Building huge but stock just isn't there. Which means out in the country, goods are even scarcer."

He also visited a special, "no-wheel traffic" street where the tour group mingled with Soviet citizens. The street was crowded with peo-ple selling arts and gifts, and exchanging money, and he noted "a pro-

66. Yeltsin, who spoke openly against communist hard-liners, would become President of the new Russian Federation in 1991.

Benitz's photos of St. Basil's Cathedral, 1989.

nounced difference from my last visit in younger people's dress, hair color, music—rock 'n roll very much in evidence…*Glasnost*[67] *was in full operation, but…As* we mingle with the Soviet citizens, the men and women have nothing to smile about whatsoever."

After four days in Moscow, Benitz's tour group departed for Odessa in the southern U.S.S.R., on an Aeroflot (Soviet state-run airline) plane. The bathrooms were "filthy," he said, but conditions were worse in Odessa. "10x12 hotel room including bathroom. A city of over a million people with no hot water! Heated water is from a central system that will be started 'later.' When tourists complain, guides answer: "Don't complain too much, there may be no water tomorrow." From Odessa, they traveled by bus to the Black Sea area, home of Soviet state-run resorts. He saw thousands of heavy wooden beach chairs, but only four were occupied. They then toured several farms. A state-run grape vineyard, he found, had been built on a "heavy gumbo" soil on flat terrain – "not typical soil or terrain for grapes," he observed dryly. "Not too well cared for. Concrete posts about 6 feet long held the wires. A great amount of Bordeaux spray on leaves indicated mildew and rot problems."

67. Glasnost means openness or freedom of expression, and was a trademark policy of then Soviet Premier Mikhail Gorbachev.

Benitz's photo of Lenin's Tomb, 1989.

Leaving Odessa, the group waited five hours at the airport for the flight to Minsk. There was "no sense of obligation to the customer by Aeroflot," he reported, but in Minsk they did have warm water. They toured farms and saw "*large* fields of radishes in full bloom to be used as green-chop for cattle, many sugar beet fields have same purpose." At Lunch, a local communist party leader proposed a toast to "peace in our time." In his private notes, Benitz couldn't contain his sarcasm: "*War* should not be their concern, it should be a system that doesn't produce." After just a day in Minsk, they flew to Leningrad, the Soviet Union's second largest city at slightly more than four million people at that time. Their hotel, the Pribaltiyskaya, had been built in the 1970s by the Swedish construction company Skanska,[68] and was "the best I've ever seen," Benitz said. The next day they visited the summer palace of the czars on the Gulf of Finland. It was "huge, beautiful, but cold," he said. On their last day in Leningrad they visited the Cathedral of St. Isaac, which he described as "inside the most beautiful building I've seen." Heading on to the European part of his tour, Benitz stopped in Berlin to view the Berlin Wall once again, seeing it less than two months before East and West German citizens tore it down.[69]

68. Skanska is a global corporation headquartered in Solna, Sweden.

Benitz's photo of street scene in Moscow, 1989.

Benitz's photo of GUM department store in Moscow, 1989.

Benitz's photo of unhealthy grape vineyards in southern Russia, 1989.

As always during and after his visits to foreign countries, particularly communist nations and other dictatorial regimes, Benitz reflected on the look and feel of repression, and the lessons for Americans. "The Soviet Union is a nation characterized by contradiction: Emboldened citizens stand poised for change, their hopes buoyed by greater tolerance of individual expression and the promise of social freedom and economic opportunity," he wrote when he returned home. "But their hopes are tempered by poorly managed, unproductive economy and a total lack of experience in building a free, democratic society." President Gorbachev had risen through the ranks of the Communist Party to become Secretary of Agriculture and later President. In his agricultural position, he had seen starvation first-hand as a result of the collective farming system that motivated no one and wasted resources through misallocation and centralized decision-making that did not account for conditions and needs in the field. He had introduced first a farm co-op system that allowed workers to divide among themselves any profits remaining after meeting state quotas. Then, he had allowed the "backyard farms" that actually allowed people to act as small entrepreneurs. By the late 1980s, despite their small size, backyard farms were producing nearly one/third the entire agricultural output of the Soviet Union. In October 1988, Gorbachev had shocked the world by announcing that government collective farms will be leased to private individuals to expand production and curtail massive subsidies.[316]

As President, Gorbachev had signed the Intermediate Nuclear Forces Treaty with U.S. President Reagan in December 1987, as a way to cut Soviet military expenses direct more resources at food production and other domestic needs. With "glasnost" he allowed some individual expression and dissent, but still he could not keep the dying Soviet system

69. The Berlin Wall was torn down on November 9, 1989.

Benitz's photo of the Berlin Wall, from Potsdamer Platz on the West German side, September 1989.

YOU ARE INVITED TO COME TOUR RUSSIA WHILE SAMPLING SOME WASHINGTON WINES.

SOVIET UNION

TIME: 5:30 Today 3/7/90

PLACE: Senate Hearing Room 1

HOST: Senator Max E. Benitz-
will be showing slides of his
September 1989 Agri-Tour of the
U.S.S.R.
20 min. program

Back home in Washington State, Benitz gave a series of slide shows and talks on his U.S.S.R. visit, often serving Washington wines to his colleagues.

afloat.[317] However, at the time of Benitz's visit in September 1989, events that would cause the Soviet Union to dissolve were two years away, and he could not know what would happen. However, presciently, he was positive that change was *"imminent...Mikhail* Gorbachev's efforts to promote a more open society are very apparent in the Soviet Union . . . he is on the right track with his efforts to provide opportunity for his people and to instill in them hope, ambition and leadership. His 'westerniza-tion' of the Soviet Union is the right medicine to cure a system that does not produce. But he faces an enormous task . . . There are many in po-sition of power in the USSR who would like to see Gorbachev fail. The deciding factor in the Soviet Union's future will be the actions of the dissatisfied masses. These people desperately want things to be better, but don't quite know how to make it happen, the result of generations of restrictive rule...great change [is] imminent... We can only hope the Soviets are able to make the transformation to a free, open society."[318]

1990 Brings Busy Agenda and Election Challenge

As the 1990 session of the State legislature opened, Max Benitz had a lot on his mind. He was now involved in pressing energy issues on a national level, and spent increasing amounts of time traveling and writ-ing proposals and issue papers on those subjects.[70] In addition, he told constituents early in the year that he wanted to push a telephone assis-tance program to "focus on getting more benefits to senior citizens," re-new the program providing telecommunication devices to the deaf and extend the program to the speech-impaired, require alternate operator services to register and be regulated, "possibly [add] some additional legislation on telephone solicitation and on telephone credit card fraud," and "renew the program that puts restrictions on shutting off heat [for low income seniors] in the winter months."[319]

Early in the session, Senate Republicans unveiled a supplemental budget for the 1989-91 biennium, including direct appropriations from the motor vehicle excise tax to help counties perform criminal justice work. Benitz co-sponsored the bill, which specifically directed counties to use the funds, in part, for the "preservation of public health," as fight-ing against the spread of illegal drug use had become an increasingly important cause to him.[320] (Disappointingly to Benitz, the bill did not pass.[321]) He coordinated a drug-awareness program called "Grandpar-ents Against Drugs," because, he said, "There's so much talk about dam-

70. Energy issues will be discussed in Chapter 4.

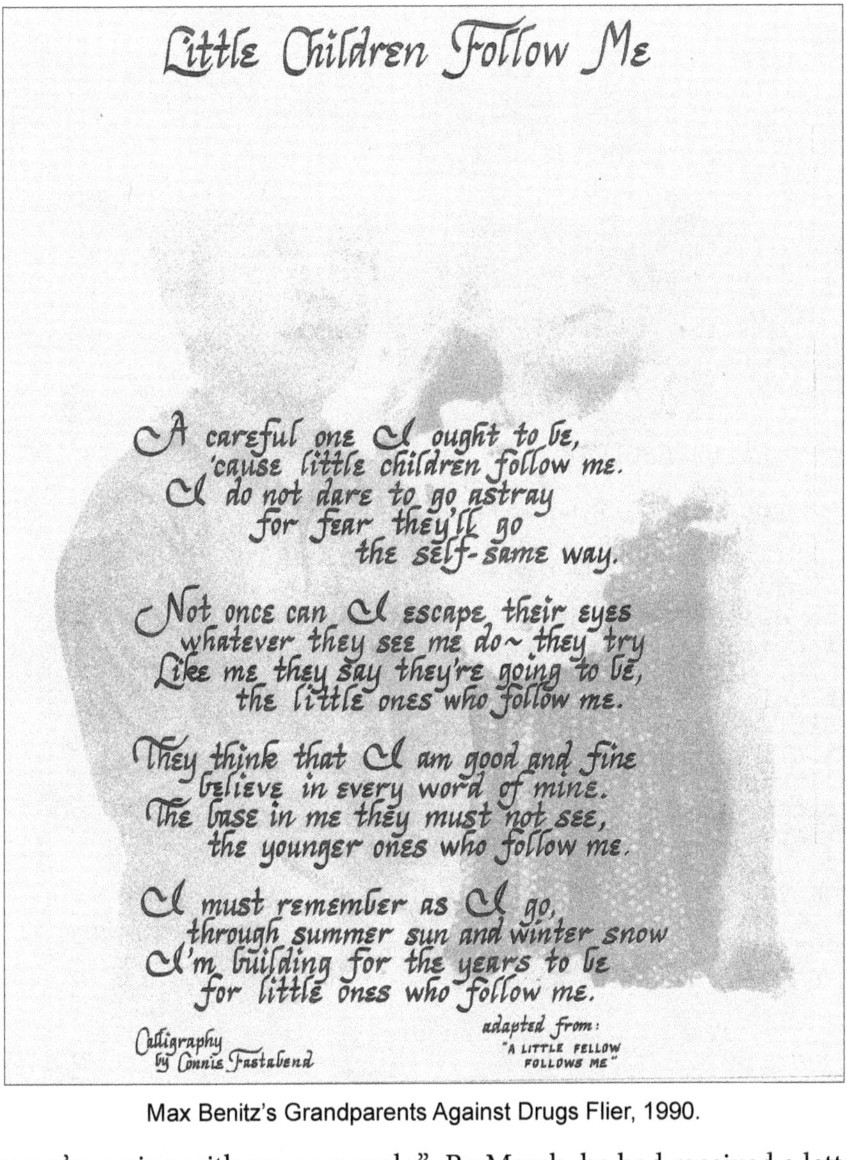

Little Children Follow Me

A careful one I ought to be,
  'cause little children follow me.
I do not dare to go astray
    for fear they'll go
      the self-same way.

Not once can I escape their eyes
    whatever they see me do~ they try
Like me they say they're going to be,
    the little ones who follow me.

They think that I am good and fine
    believe in every word of mine.
The base in me they must not see,
    the younger ones who follow me.

I must remember as I go,
    through summer sun and winter snow
I'm building for the years to be
  for little ones who follow me.

Calligraphy
  by Connie Fastabend

adapted from:
"A LITTLE FELLOW
FOLLOWS ME"

Max Benitz's Grandparents Against Drugs Flier, 1990.

age we're seeing with young people." By March, he had received a letter of support for the program from President George H.W. Bush.[322]

The Republican supplemental budget also included extra funds for the WSU Tri-Cities branch campus to replace money from a grant being terminated by the federal Department of Energy, and "major enhancements for public schools," Benitz told constituents. He also introduced a vocational education bill, providing funding to lower class sizes in state

THE WHITE HOUSE

WASHINGTON

March 20, 1990

Dear Senator Benitz:

Thank you for telling me about the Grandparents Against Drugs Program and for sharing Mrs. Kraus's inspiring letter with me.

I was delighted to learn of your efforts to rid your community of the scourge of drugs.

Your unique program links together the American tradition of volunteer service with one of our nation's greatest resources -- our senior citizens. The interest, involvement, and ideas of every American, young or old, are needed if we are ultimately to achieve victory in the war on drugs.

Thank you for giving heart to our cause. I urge you to remain steadfast on the battle lines in your community. Help America fight back until we can truly claim victory over drugs.

Sincerely,

[signature: George Bush]

The Honorable Max Benitz
103 Institutions Building
Olympia, Washington, 98504

George Bush White House Letter to Benitz, 1990.

Governor Booth Gardner, Senator Max E. Benitz, Sr. , Gary Nelson, 1990.

vocational education school and place new equipment into the classrooms. "Vocational education is one of our best options for training young people who are not interested in academics, and meeting the work force needs of the future," he said. "The budget gives voc-ed a shot in the arm that should result in some real improvement." Benitz backed other enhancements for Kindergarten-12th grade education in the state, including funding for public school construction, books, classroom supplies, more teachers to reduce class sizes, and the "Fair Start" program "to help at-risk children success in the classroom. Our children are our future," he stated. "This budget makes a major investment in helping children." He also co-sponsored successful bills providing a pathway to tenure for state community college instructors and mandating the state's higher education board to study ways to ensure educational opportunities for place-bound students.[323]

Benitz also sponsored a bill to provide monies to local governments to reduce property taxes for qualifying senior and disabled citizens. "We want seniors to be able to stay in their own homes and keep up with medical expenses and other costs of living," he said. However, his bill was stopped in the House Revenue Committee. Successful bills he sponsored, co-sponsored or worked hard to pass included one requiring telecommunications devices for the hearing and speech-impaired to be provided at no additional cost above the costs of regular telephone service, one penalizing telecommunications fraud, two bills protecting the health of public water systems and assisting failing public water systems, and one giving civil investigative powers to the Attorney General to pursue consumer protection complaints.[324] The Republican supplemental budget also created a "budget stabilization account" to be used in case of an economic downturn, and, according to Benitz, "reflects the

Senator Max Benitz speaking in the State Senate, Olympia, 1990. Photo courtesy of *Yakima Herald*.

Legislature's strong commitment this year to help counties fight crime and drugs." He co-sponsored a successful bill funding the Utilities and Transportation Commission to study implementing a statewide 911 emergency system, establishing more severe penalties for air pollution violations, limiting solid fuel burning (mostly wood stoves) during air pollution episodes, regulating the safety of food products transportation, and funding a study of the effects of exempting motor carriers of recycled materials from certain taxes.[325] Benitz sponsored another successful bill to relax window tinting regulations for cars. The largest newspaper in Benitz's district, the *Tri-City Herald* called the bill "a minor issue in the grand sweep of Olympian legislation but a major one back home in the Tri-Cities.[326]

Soon after the 1990 legislative session ended, Benitz attended a three-day retreat on Orcas Island off Washington's coast to study ways to manage Washington's water resources. It was the first-ever gathering of more than 175 representatives of Indian nations and tribes, legislators, state officials and environmental groups to work together to develop a comprehensive state water policy. On the minds of everyone present was a recent statement by Los Angeles county supervisor Ken Hahn that California would like to have three billion gallons of water per day pumped from the Columbia River! Hahn's comment, said Benitz, "swept through the...retreat like a tidal wave. California has tried to hijack our water resources before and it hasn't worked. But those comments and California's drought did remind all of us just how precious our water resources are...We all agreed that we don't want to be in California's situation in a few short years – which is where we're headed unless...we learn to use those [our water] resources wisely." The session ended with a pledge to work together, and the cooperation was better than Benitz expected. He left the gathering hopeful and pleased that "perhaps...for the first time I can recall, we have all the major interests together at one table deciding how best to ensure the availability of clean pure water, now and in the future." A follow-on retreat was scheduled for September.[327]

Aside from conscientious attention to duty, why was Max Benitz so very busy in 1990? Newspapers and other state politicians speculated throughout the spring that an election challenge could be coming that year from a serious contender – two-term Democrat Representative Jim Jesernig of Kennewick. Jesernig, an attorney 40 years younger than Benitz, had gained a reputation in the State House as a fighter for Tri-Cities issues. He had been, according to the region's newspaper, "among the biggest proponents of Benitz's bills in the House," and he and Benitz had formed a legislative "team" that brought the Tri-Cities more influence in Olympia than that to which the area had been accustomed. While many Tri-Cities leaders did not want this situation to change, state Democrat leaders saw a potential Jesernig victory as a way to retake the majority in the State Senate, where Republicans had held all the committee chairmanships for three years. On May 30, Jesernig made it official, announcing that he would challenge Max Benitz in the District 8 run for the State Senate that autumn. Benitz, wary of the challenge, had already begun amassing an organization and a campaign fund. "I have news for him [Jesernig]," Benitz stated. "I'm going to run a very aggressive, straightforward, and high-profile campaign."[328]

The *Tri-City Herald* framed the dilemma for Benitz's district succinctly: "Tri-Citians have a lot to lose if Jim Jesernig decides to try for Max Benitz' seat in the Senate this year. They will lose Max, or they will lose Jim. Neither alternative is at all appealing...If Rep. Jesernig's associates are telling him that he's a sure winner, they are telling him wrong. The widespread support the young Kennewick attorney enjoys

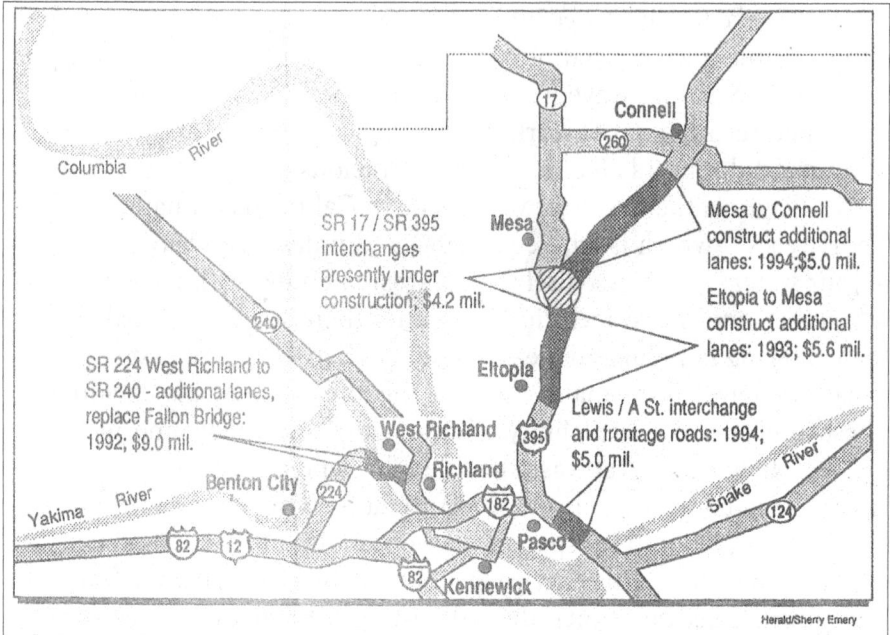

Newspaper depiction of $40 million worth of highway work scheduled for Tri-Cities, July 1990.

as a scrapper for the Tri-Cities' interests may not follow him into battle against Sen. Benitz...Few voters...will abandon an old friend who wants to keep his job just because a new one comes along who'd like it, too... Benitz is no push-over. And Jesernig, who has been so successful in Olympia on his own, could find the party's thinkers maneuvering him not into the Senate, but back to private life."[329]

By mid-summer, $40-million in road work was scheduled for the Tri-Cities and areas just to the north and east. Max Benitz had worked for many of these road projects for years, and State Republicans were doing their best to secure funding for them to help voters see the value of his seniority.[330]

Benitz was busy campaigning, attending national gatherings on energy issues, and, along with two other Senators and two State Representatives, organizing a statewide workshop entitled "Stopping the Violence: The Community Approach." The workshop, to be held in September, would focus on "the epidemic proportion of violence in homes and communities, and will offer proven strategies to develop safe families and neighborhoods."[331]

In late summer 1990, he penned a speech to be given to a gathering

Max Benitz with former-President Ronald Reagan, Goodwill Games, Seattle, July 1990.

of vocational and cooperative school personnel in Yakima. In the talk, he recalled his long-standing and constant interest in education. "It has been my good fortune to be very much involved with educational policy matters, both in the legislature and prior to that...As a House Member and Senator...One choice has remained constant, education...I serve today on the Senate Education Committee as Minority Chairman. Several strong biases have grown out of that...First it is inescapable, that the seat of the pants approach that no longer cuts it in agriculture doesn't cut it elsewhere either. There is a vital linkage between education and economic development. Neither our current businesses and industries or any we hope to attract can remain competitive without a well prepared work force. Second, our current and future economic well being depends upon a good balance being maintained between theoretical and practical educational priorities...In additional to skills...the work ethic must be carefully nurtured or American will not survive as an economic force in global affairs, or strong within its own borders." Benitz advocated a work-study program that would give students the opportunity to work as a part of their school programs. Such a program, he believed, would develop good work habits and make students realize that "paychecks must be earned." His remarks concluded with the statement that

Max Benitz in Benton-Franklin Counties Fair Parade, Kennewick, August 20, 1990.

"in Washington State...our economic future depends on [preparing our students well]...we can romance new employers with all the good things about our quality of life here but when it comes right down to the nitty-gritty, either we offer a competent work force or they go elsewhere."[332]

On August 20, Senator Max Benitz rode in the parade that serves as the opening event of the annual Benton-Franklin Counties Rodeo. One week later, he entered the hospital in Richland, WA, to be treated for a health event first described as a virus or pneumonia. In fact, it was a massive heart attack, and he died on August 28, 1990.[333]

Chapter Four:
Energy Issues

Mr. Energy

By the end of his career in 1990, Senator Max Benitz had been called "Mr. Energy" by more than one publication. In fact, energy issues had come to dominate his time, thoughts and reputation even more than had agriculture issues in the first six decades of his life. The last decade of Benitz's career, while still productive in farm, education, law enforcement and social issues, was devoted to energy issues that still resonate – and await solutions – today. The questions that consumed him included how to secure a safe, independent energy supply for the United States, how to balance environmental concerns with energy production, how to ensure that citizens' voices are heard in these debates, and how to combat fears of unknown technologies with reasonable risks, costs and choices.

Hanford Site in District 8

Max Benitz was thrust into the middle of these debates both by his own determination and by some of the most amazing circumstances and coincidences in American history, because the district this farm-based politician represented included the largest nuclear defense production site in the nation. The Hanford Site, begun as the Hanford Engineer Works in 1943, had astounded the U.S. and the world in 1945 when announcements by President Harry Truman revealed that Hanford's product, plutonium-239, had formed the core of the atomic weapon dropped on Nagasaki, Japan, ending World War II. Hanford had also produced the core material in the world's first atomic explosion, the Trinity bomb test in New Mexico in July 1945. The huge site – 640 square miles during World War II – had been located in the dry Columbia Basin of eastern Washington because of access to the Columbia River, rail transportation, gravelly soil and sunny climate for building, and most of all because of its remoteness and seclusion. Only 1,500 people, and about 20,000 sheep, inhabited the behemoth tract when it was chosen in secret in the depths of the war. Built quickly and under heavy press censorship, the site was producing nuclear defense materials almost before anyone took notice of it.[334] Max Benitz was milking cows in Ellensburg, about 80 miles away, and saving money with his wife for a down payment on a farm they could call their own. Good prices and new irrigation water brought him to Prosser, Washington in 1946, just 28 miles from Hanford's western border. The Benitz's were so busy raising their growing family and working their new land that they, like most others in the region, paid virtually no attention to Hanford.

By 1963, eight nuclear reactors operated along the banks of the Columbia River at Hanford, forming the largest collection of defense power in the nation. When the dynamic, aggressive President John Kennedy challenged the Soviet Union's play for world dominance in his inaugural address in 1961, it was Hanford's might that stood behind him and enabled his hubris. Without the nuclear weapons – by then numbering in the thousands – that contained Hanford's plutonium, U.S. boasting would have been just that and nothing more. Following the Soviet launch of Sputnik in 1957, the United States embarked on building the biggest war machine in history up to that point. It was the massive N Reactor at the Hanford Site. It was a special, new type of reactor, that would be not just a potent plutonium producer, but a domestic electricity generator as well. N Reactor was so complex that it took nearly six years to design and build. By the time it was ready for its inauguration, events in the world and the Columbia Basin were colliding.[335]

In Autumn 1963, Washington State Farm Bureau President Max Benitz toured the Soviet Union, Poland, Hungary, Germany and seeing socialism and communism first hand, he came back appalled at the corrosiveness of the Soviet system on the human spirit and farm productivity. Public service and outreach were becoming more important to Benitz, as he spoke to numerous groups about his tour and appeared on the *CBS Evening News*.[71] On September 14, he hosted a visit by 90 Hanford personnel to his farm, sponsored by the Benton County Farm Bureau, Benton County Wheat Association and other farm groups. The visit was in return for a tour of the Hanford Site by a group of farmers the previous year.[336] Hanford tours were extremely rare at that time, and the exchanges represented a bridge between two very different worlds. Just two weeks later, on September 26, President Kennedy spoke at the dedication of N Reactor, and broke ground for the steam generating plant

---

71. See Chapter 1 for a full discussion of Benitz's 1963 tour of the U.S.S.R and other nations.

President Kennedy at Hanford, September 26, 1963.
Courtesy of U.S. Department of Energy

that would connect the huge war horse to the commercial electric grid to power homes and businesses.[337]

By 1970, Benitz was running for his second term as a State Representative, and he had introduced a bill to remove the tax exemption the steam plant enjoyed as it had been running alongside N Reactor since 1966. His opponent, Democrat Joe Shipman, accused Benitz of "a complete disregard for the economy of the Tri-Cities." Removing the tax exemption for the steam plant, Shipman said, would cause the shutdown of N Reactor and "the loss of thousands of jobs." Benitz disagreed. He believed the state, county and school districts should receive a fair share of taxes from the huge project, which by then was generating more electricity than any utility in the region.[338] Benitz defeated Shipman by a wide margin that November.[339]

Times had changed considerably at Hanford by that time. Five of the nine plutonium production reactors had closed, and two more were slated to close in 1971. Even N Reactor, the ninth, was scheduled for closure, and did close briefly in 1971, but was re-opened for electric power production only.[340] President Lyndon Johnson had scaled back the nation's plutonium production mission and sent it to the Savannah River Site in South Carolina in the mid-1960s, just after the Senate began questioning the overproduction of plutonium. In return, Washington's powerful Congressional delegation had captured a promising new mission for the Hanford Site in modern, high-flux reactor technology. In 1968, the Atomic Energy Commission (AEC) – the federal agency managing atomic energy – had chosen Hanford as the location for the Fast Flux Test Facility (FFTF), the largest experimental reactor in the U.S. The FFTF would pioneer development of new nuclear fuels, fuel fabrication methods, fuel claddings, and other in-reactor materials. It would also be able to "breed" new reactor fuel as it operated, leading to a virtually endless fuel supply and a nuclear fuel cycle that could destroy excess plutonium and fuel the reactors of the future.[341] While Hanford's old production mission was shrinking, it was a heady time in terms of commercial nuclear development. Glenn Seaborg, then-current Chairman of the AEC and brilliant discoverer of plutonium back in 1941, predicted that, with the FFTF as the anchor, Hanford would house a giant industrial complex generating electricity and recycling the waste from that production in a perpetual chain. This "nuplex" would usher in a "junkless society" with an unlimited energy supply.[342]

Washington Public Power Supply System

At nearly the same time, the Washington Public Power Supply System (WPPSS), a municipal corporation chartered by the State Legislature that allowed publicly owned utilities to combine their resources and build power generation facilities, authorized construction of nuclear power plant on the Hanford Site. It was 1971, and planners expected that demand for electricity would double every 10 years and outpace the capacity of hydropower.[72] In 1972, Governor Dan Evans signed the site authorization for the plant at Hanford. That same year, two more nuclear power plants –one at Satsop in Grays Harbor County in western Washington and another one at Hanford — were proposed.[343] Max Benitz, long a proponent of expanded water use for irrigation and regional growth, firmly supported the new power plants. Agriculture in his district was too much at the mercy of droughts, he believed, and energy sources had to be found outside of area rivers. In early 1973, he sponsored House Bill (H.B.) 502 to expedite financing and construc-

---

72. Hydropower refers to electric power generated by damming rivers.

tion of the third plant.[344] The project was authorized, and within the next 15 months two more nuclear plants were proposed. The last two plants would also be at Satsop and Hanford, and would be "twinned" with the plants already authorized in order to save certain construction costs. The WPPSS Board enacted the resolution calling for construction of plants four and five in May 1974.[345]

In the meantime, power needs had become more urgent, as an oil embargo by the Organization of Petroleum Exporting Countries (OPEC) hit the United States in late 1973. The embargo was announced on October 16, after Israel had rapidly defeated the armies of Egypt and Syria who invaded it on October 6. Consumer prices rose throughout the U.S., and long waiting lines, along with rationing, developed at gasoline stations across the nation. The embargo lasted until March 1974, but shortages lingered. Americans, who had been the world's foremost oil producers at the end of World War II, faced the new global reality that their consumption could not be sustained by their own oil resources. Benitz, by now a State Senator, told his constituents that the fuel crisis would not be temporary, but was a new fact of life. "I am convinced that there really is a fuel crisis," he stated in early 1975. "We've been using more fuel than we're producing. Fuel has been cheap and oil companies have not built refineries or started new exploration...The use of fuel has increased. Between 1965 and 1972 fuel used for recreation alone increased 1 and ½ times. The two factors, non-production and increased use, have run into each other."[346]

In 1976, ground was broken on the first WPPSS nuclear plant on the Hanford Site. However, the project was already experiencing problems. In 1974, participating utilities had to sign option agreements underwriting project bonds in order to continue planning and design work on the endeavor. In 1976, major utility Seattle City Light voted not to participate in building the fourth and fifth plants, and construction cost estimates were escalating for the entire undertaking.[347] In fact, in the first decade, cost estimates for the WPPSS nuclear projects climbed for 400 percent.[348]

Seeking to smooth the way for energy projects in the Washington, Benitz co-sponsored legislation in 1977 to "expedite the certification of sites for energy facilities...and provide abundant energy at a reasonable cost," while still protecting the environment. It sought to prevent duplicative siting studies, which were being used by environmentalists to slow approval of energy projects such as the fourth and fifth WPPSS nuclear plants.[349] He also helped pass legislation transferring responsibilities for development of nuclear power in the state from the Department of Commerce and Economic Development to the State Energy Office. The new law helped clarify insurance regulations for a low-level radioactive waste (LLW) disposal site operated by a private contractor on leased land on the Hanford Site. Benitz wanted to clearly separate the issues of power plant waste disposal from commercial LLW disposal, and not let the latter be bound up in the tighter regulations that would be imposed on the former.[350] As the Senate Republican Caucus drily observed, "during the 1977 legislative session, one of Benitz' primary concerns...[was] the increasingly controversial subject of nuclear waste disposal."[351] That same year, Benitz and Oliver teamed to pass legislation that gave tax revenues from the region's nuclear projects to local governments in the Mid-Columbia area (the Hanford, Tri-Cities and surrounding areas). The revenues would be distributed 50 percent to schools, 22 percent to counties, 23 percent to cities, three percent to fire districts and two percent to libraries. Governor Dixie Lee Ray soon approved the legislation.[352]

Biomass and Other Energy Interests Grow

While Max Benitz remained a firm proponent of nuclear power, he also believed it prudent to explore other energy sources. He was an early proponent of the "all of the above" energy strategy that became prevalent decades later. Looking at the vast Hanford Site in his district, which contains hundreds of square miles of buffer land that is not used for any purpose other than providing distance between facilities, Benitz began investigating biomass fuel production in 1977. Working with Republican Representative Claude Oliver of Kennewick,[73] he asked Battelle Northwest Laboratories, the science and environmental contractor at the Hanford Site, to examine the potential of two plants to produce a liquid product similar to crude oil. They wanted to build on the research of University of California chemist Melvin Calvin into the Aveloz tree of Brazil and the gopher plant of California, and possibly grow the plants on unused areas of the vast Hanford Site. Benitz and Oliver urged support for an immediate horticultural research project to examine the feasibility of growing and harvesting such plants for energy. "We are pleased that one of Governor [Dixie lee] Ray's major goals was to lessen our dependence on any one source of power. We think this [plant

73. Kennewick is one of the Tri-Cities.

project] could fit into her goal of finding long range solutions to energy problems," said Benitz and Oliver.[353]

In 1978, Benitz attended a Bioconversion Workshop in Portland, Oregon, that examined the future potential of wood and grain byproducts into energy. The purpose was to develop recommendations to be used by state and federal officials in budgeting bioconversion programs. While he remained interested in biomass as an energy source after the conference, he stated that investigations into it and nuclear energy clearly showed that nuclear was still the cheaper source of power as an alternative to oil.[354] The conference is expected to develop recommendations to be used by state and federal officials for budgeting bioconversion programs.

During 1978, Benitz, as a member of the Senate Energy and Utilities Committee, became interested in the committee's study on nuclear waste disposal. The topic was timely, as President Jimmy Carter had recently terminated the nation's "breeder reactor" program due to proliferation concerns. Carter indefinitely "deferred" spent nuclear fuel (SNF) reprocessing (also called recycling) and vetoed federal legislation that would have appropriated funds to construct a federal reprocessing facility. The federal Nuclear Regulatory Commission (NRC) then suspended license proceedings relating to SNF recycling.[355] These actions effectively put an end to the nuclear waste disposal path that the nuclear power plants and most policymakers had been counting on – namely reprocessing. Now another disposal path had to be found, in order for the nuclear industry to grow. Benitz was selected as the Washington State Senate's representative to a national nuclear waste disposal conference being held that autumn in New Mexico.[356] Shortly after returning from this conference, he invited the NRC to hold one of its 1979 meetings in the Tri-Cities. Because many facilities at the Hanford Site were now closed and would have to be decommissioned, Benitz wanted the NRC to discuss decommissioning plans and policies with the population of the closest cities. Important issues, he said, were the safety of the decommissioning process, costs, environmental impacts, the freedom of operators to choose the actual method of disposal, and residual contamination left behind. "I think a meeting in the Tri-Cities area would serve both the NRC and the Hanford facility operations in examining all facets of the decommissioning process," he stated.[357]

Senator Benitz also made it a point to tour and learn about the FFTF in 1978, newly constructed but not quite yet ready to operate. President Carter's decision to terminate the U.S. breeder reactor program the previous year had removed one key purpose for the FFTF. However, many other future missions were envisioned, and the reactor was still seen as a crucial asset in securing a role for Hanford and the Tri-Cities in expansive nuclear technology development.

Energy Issues
Become More Pressing in Second Senate Term

In November 1978, Max Benitz won re-election to his second term in the Washington State Senate. He was re-appointed to the Energy and Utilities Committee, along with his assignments to the Agriculture and Higher Education Committees. Almost as soon as 1979 dawned, major changes occurred in the world and the nation, shaking the entire energy picture. In January, the Shah of Iran, keeper of a great reserve of oil and a ruler who had been very friendly to the U.S. fled into exile. Just weeks later, the new ruler of Iran, the Ayatollah Ruhollah Khomeini proclaimed Iran an Islamic Republic and imposed a severe cutback of oil shipments to America.[358] In March, a pump and a valve failed at the Three Mile Island nuclear plant near Harrisburg. Pennsylvania. Operator error compounded the event, and the reactor heated to levels beyond allowable safety limits. Small amounts of radionuclides were released, but the public relations effect was disastrous.[359] Nuclear power suffered a major setback in perception, and all orders for new reactors were cancelled in the U.S. in the next few years.

Additionally, throughout 1979-1981, inflation stood at near-record highs in the U.S., and the American economy slumped into the worst recession up to that point in the post-World War II period. Interest rates soared, making borrowing and electric rates very expensive and dampening energy demand. These economic factors, along with schedule delays, cost increases, and contracting and labor problems caused the entire WPPSS building program to wobble toward collapse. By February 1979, WPPSS had borrowed more than $1-billion in less than two years, and anticipated needing more than $3.5-billion more. By October 1980, the consortium was quietly studying scrapping or delaying the fourth and fifth plants. In January 1981, the State Senate Energy and Utilities Committee issued a scathing report on WPPSS cost overruns and construction delays. In May 1981, WPPSS had to announce a decision to stop construction on the fourth and fifth plants[360]

Benitz stepped into the growing mess to try some legislative measures. He supported an investigation of some of the actions of the Bonneville Power Administration (BPA), a federal agency that markets power to utilities. He believed that BPA decisions had exacerbated, rather than helped, WPPSS's problems, and helped slow down construction. He helped pass legislation that overhauled the "confusing" board structure of WPPSS, and "streamlined procedures for getting work and material for the remaining plants in a timely and cost-effective manner." He told constituents that, with this legislation, "public power ratepayers now have a greater voice in the management of WPPSS because of legislation...which increases the accountability of WPPSS management and allows more participation by nuclear power experts...We also passed legislation giving WPPSS officials the authority they need to keep the system from total collapse."[361]

During the same period, Benitz sponsored, co-sponsored or helped to pass legislation requiring any persons operating a uranium or thorium mill in Washington State to be perpetually responsible for all mill tailings and other wastes, promoting fuels containing alcohol through tax exemptions, and enumerating and enforcing regulations and penalties for transporters of hazardous wastes.[362] In August 1982, while running for re-election to a third term, Benitz became Chairman of the Senate Energy and Utilities Committee.[363] That November he beat Democrat challenger Ed Alden to secure his third term in the State Senate.[364]

Nuclear Energy and Waste Issues
Grow Throughout Third Senate Term

In the last days of December, 1982, the U.S. Congress passed a landmark bill to deal with the nation's growing stockpile of SNF and radioactive high-level waste (HLW). The Nuclear Waste Policy Act (NWPA) was signed into law by President Ronald Reagan on January 7, 1983.[365] Ever since the first nuclear power reactors began operating in the United States in the late 1950s, the highly radioactive byproducts (SNF and HLW) have been stored at the plants where they were created. After President Carter terminated the reprocessing option in 1977, policymakers had struggled to define a new, safe and sensible way to deal with and dispose of these materials. The NWPA represented that new method. It mandated that centralized places should be designed and built to store and dispose these nuclear wastes and byproducts. The repositories, and some interim retrievable storage sites, would be paid for by imposing a tax on ratepayers who used electricity generated by nuclear plants. President Reagan, in signing the new law, summarized its purpose: "The Nuclear Waste Policy Act…provides the long overdue assurance that we now have a safe and effective solution to the nuclear waste problem. It's an important step in the pursuit of the peaceful uses of atomic energy… This act…clears the barrier that has stood in the way of development of this vital energy resource…The step we're taking today should demonstrate to the public that the challenge of coping with nuclear waste can and will be met."[366] The NWPA directed the Department of Energy (DOE – a successor agency to the AEC) to select several potential sites for geologic repositories to place the waste, and then down-select the most suitable for further study.

In December, 1983, DOE nominated sites in Washington (Hanford), Nevada, Texas, Mississippi and Utah. These nominations were accompanied by Draft Environmental Assessments (EAs) that evaluated each site against general suitability guidelines. By early 1984, DOE was out in the communities neighboring the sites holding briefings and hearings on the EAs, and taking public comments. At Hanford, the Basalt Waste Isolation Project (BWIP) had been underway since 1977, drilling and exploring the geology and hydrology of an 18-square mile tract underlain by thick basalt near the center of the vast site. Scientists and policymakers already agreed that basalt, clay/rock or salt formations would be the likely places to place nuclear waste, and the DOE, manager of the Hanford Site, had authorized pre-work. As it happened, BWIP's first Site Characterization Report was issued in November 1982, a month before the NWPA was passed.[367]

Additionally in 1983, WPPSS made news when it defaulted on its bonds on July 22, making this case the largest bond default in American history up to that point. Member utilities, and ultimately the ratepayers, were obligated to pay back the borrowed money. In some small Northwest towns already struggling with high unemployment, the amounts owed equaled up to $12,000 per customer. The bondholders sued, and the matter wound its way through the courts for the next 13 years. Plants Four and Five were terminated, while Plants One (at Hanford) and Three (at Satsop) were "mothballed." (Construction stopped, but the ultimate fate of Plants One and Three were left in limbo.) Plant Two at Hanford was the only one of the five planned nuclear facilities to be completed. It began operating in 1984.[368]

At the Hanford Site, defense production was once again bustling in 1983, after President Reagan announced his Strategic Defense Initiative (also known as "Star Wars") in March. Long dormant weapons production facilities such as the Plutonium Uranium Extraction (PUREX) Plant, and the Plutonium Finishing Plant (PFP) were upgraded and restarted. The giant N Reactor was re-tooled for plutonium production once again, as Reagan pressed the failing Soviet economy in the final push of the Cold War.[369]

By early 1984, it was an open secret that three front-runner sites to become the nation's first HLW and SNF repository were Yucca Mountain in Nevada, Deaf Smith in Texas and Hanford in Washington. Max Benitz was very interested and engaged. He commented in January 1984 that "the controversy, surrounding the siting of power-generating facilities and the location of a repository for high-level nuclear waste, gives my service on the Energy and Utilities Committee added significance... It will allow me to maintain my influence on the future direction of these issues."[370] That February, he missed a meeting in Denver of the National Conference of State Legislatures (NCSL) Working Group on High-Level Waste, due to his heart attack. However, he followed the meeting closely, as he wanted to make sure the candidate states maintained an active role in decisions. The NWPA guaranteed a collaborative, inclusive process, and the five states insisted that that process be meaningful. Although Democrats had won the majority in the State Senate in the 1982 elections, and assumed the committee chairmanships, Benitz still supported a bill by Senate Energy and Utilities Chairman Al Williams (D-Seattle) that required Washington's State Nuclear Waste Board to monitor and evaluate research conducted by the DOE with respect to the Hanford Site's BWIP and that authorized the Board to conduct independent research if it was dissatisfied with the DOE process and findings.[371]

In December 1984, the DOE announced that the three top candidate sites for the nation's first geologic repository for HLW and SNF were indeed Yucca Mountain in Nevada, Deaf Smith in Texas and the BWIP site at Hanford. Benitz immediately welcomed the news, saying that it meant that Hanford would now undergo at least $500-million worth of testing. "We were glad to hear the news from the Federal government that Hanford was selected as one of three possible sites in the nation," he stated. "We welcome the opportunity to test the Hanford site completely and thoroughly -- to find out if it is indeed the safest place to store high-level nuclear waste...Hanford has sought this selection because they feel it is the safest place for the storage facility. If they can prove that be the case, the repository should be here. If they can't prove that -- positively -- then we don't want the waste stored here...we don't want to endanger our environment." He also said there should be independent state monitoring of the DOE's characterization process, to remove any doubt about the findings and to ensure that people knew the federal government was not "pushing this down our throats." If Hanford was selected as the final site for the repository, he pointed out, it would mean perhaps $25-billion "in development and a drilling and disposal process lasting well into the next century."[74-372] While Benitz enthusiastically supported a nuclear waste repository at Hanford, he also believed that nuclear waste might have hidden value. "Vitrifying" or hardening the waste into an impervious glass form, might prevent future generations from reclaiming useful isotopes. Therefore, he favored waste research in parallel with planning for disposition.

Another energy issue important to Benitz throughout 1983-84 and into 1985, included the formation of the Northwest Low-Level Radioactive Waste Compact. The Compact grew out of the federal Low-Level Radioactive Waste Policy Act of 1980, which authorized states to form interstate compacts and develop new regional disposal facilities for LLW. Washington, Alaska, Hawaii, Idaho, Montana, Oregon and Utah quickly formed the Northwest Compact, with the disposal site located on leased land on the Hanford Site and operated by a private contractor.[75] The Washington State Legislature approved the compact in 1983, but other regions of the country were slow to form compacts. As a compromise between states with and without compacts, the LLW Policy Act was amended in 1985. Sited states agreed to accept waste generated nationally until January 1993. In return states and compacts without disposal capacity agreed to acquire it by January 1, 1993, either through the siting of disposal facilities of their own or through disposal contracts with other states or compacts. By that date, all states and compacts were to have either operational disposal sites or storage, or other interim waste

74. The DOE selection process for the three sites in 1984 was questioned, and a new, more inclusive process ensued. In May 1986, it was announced that the new process had selected the same three, top candidate sites.
75. Wyoming joined the Northwest Compact in 1992.
76. Accordingly, the Hanford, Washington, disposal site stopped accepting out-of-region LLW as of January 1, 1993, except for small volumes agreed to in a separate contract with the Rocky Mountain Compact.

management programs in place.[76-373] Max Benitz was a firm supporter of the Northwest Compact and the disposal site at Hanford, and worked closely with Republican Senator Sam Guess of Spokane to ensure its passage.[374]

Benitz also supported a non-nuclear disposal site at Hanford for hazardous wastes including chemicals, solvents, certain metals, corrosives and other toxic materials. However, such a facility was not located. [375] He sponsored, co-sponsored or worked to pass legislation fostering but regulating oil and gas exploration, development, production, reclamation and conservation in Washington, and permitting irrigation districts of cities, towns and/or public utility districts to construct or acquire and operate hydroelectric facilities.[376] He opposed a bill in the State Legislature that proposed $27,000 to study plans for long-range uses of 1,000 acres of leased land on the Hanford Site. He called the study "needless," and said the "plan proposes to throw away $27,000 of taxpayers' money that could be spent for better purposes, such as improving the employment climate...The federal and state governments are doing very adequate jobs of planning uses for this land. This study would do nothing more than scare potential lessees from settling in the area...The fewer lessees, the less revenue to the state."[377] Near the end of the 1984 legislative session, Benitz remarked that "I've been scrapping like hell all session to try to keep the nuclear industry alive...I fret about it at night."[378]

In February 1985, he attended the annual meeting of the High-Level Nuclear Waste Working Group of the NCSL in Denver – the meeting he had missed the previous year due to his heart attack. Texas, Nevada, Utah, Pennsylvania and Washington were represented. Benitz reported to his constituents that, after much discussion, the Working Group agreed on three key points. First, they would not try to challenge the basic concept of having a national nuclear waste repository, because a duly elected, representative Congress had passed the NWPA mandating that the U.S. would have such a repository. Second, they would work with the DOE in every developmental and characterization step, so as not to be in the position of challenging decisions after the fact. Third, they wanted the Price-Anderson Act amended to directly address and cover accidents at nuclear waste repository sites.[379] The Price-Anderson Act, originally passed in 1957 and amended several times, was meant to ensure the availability of a large pool of funds to compensate those who incurred damages from nuclear or radiological incidents, no matter who might be liable. The Act provided "omnibus" coverage - essentially the same protection available for a covered licensee or contractor extended through indemnification to any persons who might be legally liable, regardless of their identity or relationship to the licensed activity. Essentially it was a huge subsidy for the nuclear industry, but was deemed necessary because no insurance company would underwrite a nuclear power plant to the full extent of possible damages.[380]

There was much discussion of nuclear waste issues during the 1985 session of the Washington State Legislature. According to Benitz, "a host of proposed legislation has been introduced most generally by legislators not considered to be friendly toward nuclear energy (ex. PUREX emissions, monitoring USDOE research at Hanford, and assessing fees on radioactive shipments)."[381] The worst act, in his view, was joint House-Senate Bill 723, that extended the Business and Occupation (B&O) tax at a whopping "33% to all disposal activity of radioactive waste. Paying this tax will be the state low level site operators and the federal government operating high and low level sites at Hanford. All *activities* of the potential high level radioactive waste repository for the nation would also be taxed...SHB 723 singled out nuclear waste activities at the highest rate imposed by the state. The cost will be an additional $75 million for all radioactive waste generators. Directly affected will be all hospitals, utilities, manufacturers and other radioactive waste related businesses. Low level waste generators already pay the state over $13 million per year in taxes, fees and other costs. Previously, B&O taxes were not assessed on the federal government's radioactive waste disposal at Hanford. It is my hope this unwise and anti-business legislation will be challenged in court."[382] Benitz met with Governor Booth Gardner to discuss nuclear issues, animosity, balance and compromise. In the end, the Governor vetoed the high tax on radioactive waste activities, but, said Benitz, he did so "for the wrong reasons....While I am pleased that the Governor vetoed this tax...[he] indicated that if we collected the $75 million in taxes, that would have given the federal government the license to build a high level waste repository at Hanford as they would feel, 'the price is right.' I don't agree with that reasoning, as safety is the number one concern."[383]

In March 1985, Washington State's Nuclear Waste Board sued the DOE in two different cases, one initiated separately and one in conjunction with Nevada. The Nevada-Washington suit asked that the federal government provide state funding for further research of the sites selected. The singular Washington lawsuit alleged that DOE failed to live up to the provisions of the 1982 NWPA in the site selection process. In May, Benitz attended the Spring Information Meeting and Briefing on the planning process to choose and characterize the nation's first geologic repository, held in Kansas City and sponsored by the U.S. DOE and its Office of Civilian Radioactive Waste Management (OCRWM). The OCRWM office within DOE was responsible for power plant SNF and HLW, and their disposition. Representatives from more than 15 states attended the Briefing, many of which contained nuclear power plants that would need a repository for disposition. Benitz observed that "both DOE officials and many state officials continue to be disappointed by the negative attitude taken by some representatives of the possible host states." He also affirmed that "the ultimate decision of what we do with high level radioactive waste is most important...The problem must be solved, and... it will not be by the customary federal government approach of 'trust us.' We must prove that we have the technology and other know-how to provide a solution... "If in the near future Hanford is chosen for 'site characterization'...not only the respective state governments need to continue to be involved but many areas of local government will need to be activated so that the DOE and state and local governments can come together in a positive agreement." At the Meeting, it was announced that nuclear defense wastes and civilian (power plant) HLW would be "co-mingled" in the same repository. Benitz stated that utility representatives seemed to like this approach, as they believed it would "help hold down costs to ratepayers and taxpayers."[384]

In June, he met in Olympia with members of a Japanese Survey Mission visiting the United States to discuss SNF handling and disposal. Benitz was impressed that Japan was actively building and expanding its nuclear capability. "These representatives made it plain that nuclear generated electricity is the chief future power in Japan," he stated. The Japanese also intended to build a reprocessing plant to recycle their used fuel, and to site disposal facilities for LLW and HLW. "This kind of progress in the nation of Japan to me is a positive indication of the future of nuclear energy," he concluded.[385]

If the previous few years had been eventful in terms of nuclear news and developments, 1986 would prove to be even more so. As soon as the State Legislature convened, Benitz signaled his intent to become even more involved in energy issues by announcing that energy expert Larry

Washington State Senate Group Photo, January 1986; Benitz first row, fifth from right.

Bradley was becoming his administrative aide. Bradley had been Director of the Washington State Energy Office from 1976-1980, and Executive Director of the state Office of Nuclear Energy Development for six years prior to that post. On other qualifications in the energy field, he was a member of the American Nuclear Society, American Association for Advancement of Science, the Bonneville Power Administration Advisory Council and had been one of the original directors of the Hanford Science Center.[386]

Almost immediately, Democrats in the legislature, many of whom opposed siting the first national HLW repository in the state, proposed bills that would severely restrict the transportation and storage of nuclear waste in Washington.[387] "Western Washington lawmakers have stepped up their efforts to 'regulate the shipment and storage of nuclear waste to death'... [they] have launched what amounts to an all-out attack on the transportation and storage of nuclear waste in Washington," Benitz observed. He fought their plans with a major bill of his own that would comprehensively regulate hazardous and dangerous wastes.[388] In his view, the anti-nuclear legislators had "done nothing to train and support public safety personnel for accidents associated with the routine shipments of other dangerous chemicals...The situation borders on criminal negligence. We have dangerous substances traveling up and down our highways...[while] the Legislature directs all its efforts toward the shipment of nuclear waste and the record shows that nuclear waste is a small fraction of the potential safety problem... [Many] politicians in Olympia respond only to the irrational fears of those who refuse to acknowledge the nuclear industry's record of safety." He pointed out that in 1984, there had been 118 accidents involving heavy trucks carrying hazardous materials such as explosives, flammable gas, non-flammable gas, poison, corrosive materials, and flammable liquids in Washington State. However, he added that *"none of the accidents involved low level radioactive waste."* Benitz also stayed involved with planning and regulations for the LLW disposal facility on the Hanford Site during 1986.[389]

Additionally in 1986, as multiple trials and other legal proceedings went forward to settle the WPPSS bond default cases, the State legislature approved a bill that would require WPPSS bondholders to prove that public utilities knew the bonds they sold were worthless, in order to collect damages. Under existing law, Benitz explained to his constituents, "bondholders would have to prove only negligence and not the tougher "knowing-intent" standard... to collect. Ratepayers back this [new] measure since any damages paid to bondholders by public utilities would translate into higher rates for them." Benitz strongly disagreed with this bill. "As written is retroactive," he said, "and if finally passed into law would probably be found unconstitutional in the courts."[390] Later in the year, he told his constituents that he and fellow legislators had finally passed "several major laws to help straighten out the WPPSS situation in the face of seemingly endless stall-tactics and political posturing on the part of people who do not understand or care about the need for nuclear power."[391]

On April 16, 1986, two powerful explosions destroyed Unit 4 of the Chernobyl nuclear power plants, located in the Ukraine (then part of the Union of Soviet Socialist Republics). Highly radioactive nuclear fuel burned through the reactor core, after it failed to receive adequate cooling water. The burning fuel released large amounts radioactive gases into the atmosphere, eventually contaminating thousands of square miles of Russia, Belarus, Ukraine and neighboring areas. The accident was by far the worst in world nuclear history.[392] In response, 56 Democrats in the Washington State Legislature petitioned President Reagan to shut down Hanford's N Reactor because some features of its design (primarily its graphite core and "light" water cooling system) were similar to those of the Chernobyl reactors. The petition also asked Reagan to cease production of all military radioactive waste and halt the national repository selection program. Max Benitz led the opposition, stating that N Reactor was safe and contributed clean energy to the region, and that shutting it would damage national security and cost up to 14,000 jobs.[77-393] He chastised the petitioners, saying that "the people of the state do not deserve the divisiveness and acrimony dispensed by some of our leaders."[394]

In early May, Benitz announced that he was running for a fourth term in the State Senate, and said he hoped for a Republican majority so he could become Chairman of the Senate Energy and Utilities Committee.[395] As if things could not get more rancorous, the DOE announced on May 28, 1986, that its new selection process, underway since 1984, had once again recommended the three candidate sites for the national SNF and HLW repository to be Yucca Mountain, Nevada, Deaf Smith. Texas, and Hanford. Washington. At the same time, exacerbating matters further, the Energy Secretary announced that DOE was indefinitely suspending its search for a second repository site east of the Mississippi River. The 1982 NWPA had mandated two sites, one east and one west of the Mississippi. The new decision seemed especially unfair to opponents of the sites in candidate sites in the west, since the vast majority of SNF and HLW is generated by power plants east of the Mississippi.[396]

Within weeks, some Washington legislators called on the Governor to call the State Legislature back into special session to protest the selection of the BWIP site at Hanford as a finalist candidate. Max Benitz thoroughly opposed such a move, and sent to all his fellow legislators an eastern Washington editorial that condemned such a special session. "Nuclear energy is a blessing to mankind," the editorial stated. "It will do no good for the Washington Legislature to get together to...pontificate against the federal government's decision...and play upon the unwarranted fears of the public...The storage of waste is a serious matter, but one which science can manage well. We already have over half the U.S. military 'waste' at Hanford where it has been for 40 years."[397] As Benitz quipped, "I don't feel I could have stated it better than...in this well writ-

---

77. 14,000 people did not work at N Reactor, but the figure included the "multiplier effect" of other jobs that would be lost at other Hanford plants and in the surrounding communities if N Reactor products and paychecks stopped flowing.

ten editorial."[398]

The Governor did call such a special session, which lasted exactly five hours on August 1, 1986. The Legislature voted to put Referendum 40 on the November general election ballot, which asked the people of the state to determine whether they believed the DOE's selection process had been accurate or politically motivated. In July, Gardner introduced a resolution before the Western Governor's Conference in Colorado Springs, condemning DOE's process and calling on Congress to "suspend further work on site characterization for a first repository." The resolution passed unanimously and was transmitted to the President, the Secretary of Energy and members of Congress. In September, Gardner again called on DOE Secretary John Herrington to halt the nuclear repository siting process, and also admonished President Reagan's chief of staff, Donald Regan, for saying that Hanford is the most likely "winner" as the nation's first high-level nuclear waste repository. In October, Gardner sent a letter to President Reagan urging him to intervene in the selection process to "take this issue out of the political arena and put it into the hands of those qualified to make sound, scientific decisions...I must appeal to your sense of fairness and equity and urge you to intervene in this matter," Gardner wrote. "There is a great injustice being done to the people of Washington." Later in October, Gardner submitted a statement protesting the site selection process to the NRC, saying that "the ranking methodology used by USDOE was seriously flawed... It is clear to me that the effort to site a high-level repository is on the wrong tract. The Department [of Energy] seems obsessed with its time lines and not conscious enough of our safety concerns." The Governor also issued a chronology detailing his long-standing opposition to the repository siting in Washington State.[399]

In November, state voters approved Referendum 40 overwhelmingly, telling state officials to "continue challenges to the federal selection process for high-level nuclear waste repositories and...provide [a means] for voter disapproval of any Washington site."[400] At the same time, Max Benitz was elected, also by a large margin, to his fourth term in the State Senate.[401] The 1986 elections gave the Democrats a 25-24 majority in the State Senate, and they retained control of the House.[402] Benitz had received approval to attend the HLW Working Group meeting of the NCSL meeting in Amarillo, Texas in November, but the meeting was cancelled.[403]

In the meantime, controversy was brewing for the DOE in arenas and issues even bigger than the national repository. In February 1986, in response to inquiries that were part of lawsuits opposing the repository selection in Washington, the Department released 19,000 pages of previously classified historical documents from the Hanford Site. Larger document releases would follow in 1987, becoming a virtual flood of documents during the 1990s. As soon as the first document releases occurred, researchers began requesting documents from other nuclear defense sites around the country. In July 1986, a national news syndicate company penned an article that described health problems in nuclear workers at the Rocky Flats Plant in Colorado, the Fernald Site in Ohio, the Nevada Test Site, the Idaho National Engineering Laboratory and the Hanford Site. The article alleged further that data on the health of nuclear workers had been deliberately suppressed by the DOE. The *Yakima Herald-Republic* reprinted the article, enraging Max Benitz. In an open letter to the editor, he stated that "many people are understandably concerned about radiation because it seems so mysterious to them and because it usually receives sensational news treatment. However, they do not deserve to be frightened needlessly by mistaken reports."[404]

Others in Washington State weren't so sure. In 1986, to study the information in the first batch of released historical documents, a coalition of Hanford's home state and neighboring Oregon, along with four Indian nations, had formed the Hanford Health Effects Review Panel. They hired a medical doctor from the U.S. Centers for Disease Control (CDC) and an official from the Office of Radiation Protection of Washington State's Department of Social and Health Services to examine the information in the documents. They formed the Washington-Oregon Hanford Historical Documents Committee the next year, to further investigate the document and request that more documents be declassified.[405]

During the spring and summer of 1986, the *Spokesman-Review-Spokane Chronicle* newspaper began publishing a scathing series of articles excerpting events from the newly-declassified Hanford historical documents and drawing very damaging conclusions. The young reporter drove south approximately 125 miles and spent time with a group of farmers living across the Columbia River to the east of the Hanford Site. They were known as "downwinders," because they lived "down the wind stream" of the prevailing winds of the region. In Washington State, winds blow from west to east, sweeping over the Cascade Mountains, down the Yakima Valley through Prosser, across the Hanford Site, and then across the river to Franklin, Adams, and Walla Walla counties. Often, due to quirks of topography, the winds will often sweep north towards Spokane. The downwinders of eastern Washington told the newspaper of unusual illnesses, cancer clusters, and most often about prevalent thyroid disease in their families and neighbors. Thyroid deterioration and disease can be caused by exposure to radioactive iodine, particularly an isotope called I-131, that was released from the exhaust stacks of Hanford facilities during the 1940s through 1960s. The region's major newspapers, Portland's *Oregonian* and the *Seattle Post-Intelligencer* picked up the interest and ran investigative stories of their own. A group named that Hanford Education Action League (HEAL) had formed in Spokane a few years earlier, and was hiring researchers to investigate Hanford and its potential connection to regional health issues in animals and people.[406]

Major Energy Developments in 1987

In January 1987, a major development shook the Hanford area and Max Benitz's district. The DOE closed the N Reactor in order to study safety issues and make safety improvements. Benitz told his constituents that "the 1987 Legislative session opened January 12th. The Governor's bashing of Hanford [and certain other topics] were still very popular issues." Concerns for the future of the N Reactor and its safety for the people of Washington were discussed at length.[407] By February 10, Benitz was watching a veritable avalanche of Hanford-related bills introduced into the Legislature. Among these were House Bills requiring a major impact report on N-Reactor conversion, providing for an income tax on businesses involved in disposing HLW and extending a 30 percent tax to any federal repository projects, changing provisions relating to issuing permits and site certifications for energy facilities, establishing procedures and limiting ports of entry for radioactive materials, creating a state Department of Nuclear Safety, requiring special training for truck drivers carrying hazardous materials, transferring responsibility for nuclear safety for government production reactors to the NRC and stopping food irradiation until further study. He was also monitoring Senate Bills allowing the State Department of Ecology to regulate all hazardous and radioactive wastes, establishing a western states compact on the transport of radioactive materials, expanding state regulation of radioactive shipments, and duplicating House efforts to designate limited ports of entry for radioactive materials and tightening regulations for permits and site certifications for energy facilities.[408]

At the same time, the Tri-Cities, in Benitz's district, were experiencing job losses, declining home prices and sales, and other economic hardships associated with the shutdown of N Reactor. A group called the Hanford Family formed in the Tri-Cities to advocate for the reactor's re-start. Group members visited to lobby in Olympia in February, and Benitz praised their efforts.[409] He held a hearing on N Reactor safety in the Legislature on March 2.[410] By April, Benitz and other Tri-Cities legislators had been able to secure funding for a study of the Tri-Cities economy by the state Department of Trade and Economic Development. The study was designed to look for ways to diversify the area's economy, and thus lessen its heavy dependence on Hanford for employment. According to the DOE, Hanford jobs accounted for 27 percent of all non-farm jobs and 45 percent of non-farm payroll in the Tri-Cities area. Excluding service jobs, which depended on a healthy local economy, Hanford workers made up about three-quarters of the Tri-Cities industrial labor base.[411]

Benitz continued to fight what he called "Hanford bashing" throughout the 1987 legislative session. Radioactive shipment fees, designed to discourage the repository, easily passed the Legislature, even though Benitz pointed out that "we haven't killed a single soul, we haven't endangered a single road outside the [Hanford] reservation. We have more important things to do than continue Hanford bashing."[412] He succeeded in amending a Senate bill on nuclear energy violations for LLW facilities, to lower civil penalties from $10,000 per day to $2,000 per day, with a total cap of $10,000, and to require the state Department of Social and Health Services to develop regulations to implement the penalty authority.[413] He was discouraged that a bill entering Washington into a compact with Oregon and Idaho to strictly regulate the transport of radioactive materials was successful, while the issue of the transport of hazardous materials was overlooked. "Because of the emotional factor, the legislature continues to place nearly all emphasis on radioactive materials transport, when in fact less than 1/10 of 1 percent of all highway accident involve radioactive waste transport," he said. "There has never been a release of radiation during transportation in the state of Washington, nor have there been any fatalities that could be related to the transportation of radioactive waste within the state."[414] Benitz subscribed to the

American Nuclear Society's position that "concern [about shipping radioactive materials through populated areas] is unwarranted because almost three decades of transporting radioactive materials has had no detrimental impact. This record demonstrates there is an excellent basis for continued safe transport of radioactive materials. The extremely low risk and consequences result from the safe practices conducted under an extensive body of federal regulation governing radioactive material transportation, and the use of design, testing, and packaging technologies that provide protection to assure public safety."[415]

In late March, Benitz told a Kennewick Town Hall meeting that about 15 of 25 bills he described as "anti-Hanford" had been defeated in the Legislature. He credited fellow Republicans, Tri-Cities freshman Democrat Representative Jim Jesernig, and Democrat Senator Lois Stratton of Spokane for helping overcome these bills. "As of now, we're having the best session, as far as Hanford goes, that we've had over in Olympia for many years," he said.[416] At the end of the 1987 legislative session, he stated that "overall I was very pleased with the treatment given the nuclear industry this season. I think lawmakers are beginning to realize that a lot of the complaints against the nuclear industry and Hanford have no basis in fact. For this reason, some blatantly anti-nuclear bills that were brought up this session went down to defeat." He said that testimony from nuclear experts at Hanford had "made a good case" for re-starting N Reactor. "I think the message is getting through that safety does not take a back seat at Hanford," he affirmed. He was disappointed that the Washington-Oregon-Idaho pact regulating transport of radioactive materials had passed, because he believed it would "simply add another layer of state-level regulation to an industry that is already monitored very closely." He also remained unhappy that the bill limiting ports of entry for radioactive materials had passed, because, he said, "the Legislature is not well-qualified to make port of entry decisions—special interests will be able to block good locations, regardless of their merit." However, he was especially pleased that a memorial was passed unanimously by the Legislature asking Congress to provide sufficient funds to meet "the extensive cleanup needs...at Hanford...cost estimates for taking care of the 40-years of accumulation of wastes range from $5 billion to $15 billion."[417] Clearly, Benitz, although he admired and supported Hanford, was a realist. He knew that concerns about the wastes generated and disposed at the Hanford Site throughout its plutonium production years were real and needed to be addressed.

Max Benitz also showed his ability to speak for Washington state interests as a whole when he signed a letter from 135 members of the State legislature to Democrat U.S. Senator Brock Adams in May 1987. The letter bluntly began: "There is now substantial evidence that the Nuclear Waste Policy Act is not working as planned. . . the time has come to revise the Act." Benitz could see that the debate over whether Hanford, Washington would become the nation's first HLW and SNF repository was tearing apart the state. The many anti-nuclear bills that took time and energy in the legislative session had been evidence that the state's anti-repository faction would keep introducing any bills it thought could hamstring nuclear operations in the state. He knew that this struggle could never produce a good climate in which to grow the nuclear industry, and so he signed up for an idea that might bring compromise. The 135 signatories of the letter to Adams proposed that "we believe it might be fruitful to focus on a shorter term solution which keeps our long term options open. This solution could be a national regional system of Monitored Retrievable Storage (MRS)." An MRS study would benefit Washington in many ways, they said. "Despite the best congressional intentions, defense waste cleanup is proceeding too slowly," the letter stated. "Siting of an MRS facility at Hanford would provide leverage for cleanup on the defense wastes located on the reservation." An MRS accepting regional waste from Washington, Oregon and Idaho, would also provide production jobs expected to be lost in the coming decade, break the current "impasse" in repository siting and show that Washington wanted to cooperate in a positive manner, avoid public outrage, and serve as model for siting other regional MRS facilities. "Regional storage of high-level waste has the simple, but compelling, notion of equity," the letter continued. "Those parts of the country which benefit from nuclear power, and also generate wastes, should also own the responsibility for the safe storage of those wastes." The letter concluded that "the country just does not seem ready for the siting of a permanent repository.[418]"

In September, Benitz traveled to Europe as part of a delegation of the NCSL, to look at European nuclear waste disposal facilities and practices. In 11 days, they visited France, Switzerland, Sweden and Germany. France was the most intriguing to Benitz. That nation generated about 70 percent of its electricity from nuclear energy and routinely performed the entire fuel cycle, including reprocessing, using nuclear fuel sever-

Max Benitz with Senator Jeannette Hayner, Olympia, late 1987

al times before considering it waste. Benitz stated that the nuclear nations they visited "were all extremely envious that we [at Hanford] had an arid site with perfect soil conditions where we could dispose of low level waste. Some of these foreign officials told me it was the most ideal disposal site in the world for this type of waste."[419]

The end of 1987 brought important changes in Washington State. In a special election that November, the victory of Republican Senate candidate Linda Smith of Clark County gave the Republicans a majority of 25-24 in the State Senate.[420]

Max Benitz assumed chairmanship of the powerful Energy and Utilities Committee, from one of his chief adversaries, Democrat Senator Al Williams of Seattle. In a move toward compromise, Benitz named Democrat Lois Stratton of Spokane to chair a subcommittee on nuclear waste transportation. Benitz was also appointed to the newly formed Senate Environment and Natural Resources Committee, which was created by joining the Natural Resources and the Parks and Ecology committees. Republican Senator Jeannette Hayner of Walla Walla, with whom Benitz worked closely, was named Majority Leader.[421]

At the same time, Benitz cooperated with Governor Gardner by preparing legislation for the upcoming 1988 session requesting additional funding for the state to monitor radiation emissions from Hanford.[422]

On December 8, 1987, President Reagan and Soviet President Mikhail Gorbachev signed the historic Intermediate Nuclear Forces (INF) Treaty.[423] It was the first arms control agreement of the nuclear age that actually limited the numbers of nuclear weapons the U.S. and U.S.S.R. could possess. Previous agreements had simply moved nuclear weapons around into different categories, but had not actually reduced total numbers. The treaty needed verification and transparency. As a result, all plutonium production at Hanford came to a screeching halt. In some cases, radioactive processes were interrupted right in their midst, leaving unique waste collections and forms to add the defense waste collections already at Hanford. Then, just before Christmas, the U.S. Congress passed major amendments to the NWPA, selecting the Yucca Mountain, Nevada site as the only one to continue characterization as the nation's first repository for HLW and SNF.[424] Already, $1.1-billion had been spent studying nine potential sites.[425] From then on, all efforts and funds would go to the Yucca Mountain site, and future citizens could decide whether and where more repositories were needed.

Energy Battles in 1988

The huge events of December 1987 spelled almost certain disaster for the economy of the Tri-Cities. The INF Treaty put the writing on the wall for Hanford's N Reactor. Still closed for safety upgrades, the reactor now was almost certainly destined to stay shuttered. With Nevada's selection as the site of the nation's geologic repository, the BWIP program closed quickly. Despite urgent pleas to President Reagan and candlelight vigils, the DOE announced on February 16, 1988, that N Reactor would be placed in "cold standby," meaning that essentially it would never restart.[426] About 3,300 jobs were expected to be lost by late 1989 at N, and about 1,200 more would be lost at BWIP. The trickle-down effects of other job losses in support services and businesses in the Tri-Cities were predicted to be enormous.[427] Clearly, Max Benitz's seniority in Olympia would be needed to find ways to offset the losses.

Soon after the closure was announced, Benitz introduced a memorial into the State Senate urging federal support for the Tri-Cities and its workers. "The Tri-Cities and its workers have given our country many years of outstanding service," he said, "and I believe the federal government should stand behind them after the N Reactor shutdown." The State Legislature also passed a bill funding efforts to diversify the economy of the Tri-Cities. Funding would go towards business development programs, job retraining, WSU's Tri-City University Center, and the Tri-City Industrial Development Council.[428] The real prize, however, that could boost the Tri-Cities economy would be if Hanford was chosen as the location for the nation's New Production Reactor. The DOE was pursuing selection of a site to construct a new reactor to produce tritium – an ingredient in modern nuclear weapons -- to "reduce national security risks," after shutting down the K Reactor at the Savannah River

Pro-nuclear rally in Walla Walla, February 1988. Front Row from Left: State Representative Peter Brooks (R-Edmonds), Representative Shirley Hankins (R-Kennewick), Senator Max Benitz (at podium), Representative Jim Jesernig (D-Kennewick) slightly behind.

Site in South Carolina for safety reasons. Hanford was one site under consideration.[429] Benitz considered the possibility of a new production reactor at Hanford to be the "number-one priority" for rebuilding the Tri-Cities economy. To him, finishing construction of the WPPSS Plant One at Hanford (known as WNP-1) as the new reactor was the obvious sensible choice. He noted that "many Senate members are taking a more positive approach to Hanford than they have in the past." He attributed this new support to a series of Hanford tours that he had helped to arrange. However, when Benitz approached Governor Gardner for support for the new production reactor, Gardner told him he could not offer his support due to adverse political implications. The Governor stated he could only help with transitional funding to diversify the Tri-Cities economy.[430]

In March, Benitz testified at a DOE hearing on the environmental impacts of a new production reactor. He was outspoken and persuasive in his arguments as to why the completion of WNP-1 at Hanford wads the "winning situation for all involved." However, he stated that he first wanted to discuss the "State's role in the decision." He pledged that, "as

Chairman of the Energy and Utilities Committee, and as a member of the committee on Environment and Natural Resources, that I will work to assure that the State takes a reasonable, positive and productive approach toward waste cleanup. I will not tolerate a State agency attitude which is punitive and negative." He was clearly signaling that the DOE should not regard Washington State as hostile to nuclear endeavors. He emphasized that "all groups concerned about the future of Hanford" agree that Hanford's defense wastes needed attention – they needed treatment and immobilization from the environment. The best way to ensure adequate waste cleanup, he said, was the site a positive, future mission at Hanford. "Common sense clearly dictates that defense waste cleanup at Hanford will be given more attention if an ongoing defense materials production mission continues at the site."

He then pressed his argument for completing WNP-1 as the nation's new production reactor. "The WNP1 option is like a contest with four winners and no losers," he said. The first winners would be the electric ratepayers and electricity users in the Pacific Northwest, who would receive abundant, cheap and clean power. "The second group of winners," he said, "are supply system [WPPSS] bondholders. As WNP- stays uncompleted, it remains a valuable but unproductive device. Completing the plant turns optional value to real value." The third group of winners would be all of the citizens of the U.S., who would gain "the safest, fastest, and most efficient, and least expensive means for producing the tritium we need to maintain peace and stability in the world. WNP1 can be operable in six years --several years before other options. It can save the taxpayers of this country several billion dollars...America's nuclear deterrent has ensured world peace for over 40 years. We cannot afford to unilaterally disarm ourselves by not having adequate supplies of domestic Tritium." The fourth group of winners would be the citizens of Washington State, who would "gain economic stability and millions of dollars of increased revenues from completion of WNP1."[431]

Shortly after offering this testimony, Benitz wrote a letter admonishing the State Department of Ecology and its director, Christine Gregoire, for presenting an anti-business, anti-nuclear stance that could undermine that state's chances to win the new production reactor. While he acknowledged that environmental concerns were important, he said that "radical environmentalists have seemingly removed themselves from reality...It seems as if many of the hard core environmentalists like to view all businesses as evil and totally uncaring with regards to the environment. Farmers get grouped into that category as well...It really comes down to some people want to create an enemy, and business and farmers are the ones they point to...It is not only disappointing, it is dangerous." He went on to defend Hanford, stating that "the Hanford reservation defense efforts contributed to ending World War II and saving a million American lives. Apparently some people feel they have to apologize for this fact. Although nuclear weapons have a horrible potential for destruction, we have had 40 years of peace in Europe because of them." A pragmatist, he definitely realized the need for waste cleanup at Hanford, but asserted that "the job ahead is to assure that this happens by working in a cooperative spirit, not allowing the issue to become politicized. Unfortunately, some members of your department have characterized Hanford as possibly the most contaminated place on the planet. Not only is this irresponsible, it's incorrect." Benitz concluded his letter by saying that the 33 and 1/3 percent B&O tax rate on the private, LLW disposal facility on the Hanford Site was punitive and would drive away business, eventually lowering state revenues. "Unfortunately, your department has a reputation of preferring that the site did not exist. This attitude has manifested itself in a very combative and adversarial relationship with the operators of the" private LLW facility. "A sad and somewhat ironic point," he stated, "is that when some people lump together everything 'nuclear,' and come out totally opposed to an operation such as the low level waste site, they never consider those who benefit...[such as] people whose lives were saved from cancer by radioactive medicine techniques." In conclusion, Benitz advised, "I believe there is one message which comes through: beware of the extremists, the ones who are anti-everything, especially anti-progress. There is a role for regulation in many of these issues, but reason should prevail."[432]

The tide of anti-nuclear public opinion in much of Washington State was hard to hold back at that point. In 1987, the DOE had tasked its Hanford Site environmental contractor with beginning a study to estimate the environmental doses of radionuclides that had been released from Hanford in the production years. By 1988, the Hanford Environmental Dose Reconstruction (HEDR) Project had acquired an independent panel of technical experts (the Technical Steering Panel – TSP) from outside the region, to give the study academic credibility. The TSP was holding public meetings throughout the state.[433]

Aside from his letter to Gregoire, Max Benitz was mostly quiet on the subject, watching developments, waiting for solid information, and continuing to fight for nuclear power. In mid-1988, he told an acquaintance that ""here in the Northwest, it would appear we have reached the bottom of the so called nuclear bashing and if our record is good and we work at informing the public more than we have in the past, the public will accept the need for nuclear power."[434] That September, he wrote Governor Gardner urging him to support, or at least not tax out of existence, the LLW disposal facility at Hanford. Benitz pointed out the revenue stream to the state generated by the disposal site, and the difficulties that LLW generators such as hospitals, industrial, research and power facilities would have in disposing their waste if the Hanford LLW site closed.[435] In November, he was appointed Vice Chairman of the Energy Committee of NCSL. One of the main challenges was to develop an energy policy that was broadly representative of the needs of all 50 states and to persuade Congress to address the issue of a national energy policy. "The stability of the world's economy depends upon just such efforts," said Benitz.[436]

In November 1988, he was appointed as Vice-Chairman of the Energy Committee for the NCSL. His term began December 1, and would run for one year.[437]

Pushing for a Sensible Energy Strategy in 1989

Back in Olympia for the start of the 1989 legislative session, Benitz hired an energy analyst for the Senate Energy and Utilities Committee, to help develop the key elements in compromise energy code legislation. During the 1988 legislative session, had sponsored a successful energy conservation bill in the State Legislature.[438] In January 1989, working hard on the code, he praised preliminary legislative agreement on a new Washington State Energy Code. "This is a critical step for all of us who want to see WNP 1 completed someday," he said. Federal law required the Northwest to address energy conservation before it developed certain new energy resources such as WNP 1. "The Northwest is the only area in the nation that has been specifically required by the federal government to address conservation, which is ironic considering the energy deficit we will soon be staring in the face," Benitz stated. "I still believe WNP 1 is our quickest, most cost-effective and reliable electric resource to bring on line. Once we have addressed conservation, I hope we can finish WNP 1 to help meet our region's growing energy demands."[439]

At the same time, he was out speaking about the greenhouse effect and depletion of the ozone layer, relatively new issues at the time. He said these effects "may be before us sooner than we realize." He worried about decreased agricultural production due to weather disturbances caused by burning fossil fuels, and he unabashedly "made a plug... for nuclear power...we have worlds of people scared of nuclear energy, mostly because of the irresponsible reporting by the news media, but it is clean energy and should be used much, much more. I don't think it is even practical to think about building more coal plants." However, he said, some anti-nuclear activists were re-thinking their positions based on the greenhouse effect. "It should be a priority of governments to spend more money on research aimed at lowering the cost of safe nuclear and solar power and making them primary energy sources," he stated. "Otherwise the global warming that results from over-reliance on fossil fuels could produce an increasingly uncertain, potentially bleak future."[440]

Interestingly, Benitz was open to new facts showing that federal weapons sites, including Hanford, spread radioactive and chemical wastes into their surrounding environments during the production years. In January 1989, he stated that nuclear power was controversial with "good reason, considering the accidents at Three Mile Island and Chernobyl, the problem of radioactive waste and the horror stories about U.S. weapons plants." However, knowing that defense waste is quite different from commercial power plant waste, he hoped and worked for a nuclear "comeback...we have to hang in there and continue to do the best job we know how."[441] By that time, tentative plans for long-term cleanup of the Hanford Site were being discussed among the DOE, Washington State officials and the U.S. Environmental Protection Agency (EPA). By the end of February, having been briefed about the preliminary plans, Benitz stated publicly that he was "cautiously optimistic...It seems to be a real good agreement, but any conclusions right now are preliminary," he said. "We still have to sit down and go through this complex agreement with a fine-tooth comb...Clearly, this route is better than going to courts; so I that sense I strongly support the agreement." He said that his main concern about the tentative agreement was whether it could "fend off 'roadblocks to cleanup' that could be thrown up by special interest groups. . . My fear is that one of these groups could file a lawsuit . . . bring the cleanup to a grinding halt."[442]

At the same time, he was sponsoring or co-sponsoring several bills designed to promote nuclear energy, energy conservation, hydropower as a clean resource, and keep the LLW disposal viable at Hanford. He reported to his constituents in early march that his bill to "actively promote" 1,000 acres of leased land on the Hanford Site "for nuclear-related industries has passed the State Senate on a vote of 45-1 . . . Actively promoting this land could pay big dividends for the Tri-Cities and Washington State. We have the land and we have the skilled workers; now we need to focus on attracting new businesses to Hanford." At the same time, the Senate approved his bill to develop energy education for public school students. The bill directed schools to offer curriculum that teaches the fundamental role of energy in the Northwest and national economics, describes the various form of energy, explains their advantages and disadvantages, and teaches energy use efficiency. "I am pleased the Senate passed this bill, and took a step toward ensuring sound energy policies in the future." Said Benitz. "Education is the key to making informed energy decisions." Additionally the Senate passed his bill setting carbon dioxide (CO_2) emission for power plants, by a vote of 48-0. Benitz introduced the bill in response to concern about the greenhouse effect, stating "global warming is a real concern to many people, and it makes sense for Washington State to promote clean energy sources... Frankly, I hope the concern over global warming promotes people to take a more objective look at nuclear power, which is much cleaner and less environmentally damaging than fossil fuel plants or hydroelectric dams."[443]

Benitz also passed bills convening a state task force to plan hydropower comprehensively in Washington, setting state surveillance fees for LLW disposal, assisting owners of structure or equipment in finding and financing energy conservation measures, specifically delineating the duties of the State Department of Ecology in radioactive waste management, and assigning cleanup responsibilities for spills to transporters of hazardous materials.[444]

At the same time, Benitz kept close watch on studies and statistics showing the costs and time frames that might be required to complete WNP-1. A study by a Hanford contractor in Spring 1989, estimated that construction could be completed in three and one/half years, with the reactor operable in six years. Costs would total about $1.6-billion, including support and electricity generating facilities. By these calculations,

WNP-1, because it was already 63 percent complete, could be ready 5-7 years before any new reactor DOE might build, at a cost of $600-million to more than $1-billion less than any new reactor. In addition, WNP-1 would be able to produce electricity, unlike most purely defense reactors.[445] "Conversion is the fastest path to a New Production reactor that will serve the government's need for nuclear materials," Benitz wrote in his notes. "Conversion of WNP-1 is the lowest cost option for the NPR [new Production Reactor]."[446]

May 1989 was eventful. Early in the month, Benitz and other officials were notified that the Hanford Site was a finalist candidate to locate the Superconducting Magnetic Energy Storage Engineering Test Model (SMES-ETM) Project. The Defense Nuclear Agency, part of the federal Department of Defense, was the client that would test SMES technology as a dual-purpose energy system for defense and electric utility applications. The SMES device would store electrical energy much like an automobile battery, in a magnetic field created by an electric current circulating in a coil of superconducting cable. The coil, slightly larger than a football field in diameter, would be buried in a circular trench 30 feet deep in solid rock to contain the magnetic forces. The SMES system and accompanying support building would be constructed within a 270-acre area on the Hanford Site, bringing potentially $200-million in funding before operability, 200-400 jobs during construction and 20-30 permanent positions during operation. The Richland Operations Office of the DOE, and the BPA had nominated Hanford for the project, and thanked Benitz for his help. "We believe that your support for the Hanford proposal was instrumental in our success in making the "short list"...thank you for your past support for the Hanford proposal and for your continued support in ongoing efforts over the next 15 to 18 months to win this important project for Hanford," wrote Mike Lawrence, Hanford's DOE manager, and James Jura, BPA Administrator.[447] Endorsements for the SMES Test Model Project at Hanford came from officials all over the Northwest, including Governor Gardner, Washington's two U.S. Senators Democrat Brock Adams and Republican Slade Gorton, Oregon's Republican Senator Bob Packwood, U.S. Congressman Tom Foley (Democrat–Spokane), many other Washington and Oregon Congressional Representatives, State Senators and Representatives, the Presidents of Washington State University and the University of Washington, Indian tribal leaders, mayors, public utility district officials, the Tri-Cities Development Council, and many others.[78]

On May 15, the Hanford Federal Facility Agreement and Consent Order, better known as the Tri-Party Agreement or the TPA, was signed by the DOE, state of Washington and the U.S. EPA, becoming the first such comprehensive waste cleanup agreement in the nation. The TPA contained milestones for cleanup progress, specific end states or standards for cleanup of various Hanford waste forms, provisions for dispute resolution among the parties, mandates for public involvement, and most of all, flexibility to set further milestones and specifications as more information was learned about the wastes.[448] Within a few years, the DOE, EPA and various states would sign similar agreements governing waste cleanup at DOE weapons sites across the nation. Mike Lawrence signed the agreement for the DOE, and Max Benitz liked and trusted him. Additionally, the agreement mandated in law federal money and jobs for Benitz's district for many years to come. He was still "cautiously optimistic" about the historic agreement. At the same time, he was speaking on the subject of "Energy Strategies for the 21st Century," at a Legislative Leaders Conference sponsored by Arizona State University in Tempe. Benitz once again took the opportunity to advocate for nuclear power.[449]

In August, Max Benitz testified before DOE Secretary Admiral James Watkins at a hearing on National Energy Strategy, held in Seattle. Clearly, Benitz was a man sure of his vision, and not afraid to state it. He first pointed out that the Northwest, having enjoyed a surplus of electricity since the days of President Roosevelt's construction of the Grand Coulee Dam, was now facing an energy shortage. "We have hit load and resource balance. We are staring a deficit in the face," he stated. Acknowledging that energy was a serious subject, Benitz then said he was going to frame his argument in "familiar" terms. He drew a parallel with the nursery story of the *Three Little Pigs*.[79] "There's regional planning, The House of Straw; and there's energy conservation, the House of Sticks; but the only long term solution, The House of Bricks, is to generate more electricity," said Benitz. Many of the benefits of regional planning had already been achieved, he asserted. In addition, even with a strong Building Code that emphasized energy conservation standards, "we will be reaching the end

78. However, Hanford was not selected for the project.
79. Halliwell, James Orchard, (also known as James Orchard Halliwell-Phillipps), *The Nursery Rhymes of England* (London and New York: Frederick Warne and Co., 1886).

of the cost effective saving that can be achieved through energy efficient new construction...over the next five years...Now, we have to look for new generating resources...And that must be the crux of any national energy policy. What will the new energy resources be for the next century? I believe Nuclear Power is our best choice ... there's no other power source that's going to spill less oil on our coastal beaches, drop less acid rain in our lakes or contribute less to the global greenhouse effect than nuclear power." Benitz then brought up the unfinished WPPSS Plants One and Three, known as WNP-1 and WNP-3. They were more than 60 percent complete, he said, and should not be wasted.[450]

He acknowledged to Admiral Watkins that the chief drawback to nuclear power was the waste issue and fear of nuclear waste, and admonished the Admiral that "the bottom line is that the department has to get the repository program on track—soon. It can and should be done, and I'm convinced that safe storage will be accomplished." He concluded by offering four key research areas and tasks for the DOE to pursue—continue and expand study for a new generation of nuclear power reactors with passive safety systems and modular construction; expand research into alternative for spent fuel disposal; continue research into alternative fuels, including electric vehicles; and implement energy education programs, starting in the public schools. "Our entire society needs to realize the tradeoffs involved with taking different energy paths... We aren't to cry wolf this time—it's a real wolf and only expended generating facilities will prevent us from suffering real shortage in the next decade," Benitz resolved.[451]

In September, he once again traveled for two weeks with an NCSL group to Germany, France, Sweden and Switzerland to study nuclear waste storage procedures. With him were Senators Stratton, Williams, Irving Newhouse (Republican–Mabton), and Representatives Hankins and Louise Miller (Republican–King County). Officials from Texas, Nevada, Mississippi and Tennessee also joined the group. Once again, they found plans well underway for waste storage and disposal facilities, prompting Benitz to wonder at the united political will in these nations. In Germany, they were invited to ride down an elevator shaft into the Tankfahrzeuge mit Salslauge Asse II salt mine, which was being investigated as a waste site. Some of the group members were wary and declined, but Benitz, eager to see the actual workings of the design, readily accepted. The idea of reprocessing used nuclear fuel rods, already com-

Benitz in Test Waste Cavern, NCSL Trip, September 1989.

mon practice in France, prompted much discussion among the Americans. To Benitz, the fact that more energy could be extracted by reprocessing, and the ultimate amount of waste generated was smaller than in "direct disposal" after just one fuel cycle, was intriguing.[452]

Interestingly, their hotel in Berlin was very close to "Checkpoint Charlie," a main gate in the Berlin Wall. Benitz wrote that "we had the opportunity to visit East Berlin while it was still under communist rule... and in 1989 there was no sign whatsoever that the Berlin Wall was going to come down in just a couple weeks."[80]

In October, Benitz attended a Pacific Northwest Legislative Leadership Forum in Seattle. The forum brought together more than 50 legislative leaders from Washington, Oregon, Idaho, Montana, Alaska, British Columbia and Alberta to discuss regional energy planning. He chaired the work group dealing with Northwest energy supplies and sources, and said afterward that the meeting re-emphasized his belief that Washington state must rely on itself to satisfy its electricity demands. The blunt message from Canadian officials, he reported, was "don't count on British Columbia to be the Northwest's energy farm...Canada's message was loud and clear: 'We are very anxious to improve Northwest cooperation on energy matters, but don't expect us to meet your electricity needs

80. The Berlin Wall was breached, November 9, 1989.

for you." He said that there was "tremendous pressure" to keep electric power produced in British Columbia in Canada. "British Columbia is experiencing growth of its own, and its power demands are rising." A power exchange agreement between British Columbia and BPA was set to expire in the late 1990s, ending the supply of approximately 300 megawatts (millions of watts) of electric power that British Columbia then currently supplied to the BPA. "Long term renewal of this pact is very unlikely," said Benitz. The conference was just one more example that convinced Benitz that Washington State should complete at least WNP-1, calling it "our best energy option."[453]

In November 1989, Washington State celebrated the Centennial of its statehood. Writing to his constituents about "beginning of a second century in Washington," he stated that "the issue of energy is an overriding concern which I hope will be solved over the next 100 years. After several years of an electricity surplus in this state, we are now facing a time where we will soon be in a deficit condition." Once again, he took the opportunity to advocate for completion of WNP-1 and WNP-1. "Those of us who know that nuclear power is the fuel of the future have been fighting a defensive struggle throughout this decade," he said. "But I believe our efforts to tell the truth have begun to turn things around... [in] the past two years...we have seen the attitude toward nuclear power change so that now we have a majority of the committee who support the use of nuclear power. I believe we can keep this effort moving... My hope is that in 100 years all the state's citizens will realize the need for nuclear power and that nuclear is the most environmentally-benign abundant source of power. I will be working for as long as I can to educate the citizens of the state on this effort."[454]

At the same time, Benitz was re-appointed as Vice-Chairman of the Energy Committee for the NCSL. His new term began December 1, and would run for another year. "I anticipate in 1990 we will propose an energy agenda that recognizes the need for new power generating facilities in our nation, and promotes nuclear power as a clean way to meet our power needs," he stated in announcing his appointment. He said that a similar agenda emphasizing nuclear power narrowly missed being adopted at the 1989 NCSL convention. However, he added, "I am confident that should we propose such a plan this year, we will have the votes needed to approve it."[455]

He immediately plunged into the work at a meeting in December in

Washington, D.C. The monumental task before his committee was to develop and write a National Energy Plan as a policy statement from the NCSL. The plan was to state the major directions that U.S. policy should follow to create a safe, sustainable and environmentally friendly energy supply. Amazingly, Benitz's Energy Committee produced a lengthy but clear statement of its views very quickly. In many aspects, the plan was prescient in speaking to issues that would continue to plague Washington State and the U.S. for decades to come.

According to the policy statement, the ultimate goal for the nation was energy independence. The goal would be reached through multi-faceted efforts, beginning with conservation and energy efficiency. The U.S. government and utilities should promote conservation and energy efficiency through tax credits, education and funded research into conservation technologies. The statement advocated that "voluntary conservation is preferred to mandatory measures wherever possible; ...with gasoline rationing reserved for only the most severe shortage."[456]

With regard to crude oil, the policy statement advocated environmentally sound production of domestic oil supplies, especially in Alaska and on the Outer Continental Shelf in the oceans, in order to "provide supply United States consumers with a secure source of petroleum, and provide a stabilizing influence to the world price of crude oil." This policy is known as "multiple use," denoting a belief that one of the uses of the environment should be to yield natural resources for useful purpose, and not simply be preserved as pristine. Additionally, the U.S. should dialogue with oil suppliers from around the world, especially those in the Western Hemisphere. "Enhanced oil and gas recovery from known reserves shall be promoted, and a research, development, demonstration, and commercialization program for unconventional sources of crude oil shall be pursued," read the statement.[457]

The statement termed coal "America's leading fuel in terms of reserves. It holds the promise of long-term energy security for this nation." However, it had to be mined and burned using environmentally safe practices, and "Clean Coal Technology Programs...[and] coal gasification should be seriously considered as an alternative to the use of coal in a conventional manner." The use and domestic production of of natural gas should be promoted "in an environmentally-sound manner by providing tax and tax accounting incentives." Pipeline construction should be expedited. Renewable energy sources should be developed and assisted, but "must be ranked and funded on the basis of factors including energy efficiency, economic competitiveness, environmental impacts, and technological adaptability." In other words, renewables such as solar and wind should only be promoted where they made economic and technical sense.[458]

The policy statement was very clear about nuclear energy. Due to its neutral contribution to the greenhouse effect, nuclear power definitely should be "included in the development of a national energy plan, with the utmost care taken to address concerns regarding plant safety and waste transportation, storage and disposal. A federal government program for storage and disposal of spent nuclear fuel shall be finalized and implemented as quickly as is safely possible...The nuclear power plant licensing process for future plant construction must be restructured to ensure both public input and timely decisions, and federally re-approved, standardized nuclear power plant designs must be established." In addition, federal funding should be provided for research into "advanced, safe reactor designs, waste management technology, nuclear fusion, and plant retrofit and life extension." Obliquely, while not mentioning reprocessing, the plan cited "the conversion of solid and liquid waste...A resource recovery program which utilizes the waste stream should be encouraged where economically and environmentally feasible for this purpose." All aspects of nuclear energy, the plan emphasized, should be conducted with full, meaningful state involvement. "States shall continue to have the right to monitor operating conditions at nuclear power plants, waste storage and disposal facilities," the plan vowed. In another indirect reference to a positive aspect of nuclear energy, the plan advocated that a "cost-benefit approach should be applied in which the full long-term costs of an option in taxes, consumer energy bills, environmental impacts, security risks, and other national goals and weighed against the additional availability or conservation of energy and other long-term benefits it might be expected to generate." In other words, nuclear would have high initial construction costs, but would be economical in the long term because of its base-load reliability, long life and environmental benevolence.[459]

In all aspects of the policy statement, perhaps the one theme most clear and stated most often was the respect for state authority and input. "State regulator bodies are in the best position to evaluate consumer needs, questions relative to fuel choice, economic development implications, and system reliability. Additionally, the determination as to when and how competitive bidding should be employed in the expansion of electric power generation capacity or to ring on new energy efficiency resources should remain the prerogative of the states through their regulator commissions and the affected utility companies....There shall be no further preemption of state regulatory authority nor shall federal standards be established governing state regulation of utilities... the federal government shall consult closely with state legislatures, shall devise mechanisms to bring state legislatures as full participants into the energy decision-making process on a continuing basis, and shall ensure the inclusion of representatives of the legislative branch of state government in all state-federal working groups in the energy area...NCSL strongly supports and urges the adoption of the concept of primary state responsibility and final decision authority with state legislative oversight for the approval and siting of all major energy conversion facilities, subject to minimum federal standards established only after the fullest consultation with state governments, including state legislators."[460] Benitz had learned the lessons from the national repository fight very well. Without state inclusion and consent, federal decisions could be hamstrung, snarled into knots, and eventually undermined.

1990 Brings Huge Push in Energy Issues

As the *Tri-City Herald* observed, Max Benitz, always a busy man, was even more than usually active in the 1990 session of the Washington State legislature. "Much of Benitz's greater prominence has to do with his role as chairman of the Senate Energy and Utilities Committee, a key position for any legislator whose district includes Hanford," said the newspaper. "Since Republicans gained control of the Senate three years ago, Benitz has unabashedly used his committee as a showcase for nuclear power and has worked to turn back much of the legislation passed during the anti-Hanford climate of the early '80s...the logjam is starting to break."[461] In notes to himself as the legislative session began, Benitz wrote that, in terms of new bills, he wanted to enact a State Energy Code as a "first step toward WNP-1," an "attempt to revive the nuclear industry" with a bill that would allow utilities to charge construction costs to ratepayers "during certain stages of plant construction" instead of only after operability. He also wanted to "make sure carbon dioxide emissions are evaluated any proposed natural gas fired turbines." His planned bill would "mandate and analysis of any natural gas, oil or coal fired facility...[to consider] the environmental effects." He also wanted to introduce a bill to give equity bonuses to utilities when they developed generating resources "as an incentive to get them to start planning for the impending electricity deficit."[462]

He also wanted to revive and re-work several energy bills that had "died in the House" or been vetoed by the Governor the previous legislative session. He wanted to reform the State Energy Facilities Site Evaluation Council (EFSEC) and move it into the State Energy Office. The EFSEC, he noted privately, "has lost touch with reality...[and needs to take] a good look at the impending deficit." He very much wanted to develop a program from energy education in the public schools, "promote the 1000 Acres (for Hanford)...[and] establish a study to determine the feasibility of developing courses...in hazardous materials management/ treatment curriculum at CBC [Columbia Basin College, in Pasco] and the Branch Campus [WSU]...to meet the high demand for specialized waste cleanup personnel." He also wanted to revise the Northwest LLW Compact to require that meetings be held in Washington. Since it was "the host state and administers the site, compact meetings should be held here, not in Alaska or Hawaii."[463]

By February, some of his bills were beginning to pass. The bill establishing a State Energy Code was signed by the Governor, "paving the way," as Benitz said, "for revisions in the code which govern construction of new homes and apartments in Washington...to make new electrically heated homes and apartments more energy efficient." To offset the increased cost of building homes under the new code, homebuyers would be eligible for energy conservation rebates. "Besides promoting energy efficiency," Benitz stated, "the bill fulfills a federal requirement that the Northwest address energy conservation before it brings certain new power generating facilities on-line."[464] The Legislature also voted to lower the B&O tax on the Hanford LLW disposal facility, from 30 percent to 15 percent, with provisions to lower it still further in future years. Benitz had long believed it was essential to keep the site open and receiving shipments to generate user fees, and hence taxes. He felt that an unusually high tax rate would eventually drive waste shippers to other sites, and result in closing the Hanford facility. Benitz also sponsored legislation to replace the Nuclear Waste Board, a citizen advisory council to the state, with one that would advise the state Department of Ecology on Hanford waste cleanup.[465]

In March, his energy education bill became law, requiring that public schools develop curriculum instructing students about various energy forms, supplies, efficiency and environmental effects. Likewise, his bill to study the feasibility of creating waste management education and training programs at CBC and WSU-Tri-Cities, passed, as did bills specifying liability coverage requirement for nuclear operations and strict air pollution control measures. Benitz recognized that "Hanford will be laboratory for waste cleanup for many years," and he wanted the area to train its young people to become experts in waste technologies. The bill to promote the 1,000 acres of leased land at Hanford expanded to a larger effort to promote business in the Tri-Cities. However, the bills to require CO_2 emissions evaluations for new power facilities, and to allow generating facilities to charge customers for construction "along the way" were defeated. He told his constituents he would try again to pass those bills the following year.[466] "My leadership has been pretty good to me in helping my bills along," Benitz told the *Tri-City Herald*. "As chairman of the energy committee, I have considerable influence in the Senate."[467]

At the same time, Max Benitz was fighting to keep the FFTF at Hanford from closing. Since the reactor was completed and started up in 1980, it had not had a clear role, because the nation had turned away from one of its core missions when the "breeder" reactor program was cancelled by President Carter in the late 1970s. During the 1980s, the reactor supplemented its budget by performing irradiation experiments for friendly foreign governments including Japan. By 1990, the DOE said it couldn't keep the reactor open much longer. "All of us who recognize the value of Hanford's Fast Flux Test Facility are presently engaged in an all-out effort to save it from the Department of Energy's 'chopping block'," he told his constituents. "The FFTF is too good a facility to shut down, and almost everyone familiar with the nuclear industry knows it." In the 1990 legislative session, Benitz introduced S.B. 5993, promoting the FFTF to potential investors. He worked toward organizing a state-sponsored trip by several nuclear experts and state officials to nuclear officials and utilities in Europe and Japan to develop more paying customers for the FFTF.[468]

In April 1990, Benitz was appointed to the Task Force on High Level Radioactive Waste/Hazardous Materials Transportation of the NCSL. The Task Force's first meeting would be in Washington. D.C. in May.[469]

Senator Max Benitz Touring the FFTF, Hanford Site, 1985.

After the May meeting of this Task Force, as well as the NCSL's Energy Committee, Benitz reported that the Energy Committee had taken the "necessary first step" toward creating a national energy policy, by adopting a policy resolution package to put before the entire NCSL Assembly in August. The key part of the package in his mind, he said, was the infusion of the statement: "Nuclear Power is an option that should be included in the development of a national energy plan." Benitz said he "had to fight hard to keep this [statement] from being watered down by substituting 'considered' for 'included,' but in the end it was a solid victory. This positive statement saying nuclear power **should** be included in a national energy policy is important to the Tri-Cities, to Hanford and to the completion of WNP-1 ... I am very anxious to be part of creating the NCSL's recommendations to Congress."[470]

At the end of June, President George H.W. Bush announced that he would follow the recommendations of a federal Task Force on Outer Continental Shelf (OCS) drilling and oil exploration. Saying that further steps were needed to protect the coastal environment, he imposed a moratorium on oil and gas leasing and development in several areas off the coast of California, and the vast majority of Sale Area 95 off the coast of southern California, until after the year 2000. He also estab-

Max Benitz at an oil well head in the Gulf of Mexico, Summer 1990.

lished a National Marine Sanctuary in California's Monterey Bay and imposed a permanent ban on oil and gas development there. These steps meant that "99 percent of the federal area off California will be off-limits to consideration for leasing for the remainder of this century." In addition, he began buy-back and cancellation proceedings for certain drilling areas off the coast of southwest Florida, and deferred oil and gas exploration in large areas off the coasts of Washington and Oregon, and St. George Bank in the North Atlantic, until after the year 2000. This delay would allow time to address scientific and environmental concerns, he said. "Although I have today taken these strong steps to protect our environment," Bush concluded, "I continue to believe that there are significant offshore areas where we can and must go forward with resource development."[471]

Max Benitz was disappointed, as the cancellations ran contrary to the "multiple use" principle in his NCSL Energy Committee's draft energy policy statement. Characteristically, he wanted to see for himself. In the summer of 1990, he traveled to the Gulf of Mexico to go aboard on offshore oil drill rig and learn as much as he could about the operations.

That summer, Benitz also was interviewed for an article in a statewide magazine. He reiterated his core beliefs that "our economy runs on energy. Our state is growing and we will need more energy resources in the future, and as Chairman of the Senate Energy Committee, I feel a responsibility to make sure the energy is there when we need it," said Benitz. He also emphasized that "we have to make sure that energy-related issues are decided on their merits, not on emotions."[472]

In early August, Max Benitz boarded an airplane for the NCSL meetings in Nashville, Tennessee, to give the last speech he would ever deliver. He would meet with the Task Force on High-Level Radioactive Waste/ Hazardous Material Transportation, and strongly defend the safe record in transporting nuclear materials. He believed that existing radioactive material transportation regulations were adequate to assure a very high degree of public safety, the technology was available and in use to design, manufacture, and evaluate equipment used in safely transporting radioactive materials, and that the risks involved in transporting radioactive materials were very small when compared to other risks in society and when weighed against the societal benefits of those materials. He also meet with his Energy Committee, and presented the consensus Draft Energy Policy, advocating strongly for nuclear power as an antidote to the greenhouse effect.[473] "Energy will be key to our commitment to the future . . . Nuclear power is vital to low-cost energy...Some people say we should not use nuclear energy...[but] it would be so foolish to close [it] down."[474]

Chapter Five:
Establishing the Washington Wine Industry, and Max Benitz Legacy

Senator Max E. Benitz, Sr., although he is best known as a champion of agriculture, free enterprise, property and water rights, and nuclear energy, was also one of the original "fathers" of the Washington State wine industry. During his early childhood in Kansas, Max helped his father Alto harvest wine grapes.

Shortly after he took office as a first term State Representative, Max Benitz was called upon to vote on a measure that would affect the production and distribution of wines in Washington State for many years to come. House Bill (HB) 100, known as the "California Wine Bill," was signed into law by Governor Dan Evans on April 2, 1969, even though Benitz voted no.[475] The bill ended preferential treatment that Washington wines had enjoyed in the state since the repeal of Prohibition in 1933. Cheap California wines immediately swept into the Washington State market, forcing many local wineries out of business. That year, the Legislature made other modifications in state liquor laws, including allowing women to sit at bars and bar patrons to stand up with a drink. However, Benitz, with his knowledge of soils, climate and agriculture, was convinced that Washington -- particularly eastern Washington -- had the climate and conditions to produce quality wines. Also a strong proponent of the free market system, he was convinced that, given a chance, Washington wines could develop and compete successfully on the national and world market. Although he was extremely busy throughout the early and mid-1970s, learning the ways of the State Legislature and running successfully for State Representative in 1970 and 1972, and for State Senator in 1974 and 1978, the idea of fostering a thriving, high-quality wine industry in Washington State never left Benitz's mind.

In 1978, Benitz finally had time to take a personal vacation with his wife to visit the famous wine-growing region in and around Napa Valley, California. The trip signaled the beginning of his hands-on approach to learning the wine-grape industry. Two years later, he and Marie accompanied Dr. Walter Clore, horticulturist with Washington State University's (WSU's) Irrigated Agriculture Research Extension Center in Prosser. Dr. Clore had been working work with small fruits and vegetables, including grapes at the Center since 1937. He grew and tested more than 250 American, European and hybrid grape varietals. In 1960, he partnered with WSU microbiologist and former Napa Valley resident Charles Nagel to test the vines and determine optimal growing locations and conditions. His meticulous research was instrumental in assuring Washington farmers that they could grow vinifera grapes and produce fine wine. By 1981, Dr. Clore was already famous and retired, and was consulting back to the wine industry and leading tours through the world's primary wine regions, explaining techniques, learning and educating constantly, and of course tasting fine wines.

Beginning of Wine Legislation

By the time of the Clore trip through the wine-making regions of Germany, Benitz was already introducing legislation to foster a fledgling wine industry in Washington State. During the 1981 legislative session, he successfully sponsored the Family Wine Act, which allowed adult members of a household to remove wine made at home from the home for exhibition or use at organized wine tastings and competitions. Quantities were to be kept small, and the wine could not be offered for sale, but the idea was for farm families to begin experimenting with wine-making, engage in friendly competitions, and not have to purchase expensive liquor licenses.[476] He also sponsored legislation that provided research funding through a one/half cent per liter tax on all Washington wine sales, collected by Washington State Liquor Control Board and sent to WSU and the University of Washington for wine-related studies. This legislation also created an industry oversight committee made up of representatives of the Washington Wine Society. The committee was later renamed Wine Advisory Board.[477] Another successful bill allowed patrons of licensed premises serving wine to re-cap, re-cork and remove unconsumed wine from the premises, and an additional measure permitted free wine samples to be given at premises not to include state liquor stores.[478] In all these measures, Benitz was opening doors and making it easier for wine to be tasted, purchased and enjoyed in friendly competitions that would improve the accessibility and quality of the wine experience.

In the 1982 legislative session, he was successful in passing the

Here is Dad pulling more grapes out of the Dodge. Eager me at the Wagon. Uncle Irvin' easing the load and we are headed for the wine press. In those days Dad locked the wine cellar but seldom the house. I still have the padlock.

Max Benitz, Sr. with his father pulling grapes on wagon in Kansas, ca. 1924. Photo is inscribed in Max's own handwriting, commemorating his start in the wine industry.

Beer and Wine Instruction Act, which allowed breweries, wineries and wholesalers to instruct their employees "on the subject or beer or wine, including but not limited to the history, nature, values and characteristics of beer or wine, the use of wine lists, and the methods of presenting, serving, storing, and handling beer or wine."[479] Later in 1982, Max Benitz's support for the small but growing wine industry was featured in his re-election campaign. "With the severe crunch in agriculture, our bright spot is Washington's new wine grape industry. Our wineries have a potential for capturing a major share of the domestic wine market. To aid their development, we've passed measures giving wineries more of an opportunity to market their product," read his 1982 campaign liter-

Benitz's Photo of Napa Valley Wine District on first trip, 1978.

ature. "We've initiated a "one-stop" permit system, allowing wineries to apply once to the state liquor board for permits to bottle and market their product." His campaign fliers also mentioned the instructional courses in beer and wine now possible due to his legislation.[480]

He also reported to Washington Brewers Enological Society Members and Washington Wine Society Members that "the 1982 Session resulted in some very positive legislation" for breweries and wineries. Along with Senator Irv Newhouse (R–Mabton), Benitz told these beer and wine enthusiasts that "1982 legislation encompassed almost all phases of the beer and wine industry, and benefits both large and small producers. We felt that many laws had become antiquated and were deterrents to the establishment of a strong economic climate within both industries...[we] anticipate that by 1990 Washington will rank 2 nationwide in wine production. To achieve this, we must remain competitive in the education and promotion of our own products. We feel confident that the wine industry will continue to thrive in Washington as long as prohibitive and stifling laws are regularly purged and all related regulations are intermittently reevaluated and/or adjust to meet the needs of the industry." Benitz and Newhouse listed 16 new provisions of state liquor laws which they believed were beneficial to small producers, societies wishing to hold private events serving wine and beer, and persons wanting occasional or special event licenses. The new laws

Max and Marie Benitz with Dr. Walter Clore and others on tour through Germany's wine regions, September 1981.

allowed Washington wineries to wholesale their own wine without paying for special licenses at extra costs, lowered fees for small brewery licenses, eased requirements for holding wine tasting or exhibition events, allowed culinary arts classes to use beer, wine and "spirituous liquors" for cooking purposes, permitted businesses not holding liquor licenses to consume liquor on their premises for business entertaining, allowed wine donations and gifts without special licenses, empowered the State Director of Agriculture to "apply emergency measures to prevent or control plant pests and diseases," and granted many other rights not available before that time to foster the availability of wine and beer at places other than restaurants and taverns.[481] In August 1982, with Benitz's encouragement, Prosser held the first annual Prosser Wine and Food

Fair, featuring local eastern Washington wines served in an "exhibition setting" made possible by the Benitz-Newhouse legislation.[482]

Re-elected in November 1982, Max Benitz went back to the legislature in January 1983 ready to work on the issues he cared about. By this time, he was already growing a variety of wine grapes under contract to a major Washington winery. During the 1983 legislative session, Benitz co-sponsored a bill to improve the competitive position of Washington wines. Among other things, it would have permitted state wineries to operate warehouses jointly and operate tasting rooms off premises either individually or jointly. "The bill was torpedoed by lobbyist for beer and wine distributors who were angry at Benitz because he had opposed a bill to give distributors exclusive franchise areas," reported the *Capitol Press* of Salem, Oregon. However, Benitz did manage to fund $300,000 in the state Department of Agriculture budget to establish a marketing program for the wine industry.[483] He was excited that the Yakima Valley had just received its own wine appellation, and effort that took nearly four years. The appellation specified certain geographical boundaries on where wines labeled Yakima Valley could be grown, and imposed other quality control measures. He stated that Washington wines were being hurt by "tremendous competition from heavily subsidized imports. But there is no question that eastern Washington wines are unique. We need to capitalize on that...It will not happen overnight. If we get our message across, we will have a tremendous market for premium wines."[484]

Benitz continued to believe that exports were the "key to survival" for Washington agriculture. After his trade trip to Japan, South Korea and Taiwan with Governor Spellman in 1981, he was still trying to open the Japanese market to Washington apples. However, he was especially "bullish" about the wine industry. In June 1983, he toured officials from the Japanese Mitsui Company through the Port of Benton and the WSU Irrigated Agriculture Research Extension Center. Mitsui had already purchased grape juice from a Prosser firm, and expressed interest in purchasing Washington wines and wine grapes. "I am tremendously pleased and encouraged by Mitsui and Company's interest in the Tri-Cities Area products. I hope this is just the beginning of a long-term trade relationship between our region and Mitsui," Benitz stated.[485]

To Max Benitz With best wishes ~~Guy Bush~~

Max Benitz at Cerebral Palsy telethon and Republican dinner with Vice President and Mrs. George Bush, January 18, 1986. Benitz gave them a bottle of his 1984 Ice Wine.

Continuing to Foster the Wine Industry

In early 1984, Max Benitz told his district's largest newspaper, the *Tri-City Herald*, of his dream to have a Washington Wine Commission one day. "In Washington," he said, "some people say we have reached the saturation point in wines, but that's not true...What we want to do is promote Washington wines."[486] That year, he successfully sponsored the Wine and Beer Product Information Act, which allowed a brewery, winery or wholesaler to "conduct educational activities or provide product information to the consumer on the licensed premises of a retailer." Information about wine or beer could include, but not be limited to, the "history, nature, quality, and characteristics of a wine or beer, methods of harvest, production, storage, handling and distribution, and the general development of the wine and beer industry."[487] He also sponsored and passed the Wine Warehouses Act, which granted licenses to wine storage warehouses off the premises of wineries.[488]

During the 1985 legislative session, he succeeded in passing legislation establishing two new classes of liquor licenses to enable retailers to serve beer, wine and liquor by the glass to members and guests or organizations on special occasions, on premises other than those holding "regular" liquor licenses. The new class H and I licenses were priced at levels affordable to most organizations.[489] During 1986, Benitz continued fostering the Washington wine industry by sponsoring and passing a variety of laws making it easier for wineries to operate, attract customers and employees, and thrive. The Class H license was extended to hotels, and a new law allowed minor employees to stock or handle,

By 1987, Max Benitz had an impressive wine collection of his own.

A Portion of Max Benitz's Wine Cellar, 1987.

but not serve, wine and beer in licensed premises, provided an adult was present. Another law authorized a "grower's license" that permitted grower's to sell wine made from their own grapes to wineries, distilleries and liquor vendors, and to store their own wine in bulk.[490]

Washington Wine Commission Legislation, 1987

Just re-elected to his fourth term in the State Senate, he believed it was time to propose the law that could truly place the Washington wine industry on solid footing. In early February 1987, his Washington Wine Commission bill (SB 5503), sponsored by Benitz with 15 other Senators, was first read and referred to Committee. It was simultaneously introduced into the State House. Benitz told his constituents that it was "vital to Washington premium wine industry to pass these into law in the current session...The Commission would give a tremendous boost to this fast growing new industry. I'm going to work full time for legislative approval. A coordinated, professional marketing effort for the state's premium wine industry will bring us big dividends, not only in wine sales but in tourism as well."[491] SB 5503 passed the State Senate with only five dissenting votes, and went on to a conference committee with members of the State House. It passed the House in March and, as amended after revisions by the conference committee, passed the Senate on April 13. The new law, which Max Benitz counted as one of his proudest signature accomplishments, became effective July 1, 1987. "One of my highest priorities for the session was to see the Legislature establish an organization to represent the state's rapidly growing premium wine industry," he said in a radio speech summarizing the 1987 legislature's performance. "This goal was realized when lawmakers voted to establish the Washington Wine Commission."[492]

The Commission was necessary, Benitz's legislation stated, because "the sale in the state and export to other states and abroad of wine made in the state from wine grapes grown in the state contribute substantial benefits to the economy of the state...[and] The general welfare of the people of the state will be served by healthy development of the activities of growing and processing wine grapes, which development will improve the tax bases of local communities in which agricultural land and processing facilities are located, and obviate the need for state and federal funding of local services."[493] The purpose of the 11-member commission, made up of representatives from the wine business, was to "create, provide for and conduct as comprehensive and extensive research, promotional and educational campaign...[designed to] establish Washington wine as a major factor in markets everywhere; promote Washington wine as a tourist attraction. . . encourage favorable regulatory and legislative treatment of Washington wine in markets everywhere; foster economic conditions to investment in the production of vinifera grapes and Washington wine" and advance knowledge about vines and wines.[494] For producers, Benitz said, the Commission established a "one-stop permit system" to allow them to bottle and market their products. Although initially partially publicly funded, the Commission was permanently funded by fees charged to wine growers and producers. Another measure passed that year allowed wineries to conduct courses for restaurateurs "to learn how to serve Washington wines at their best."[495] He also sponsored yet an additional law that year allowed beer retailers to offer samples on the premises where sold, except in state liquor stores.[496]

Continuing to Champion — and Enjoy — Washington Wine

Although Max Benitz was extremely busy with energy and other matters during 1988-89, he watched over the budding Washington wine industry with care. He made a note to himself for the 1988 legislative session, saying: "Get 1988 Appropriation Bill for $100,000 for faculty and equipment for wine industry research." The bill was passed. In 1989, Benitz sponsored successful legislation creating a special Class P wine retailer's license that would allow gifting and delivery of wines by persons other than the producers.[497] He also actively worked to smooth and sort out issues with licensing a proposed "Wine Pavilion" at a highway

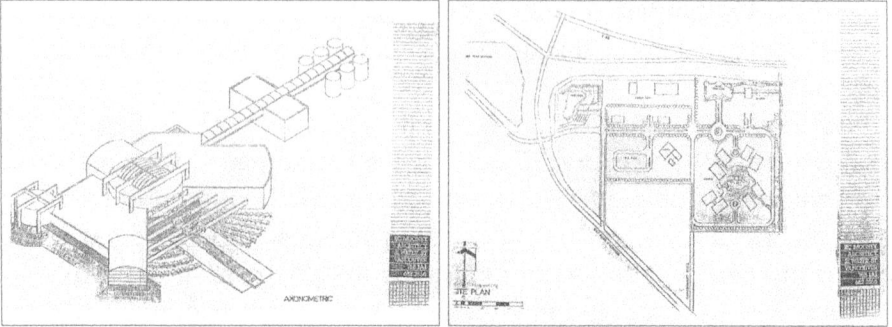

Schematic of Proposed Wine Pavilion at Highway I-82 Rest Stop, Prosser, WA, November 1988 (drawing by Prosser Land Development Company).

Poster of Benitz Entry into Grandview, Washington Wine Festival, 1989.

rest stop near Prosser. The State Liquor Control Board saw no problem with the idea, since previous Benitz legislation had established so many classes of wine licenses that a variety new arrangements for wine-tasting were possible.[498] However, the Washington Wine Institute, based in Seattle, expressed concerns to Benitz. "There is a general image problem in associating wine tasting as an activity at a highway rest stop," wrote Simon Siegal, Director of the Wine Institute. "While the actual activity

Max Benitz and his vineyard, 1990.

Leo Kocher and Max Benitz sample glasses of their wine. In the background is Benitz's's motor home, where he carried several cases of wine to sample for everyone he met.

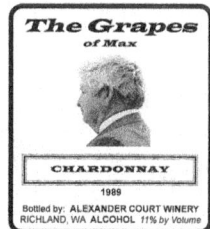

Kocher also designed several fun labels for Benitz's wine.

-ALB-R3
-ALDEN-R23
-ALICANTE-R9
-ALIGOTE-R20
-ALWOOD-R24
-AMBER RED-R16
-AUORA-R22
-AUXERROIS-R3
-AXR-R1
-BACO NOIR-R1
-BARBERA-R22
-BATH-R18
-BERGONIA-R6
-BLACK MONUKKA-R15-R18-R27
-BLACK ROSE-R25
-BUFFALO-R1
-CABERNET SAUV.-R2
-CACO-R24
-CALZIN-R1
-CAMBELL EARLY-R20
-CANDICE-R3-R23
-CANNER-R10-R18
-CARDINAL-R17
-CARIGNANE-R10
-CASCADE-R1
-CATAWBA-R23
-CHARDONNAY-R2-R24-R27
-CHENIN BLANC-R2
-CHENIN BLN Davis-R22
-CINNAMON-R14
-CLINTON-R24
-CONCORD-R2
-DATTIER ST. VAL.-R24
-DECKROT-R6
-DELIGHT-R24
-DUTCHESS-R24
-EHRENFELSER-R4
-EINSET-R25
-ELVIRA-R23
-EMERALD RIES.-R23
-EXOTIC-R25
-FRESNO SEEDLESS-R19
-FDO-R3
-FEHR LSGAOS-R24
-FESTIVAL-R18
-FLAME-R19
-FREDONIA-R20
-FRENCH COLOMBARD-R12
-FS4-R5
-GERONIMO-R20
-GEWURTZTRAMINER-R22
-GOLDEN MADERA-R15
-GOLDEN MUSCAT-R21
-GREEN HUNGARIAN-R10
-GREY RIES. #1-R22

3 -GREY RIES. #2-R23
2 -GUTDEL SLYUHNER-R23
2 -GUTDEL WIESS-R10
1 -HARMONY-R1
2 -HELENA-R26
0 -HIMROD-R13
2 -HORIZON G.V.W.-R8
0 -INTERLAKEN-R20
1 -ISLAND BELLE-R23
7 -ITALIA-R9-R10-R18-R19
0 -KIWI-R9&R10
2 -LADY FINGER-R18
4 -LAKEMONT-R25
2 -LANDOT-R24
8 -LIMBERGER CRAWF.-R11-R26
0 -LEMBERGER-R11
2 -LEON MILLOT L.S.-R5
0 -LUCIE KULMAN-R24
3 -LUCILL-R26
1 -MADELINE ANGEVINE-R22
2 -MADELINE SLY.-R23
2 -MALVASIA BLANCA-R12
2 -MARS-R25
2 -MELON-R25
4 -MERLOT-R3
2 -MEUNIER-R22
3 -MICZURNOWEIC-R21
2 -MULLER THURGAU-R16
3 -MUSCAT 487-O1A-R21
2 -MUSCAT ALEX.-R21
5 -MUSCAT BLANC-R2
2 -MUSCAT DALSACE-R27
3 -MUSCAT OTN. BEL.-R21
3 -MUSCAT OTTENEL-R21
1 -MUSCAT ROSceBLAS-R21
2 -NEW YORK MUSCAT-R21
3 -NIAGARA-R23
1 -NORAKERT PGR 2224-R4
1 -NY 44965 G.W.B.-R9
2 -NY45198-R6
3 -OKANAGAN RIES.-R23
0 -ONTARIO-R20
7 -ORANGE MUSCAT-R26
1 -OSTEINER L.S.-R4
3 -OSTEINER-R4
0 -PALIMINO-R24
1 -PEARL OF CSABA-R7
4 -PERLETTE-R19
6 -PINOT NOIR-R26
3 -RABANER-R4-R5-R9
2 -REICHENSTEINER-R3
3 -RELIANCE-R25
3 -REMAILY SLDS-R26
3 -REMAILY-R25
4 -REYNOLDS EHAENF.-R5

4 -REYNOLDS ROTOBRGR.-R7
2 -REYNOLDS WIESB.-R5
3 -RIBIER-R17
4 -RIESLING MUSCAT-R14-R21
2 -RKATZITELLI-R4
1 -ROTOBERGER-R3
1 -RUBISHEUSKI-R3
1 -RUBI RED-R9
2 -RUBY SEEDLESS-R14
1 -SALT CREEK-R1
3 -SATURN-R25
4 -SAUVIGNON BLANC-R20
1 -SCHOONBURGER-R4
2 -SCHUYLER-R23
3 -SELTANA-R26
5 -SEMILLION-R22
1 -SENCA-R24
1 -SEYVE VILARD-R1
4 -SIEGREBBE-R21
2 -SPICE-R12
1 -STAWBERRY GRAPE-R14
3 -TEXAS SPECIAL-R20-R24
1 -THOMPSON SEEDLESS-R13
3 -VANNESSA-R25
2 -VENUS-R25
3 -VERDELET-R26
2 -VINELAND-R24
5 -VOGOLDON-R16-R17
1 -WEST FREESIA-R6
2 -WHITE DIAMOND-R24
3 -WHITE MUSCAT-R21
5 -WHITE ROUGE-R23
2 -W. RIESLING-R1
3 -YATES-R4-R6
4 -ZARIA SIEWERA-R22
4 -ZINFANDEL-R13-R27
6 -ZW-R8
1 -1613-R1
1 -3304-R1
1 -5A-R1
1 -5BB-R1

| Total Number of Vines: | 407 ea | Date Printed: |
| Total Number of Varities: | 151 ea | 00-Jan-00 |

Chart of Max Benitz's 1988 grape nursery. *Courtesy of Leo Kocher*

may not be that dramatically different than what occurs at a winery facility, the more direct coupling of highway travel with wine consumption at such a pavilion becomes more blatant. Wineries utilize their facilities as an education resource and as a means to impart the 'romance' of the beverage to their visitors, which would be difficult in the pavilion." Siegal suggested that the pavilion simply offer maps, directions and information about wines, but not actual wine tasting. A wine-tasting pavilion, he said, might do better at Sea-Tac Airport. At that time, Benitz was also

Max Benitz Salutes Washington Wine Industry in the last year of his life.

Max Benitz tying up plants with grandson Carl.

Max and Marie Benitz in their experimental grape vineyard, 1990.

Marie Benitz and Max Benitz, Junior, in vineyard, 1991. *photo courtesy of Tri-City Herald*

introducing legislation to permit wineries to operate second and third facilities under their original licenses. Siegal assured Benitz that the Wine Institute "genuinely appreciate[s your] support of the Washington wine industry...[and] your initiative in reducing regulatory paperwork and increasing business opportunities for Washington Wineries."[499] Benitz planned to work on the proposal further, as time permitted.

By 1990, Max Benitz, at age 73, had cut back his own personal acreage in wine and table grapes from 160 acres to just five "hobby acres." He told a news reporter in early Summer 1990 that "grapes are my main hobby today. I love to experiment with new varieties. I have some new plants that will produce for the first time this year: Mars, Venus and Saturn. . .I think they might be out of this world." Getting serious, he added that Washington wines "can compete with California, France or any other part of the world."[500] Benitz was having fun with his wines.

With friend Leo Kocher, a Richland, Washington, nuclear engineer whom he met while trying to save Hanford's Fast Flux Test Facility, Benitz made many sample bottles of wine together in the basement wine cellar at the Benitz home.

Benitz and his friends and neighbors also thought up quirky and sometimes comical names for their wines. Benitz named one wine with a very high alcohol content as *Passionada*. One grape plant was named Geronimo by Benitz's grandson Carl. The plant had been given to Benitz's son-in-law, Curtis Wagner, by a man he helped out of a ditch on his way home from work one day. The man said the plant was a "grip," and little Carl called it Geronimo.

Ranching neighbors and friends of Benitz named one of their wines *Sadie Louise*, after a lamb with a fondness for eating grapes.[81]

Dr & Mrs. Clore in Olympia with Senator Max Benitz (left) and a student.

---

81. *Sadie Louise* is bottled by Mercer Estates Winery, Prosser, WA.

Shock, Tributes and Legacy

Max Benitz's death on August 29, 1990, was so sudden and shocking that even political opponents rushed to pay tribute to him. Democrat Governor Booth Gardner who had often sparred with Benitz, called him a "highly regarded and well-liked legislator who worked hard in service to the people of this state." Senator Mike Kreidler (D-Lacey) was state campaign chairman for the Democrat Party, working to unseat Benitz from the State Senate at the time of his death. Despite the rivalry, Kreidler said "Max was a person for whom I had the highest regard...I just can't imagine the Senate without him. We always try to win these campaigns, but . . . something like this...is not supposed to happen." Friends were even more effusive. Sam Volpentest, legendary executive vice-president of the Tri-City Industrial Development Council, stated that 'we've lost a great, dedicated public servant who worked for everything the Tri-Cities tried to achieve." Benton County Commissioner Ray Isaacson termed Benitz a "very strong, principled person and an excellent statesman. His ethics were extremely high." Another Benton County Commissioner, Sandy Strawn, said that Benitz was "a fine man who certainly cared about his community and what he did as Senator... You can't replace a person like that." Richland Mayor Craig Buchanan remembered that Benitz was "always friendly and warm to anybody who went up to him, whether he knew them or not. When he spoke, you had a tendency to listen closely because there was always some valuable advice or information in what he said." Leslie Donovan, a staff member in the State Republican office said that Benitz's "commitment and dedication was truly for the community and the state as a whole, as opposed to any personal ambition."[501]

The tributes continued unabated. The *Tri-City Herald* editorialized that Max Benitz was "really special...he was friend and a toiler for better days ahead. In the legislature as on the farm, Max plowed a straight row... he worked hard all his life to see to it that the days of poverty which he and so many others experienced during the Depression would not return... Throughout his life, Max Benitz did what he thought was right, not what he thought was popular. In the legislature, he voted his conscience, and few doubted that conscience let him sleep soundly through the night."[502] Senate Majority Leader Jeannette Hayner (R-Walla Walla) called Benitz an "uncommon man...so filled with fine qualities...He was never vindictive, not even to his opponents. He had high moral standards that endeared him to both sides. He was a sincere, hard-working legislator... who had a sincere desire to do the best he could for his constituents." U.S Representative Sid Morrison (R- WA 4th District) and Washington State Attorney General Ken Eikenberry both praised Benitz's tirelessness and enthusiasm for state projects.[503] Jim Jesernig, the Democrat who was challenging Benitz for his Senate seat at the time of Benitz's death, said that "Senator Benitz lived a life dedicated to public service and was always true to his principles and his beliefs."[504] Senator Irv Newhouse stated that Benitz "was a one-man promotion squad for Washington wines, in wine tastings, restaurants, or on any occasion he had. Developing popularity of Washington wines in our own state was really more than a hobby to him."[505] Senator Al Bluechel, President Pro Tem of the State Senate, said Benitz was "a real gentleman...[who was] so well-liked, he was extra effective for his district."[506] Dr. Walter Clore stated that "Senator Max Benitz was a strong supporter of WSU programs, especially those agricultural programs involving irrigation at the WSU Irrigated Agriculture and Extension Center at Prosser...In 1985 he was largely responsible for the legislative funding for the wine grape industry of $140,000 each year until 1987...The Senator in 1988 obtained appropriation funds of $100,000 for faculty and equipment for wine industry research. He was instrumental in passing legislation that resulted in new markets for Washington's wine grapes and up to 1,000 new jobs each year."[507]

Opening New Doors

Washington State University at Tri-Cities cordially invites you to the Ribbon-Cutting Ceremony for the New Building Addition and the Dedication of the Max E. Benitz Memorial Library

*Thursday, September 26, 1991
1:00 p.m.
WSU Tri-Cities
100 Sprout Road
Richland, Washington*

Tours and student-sponsored barbecue following

Program Brochure Dedicating Max E. Benitz Library, 1991.

Today, according to the Walter Clore website, Washington state is the second largest premium wine producer in the country and it's wine

Congressional Record

UNITED STATES OF AMERICA

PROCEEDINGS AND DEBATES OF THE 102^d CONGRESS, FIRST SESSION

Vol. 137   WASHINGTON, TUESDAY, OCTOBER 15, 1991   No. 147

Senate

TRI-CITY CAMPUS ESTABLISHED

● Mr. GORTON. Mr. President, thank you for allowing me the opportunity to commend the Tri-City community and school leaders on establishing a branch campus of Washington State University. The opening of the Tri-City campus represents the culmination of a decade of efforts to enlarge the former Joint Center for Graduate Studies.

It is especially befitting that the new library was dedicated in honor of the late Senator Max E. Benitz. Senator Benitz had always recognized the value of education and had been a stalwart supporter of the branch campus. It is largely due to his efforts that higher education will meet community needs in the Tri-City area. Senator Benitz' commitment to education has been essential to the success of the region and the State.

On behalf of the citizens of Washington State I applaud the Tri-City community and especially the outstanding service of the late Senator Benitz. ●

Benitz Library Designation Commemorated in Congressional Record, 1991.

industry contributes in excess of $14.9 billion to the national economy and supports more than 27,000 jobs.[508]

Lasting Legacy

At Max Benitz's funeral, held in the Messiah Lutheran Church in Prosser that he had helped to build more than 40 years earlier, his family asked that donations to a scholarship fund at Washington State University, Tri-Cities, in lieu of flowers. Although flowers filled the church, $17,325.12 was donated to the WSU-Tri-Cities scholarship.[509] However,

From left: Max E. Benitz, Jr., Ronald Benitz, Norma June Benitz Fortner, Representative Shirley Hankins, and Eileen Benitz Wagner, pose with portrait of Max Benitz, Sr. at Legends of Washington Wine event, Clore Center, 2007.

the most fitting tribute to Max Benitz came when WSU-Tri-Cities, which had opened in 1989, dedicated the Max E. Benitz Memorial Library on September 26, 1991. "Max will be remembered as the 'people's legislator,' one who kept making things happen for the public," said campus Dean Jim Cochran.[510] United States Senator Slade Gorton (R-Washington), wrote to Marie Benitz that "it is particularly appropriate that the new library at WSU Tri-Cities was dedicated in honor of your husband and my friend. Max had always recognized the value of education and was a staunch supporter of the branch campus concept. Max's commitment to education will long be remembered with the new, beautiful Max E. Benitz Library serving as a testimonial."[511] In September 1999 the Friends of the Library of the Max Benitz Library held a special commemorative program featuring the Benitz family. A photo album of Max Benitz's life was presented to the library by his children.

In October 1991, Max Benitz was memorialized in the *Congressional Record*, when Senator Gorton stated that "It is largely due to his efforts that higher education will meet community needs in the Tri-City area. Senator Benitz's commitment to education has been essential to the success of the region and the State."

In 2007, the Walter Clore Wine and Culinary Center held its annual gala event to honor all of its finalist nominees for membership in the exclusive "Legends of Washington Wine Hall of Fame." Max Benitz, Sr. was among the finalists, and his family gathered for the event. The nomination speech was given by Representative Shirley Hankins (R-Richland; 8th District). Hankins had served with Benitz in the Legislature since her election in 1984, through the time of his death in 1990. Her tribute to Benitz stated that "it's my honor this evening to remember and posthumously recognize one of the finalists for the Legends of Washington Wine Hall of Fame my good friend, Max Benitz, Senior...Max and I met through some of our Republican get-togethers and we became good friends...It's very appropriate that Max is honored along with the fathers of our Washington wines. On his farm he researched many different varieties of grapes and studied how they tasted when made into wine. . .he gave us each a flat with cardboard squares. And as he picked the grapes for us. He would write down the different varieties on these cardboard squares. . .Max really enjoyed showcasing Washington wines. He loved to taste other wines and see how ours compared. . .I don't think Max ever thought of himself as one of the fathers of Washington wines, even though he was instrumental in the formation of the Washington Wine Commission. He did this mostly as a hobby that he enjoyed very much . . . and although it's been 17 years since we lost Max, I think if he was able to come back here today, he would be thrilled and amazed at how our local wine industry has taken off...Thanks Max for your wonderful contribution to the Washington wine industry."

In 2013, a Wine Science Center was dedicated at Washington State University, Tri-Cities. According the Center, it "the $23 million project is designed to attract world-class researchers and students who will focus their efforts on the challenges and opportunities faced by Pacific Northwest grape growers and winemakers." At the dedication, Steve Warner, president of the Washington State Wine Commission, stated that the grape and wine industry "has experienced explosive growth since it started 30 years ago. Now with nearly 800 licensed wineries and an economic impact of $8.6 billion, Washington wines consistently outperform wines from other regions of the world," he said.[512]

Additional Testimonials to Max E. Benitz, Sr.

"Max and I were elected to the House in the class of '68, and he took a seat behind me. I saw the silver in his brush-cut hair, and it wasn't hard to imagine him in his overalls planting his "hardwood" (wine seedlings). He looked at me and thought, 'There's another Seattle "liberal.'" But we were both men of moderation, and very solid friends as the years went by. I left for the Senate after a term; Max soon followed. My admiration level continued to rise. We were on the same team in changing the out-dated leadership, although the Minority Leader was in the district adjacent to his, and on the recruiting and campaigning road in 1980, when the GOP won its second majority it the Senate in 35 years. Max was the salt of the earth, who could always be depended on to do the reasonable things, whose word was his bond...Confidence in the nation's public life would not be at a low ebb if its legislative seats were filled with charactered men and women like Senator Benitz."

SENATOR GEORGE W. SCOTT
R-Seattle, retired[513]

"I always get a great big smile when I think of Max Benitz because he consistently left me feeling that every issue we faced together was going to be OK. And he always (with a twinkle in his eye) announced as he was leaving that he had a few new ideas he was going to try. Max was too old to be my brother, too young to be my father, so he served in both capacities . . . he had special skills that fit in with the lawyers, the college Presidents, the scientists, the city slickers.

How did he do it? There may not be a simple answer, but I know it would include hard work. He just flat out gave everything he did a lot of extra effort, just as he learned from his life of dealing with Mother Nature on the farm. Max also had a personality that "drew people in". They wanted to like him, and trust him, just because he was likeable, and earned their trust... Why would a room full of PhDs dealing with higher education pay strict attention to Max Benitz? Because he got quickly down to the truth, not needing the tinsel and puffery of the fancy stuff to make his point, and he had done his homework. He was to be respected.

Max gave so much of himself. I remember one occasion when he joined Lieutenant Governor John Cherburg on a trade mission to Tiawan. Max had a case of Washington wine that he really wanted to get to potential customers, and there was no room on the plane, but Max tenaciously kept that wine under his arm and sat on it for most of the almost forever it took to get to his destination....

I was delighted when Max was willing to take on the prestigious Chairmanship of the State Republican Party. They needed help and figured they could use a guy as close to Abraham Lincoln as you can find these days. I know he surprised a lot of folks in Seattle and Bellevue because he outworked and outsmarted them and did the party a real favor . . . A friend to everyone, and a mentor to me and many others, they don't make 'em like Max Benitz anymore. Respected because he earned it, he was street smart...I cherish the moments I spent with Max Benitz, and those memories live on."
CONGRESSMAN SID MORRISON (retired)
(R-Washington; 4th District)[514]

"It was an honor, a privilege, and terrific fun to work for and with Senator Max E. Benitz. Max is still well known for being one of the essential founders of Washington State's premium wine industry, a champion of the state's higher education system, and an energy policy leader, among many other accomplishments. But highest on my list is his role as a friend and mentor to me and countless others. Max was not so much a boss for me but closer to a favorite uncle: wise, generous and fun, but discipline and integrity were expected . . .

My lasting professional images of Max relate to the work we did together promoting energy policies that continue to provide benefits to the entire Pacific Northwest. Max was unabashedly pro-energy and a big supporter of the nuclear industry and hydroelectric power. He authored legislation to promote economic development at Hanford, and even authored legislation to evaluate greenhouse gas emissions related to new power plants. But he saw the need for a balanced approach toward supply and demand. Without his leadership, the multi-year effort to enact the landmark 1990 Model Conservation Standards legislation would not have happened. More than 20 years later, this legislation--which set a new standard of excellence for the nation--continues to provide cost-effective benefits to the electric ratepayers of the Pacific Northwest.

I continue to miss Max's wisdom and humor, but think of him often as our nation's energy policy debates are often very similar to those of over 20 years ago. As I learned from him, bringing people together is satisfying, whether it's over a discussion of energy policy or whether it's over a glass of wonderful Washington state wine."

COMMISSIONER PHILIP MOELLER
Federal Energy Regulatory Commission[515]

"I lobbied for the Washington PUD Association 1987 and 1988...I remember writing this letter [during that time period]: Recently, I attended an appreciation dinner at Cavanaugh's for Sen. Max Benitz. My Client, the Washington PUD Association, sponsored the well-deserved event.

As I listened to the factual representation of Sen. Benitz's effort during the last session I had occasion to reflect on how fortunate the Tri-Cities is to have Max in the Senate. As a lobbyist with four Tri-City area clients representing Hanford issues, economic development activities and general business interests. I remembered how many times I was in Sen. Benitz's office and how many times he went to bat for his district and our needs.

As chairman of the Energy Committee, he literally caused the WPPSS settlement funds to be forthcoming...In the face of opposition within his own party, he brought out of his committee an unprecedented conservation building code because it was "right." He coaxed Sen. Saling, Spokane's chairman of the Senate Higher Education, to try once more to meet with the House leadership to reach a compromise for the Tri-City WSU branch campus. I could go on for pages about his work.

He is more quiet and more powerful than I have ever witnessed, and I've worked with him for 15 years. We are fortunate to have Sen. Benitz. There should be an "appreciation dinner" every night this summer sponsored by some interest or person helped by this productive statesman.

JIM BOLDT
The Boldt Group
Lobbyist for the Washington Public Utility Districts, 1987-1988[516]

It was well known and documented that Max promoted national programs for the Hanford project and for the Washington State College in the Tri-Cities. Following the signing of a contract with Battelle Pacific Northwest Laboratories in the Summer of 1986, Max...[asked for a reference for an amateur wine maker]. One of the Battelle managers in attendance, was L. Donald Williams [my goose hunting partner], who quickly stated, "I have the man just for you. His name is Leo F. Kocher, who lives in Richland." That evening I was privileged to receive a call from Senator Max, who asked me if I was interested in making sample wines with grapes from his vineyard; if so, [he said] "would you please come to my farm in the next day or two?"

My dad was a grain farmer but when the harvest season was over he normally made some wine from cherries, plums and grapes...Seeing my father make wine, I picked up the thought of being a home wine-maker in 1982. My meeting with Max the next day initiated an immediate friendship. We spent many an hour planting, spraying and pruning new vines and then hand-hoed the vineyard to remove every single weed. Labor in the field usually was followed with a lunch down the road a bit, at the village of Whitstran. With the passing of Max, I found my loss, like I did with my own father.

LEO KOCHER
Nuclear Engineer[517]

I'm a nuclear engineer who spent almost 20 years on the FFTF Project with Westinghouse, a long-time Republican PCO [Precinct Committee Officer] of moderate persuasion, past Richland City Council member, and currently a Presidentially appointed member of the Advisory Board on Radiation and Worker Health under HHS [the Department of health and Human Services]....I thought your father was a remarkable individual, and was delighted when the new WSU Tri-Cities Library was given his name.

WANDA MUNN
Richland Engineer[518]

Senator Max E. Benitz, Sr., 1990

Endnotes

Chapter 1

1. Jones, Aaron, "Senator Max Benitz – "Mr. Energy" – Still Going Strong," in *Washington Rural Electric Cooperative Association News* (Olympia), July 1990, p. 25, citing Max Benitz.

2. Personal Communication, E.M.B. Wagner to M.S. Gerber, October 9, 2013.

3. Benitz, Max, "Personal Profile," Transcript of Tape 1, Family Records, Prosser, WA, 1986, p. 7.

4. Ibid., p. 6.

5. Benitz, Max, "Personal Profile," Transcript of Tape 2, Family Records, Prosser, WA, 1986, p. 1.

6. Ibid., p. 2.

7. Ibid., p. 4.

8. Ibid., pp. 4-5.

9. Ibid., pp. 10-11.

10. Benitz, Max, "Education," Speech prepared for Yakima Public Schools, in Personal and Family Papers, Prosser, WA, Summer 1990.

11. Ibid., p. 11.

12. Webster, Frank, "County Agent's Column," in *Prosser Record-Bulletin* (Prosser, WA), 1952, partially citing Max Benitz.

13. Associated Press, "Truman Urges Teamwork on Inflation," in *Ellensburg Daily Record* (Ellensburg, WA), April 10, 1951 at http://news.google.com/newspapers?nid=860&-dat=19510410&id=ikkKAAAAIBAJ&sjid=9UoDAAAAIBAJ&pg=5720,2102652

14. "Truman Seizes Control of Steel Industry – April 8, 1952," Miller Center, University of Virginia (Charlottesville), at http://millercenter.org/president/events/04_08

15. "Eisenhower Ends all Wage Controls," *in Reading Eagle* (Reading, PA), February 6, 1953, p. 1 at http://news.google.com/newspapers?nid=1955&dat=19530206&id=soktAAAAIBAJ&s-jid=b5sFAAAAIBAJ&pg=4049,195542916. Benitz, Tape 2, p. 11.

17. "Moses, Benitz Top Corn Club Production Contest," in *Prosser Record Bulletin*, 1958; Thompson, Mrs. Cormac, "Bureau President Farms 410 Acres," *in Tri-City Herald* (Kennewick, WA), December 29, 1960, partially citing Max Benitz.

18. Thompson, "Bureau President Farms 410..." partially citing Max Benitz.

19. "Benitz is Voting Delegate at National FB Convention," in *Washington State Farm Bureau News*, Washington State Farm Bureau (Lacey, WA), December 1960.

20. Dimitri, Carolyn, Effland, Anne and Conklin, Neilson, "The Twentieth Century Transformation of U.S. Agriculture and Farm Policy," Economic Information Bulletin #3, U.S. Department of Agriculture (Washington, DC), June 2005 at http://www.ers.usda.gov/media/259572/eib3_1_.pdf.

21. "Action to Protect Rights Asked of Farm Bureau Members," in *Tri-City Herald*, January 6, 1961, citing Max Benitz.

22. Boycott on Apples Hit By Benitz," in *Prosser Record Bulletin,* 1961.

23. Ibid.

24. National Labor Relations Board, Petitioner, vs. Fruit and Vegetable Packers and Warehouse-men, Local 760 et al, 377 U.S. 58, 84 Supreme Court 1063, 12 L. Ed. 2nd 129, April 20, 1964 at https://bulk.resource.org/courts.gov/c/US/377/377.US.58.88.html

25. Summers, Clyde, "Freedom of Association and Compulsory Unionism in Sweden and the United States," Yale Law School (New Haven, Connecticut), Faculty Scholarship Series Paper #3918, 1964 at http://digitalcommons.law.yale.edu/cgi/viewcontent.cgi?article=4917&context=fss_papers; Muskie, Edmund, "Right-to-Work Legislation," Remarks in Congressional Record – Senate (Washington, DC), page 10609, June 16, 1961 at http://www.muskiefoundation.org/esm.index/1961/right_to_work

26. "Farm Leader Hits Compulsory Unionism; Chamber Backs FB Position," in *Prosser Record Bulletin*, March 1961.

27. Kennedy, John F., "Statement of the President Upon Signing Bill Providing for an Emergency Feed Grain Program," The American Presidency Project (University of California, Santa Barbara), March 22, 1961 at http://www.presidency.uscb.edu/ws/?pid=8543

28. "Farm Bureau Leaders Rap Feed Grain Bill," in *Yakima Morning Herald*, November 17, 1961.

29. Reading, Amy, "How a Texas Paper Brought Down Billie Sol Estes," in *Bloomberg.com*, May 16, 2013 at http://www.bloomberg.com/news/2013-05-16/how-a-texas-paper-brought-down-billie-sol-estes

30. "State Farm Bureau President Hits Administration Farm Bills," in Lynden Tribune (Lynden, WA), June 1962.

31. "Turkey Growers Reject National Marketing Order," in *Virginia Farm Bureau News* (Richmond), Vol. 22, Number 7, July 1962, p. 1, citing Shuman, Charles B. (President, American Farm Bureau Federation) at http://virginiachronicle.com/cgi-bin/virginia?a=d&d=VFBN19620701.1.1

32. "State Farm Bureau President Hits...".

33. "Max Benitz Blasts New Farm Proposals," *Yakima Morning Herald* (Yakima, WA), November 17, 1962, citing Max Benitz

34. "Freeman's Farm Plan is Attacked," in *Spokane Spokesman-Review*, February 13, 1962, citing Max Benitz.

35. Benitz, Tape 2, p. 12.

36. "Rural Renewal Plan Advocated," in *Spokane Spokesman-Review*, February 13, 1962.

37. "Freeman's Farm Plan is Attacked," citing Max Benitz.

38. "Max Benitz Blasts..."

39. "Economist From Farm Bureau Hits Kennedy Farm Bill," in *Tri-City Herald*, April 27, 1962, p. 14.

40. "Max Benitz Blasts...", citing T.C. Peterson and Max Benitz.

41. "Food And Agriculture Act of 1962: An Act to Protect Farm Income, to Reduce Costs of Farm Programs to the Federal Government...and to Conserve Natural Resources," Public Law

87-703, 87th Congress, H.R. 12391, (Washington, DC) September 27, 1962

42. Kennedy, John, "Radio and Television Report to the American People on the Soviet Arms Buildup in Cuba, October 22, 1962," John F. Kennedy Library (Boston), at http://www.jfklibrary. org/Asset-Viewer/sUVmCh-sB0moLfrBcaHaSg.aspx

43. Chang, Lawrence, and Kornbluh, Peter, *The Cuban Missile Crisis, 1962: A National Security Archive Document Reader,* W.W. Norton and Co. (New York), 1992.

44. Benitz, Tape 2, p. 13.

45. Personal Communication, E.M.B. Wagner to M.S. Gerber, July 29, 2013.

46. Eisenman, Don, "Benitz Critical of Socialized Farming," in *Ellensburg Daily Record,* March 1, 1963.

47. Ibid.

48. Ibid.

49. Daft, Lynn M., "The 1963 Wheat Referendum: An Interpretation," in *Journal of Farm Economics* (Agricultural and Applied Economics Association [AAEA]: Milwaukee, WI), 1964 at http://www.jstor.org/discover/10.2307/1236442?uid=3739960&uid=2129&uid=2&uid=70&uid=4&uid=3739256&sid=21102492287677

50. Benitz, Tape 2, p. 12; Jones, Senator Max Benitz..."

51. Benitz, Tape 2, p. 12.

52. Benitz, Max, "The President Reports," in *Washington State Farm Bureau News,* September 1963.

53. Ibid.

54. Kennedy, John, "American University Speech (Washington, DC), June 10, 1963, transcribed by Public Broadcasting System (New York) at http://www.pbs.org/wgbh/americanexperience/features/primary-resources/jfk-university/

55. Benitz, "The President Reports," September 1963.

56. "Foreign News: We Will Bury You," in *Time Magazine* (New York), November 26, 1956, citing Nikita Khrushchev at http://www.time.com/time/magazine/article/0,9171,867329,00.html

57. Taubman, William, *Krushchev: The Man and His Era*, W.W. Norton and Co. (New York), 2003, citing Nikita Khrushchev.

58. Benitz, "The President Reports," September 1963.

59. Ibid.

60. "Soviet Agriculture: Record of Stagnation: Trouble on U.S.S.R.'s Socialized Farms," in *CQ Press Researcher* (Congressional Quarterly: Washington, DC), 2013 at http://library.cqpress.com/cqresearcher/document.php?id=cqresrre1964012900#.UhE9BDrn-Um

61. Benitz, Max, Private Diary, in Family Records, Prosser, WA, September 1963.

62. Ibid.

63. Ibid.

64. "Max Benitz and His Apple Crop Featured on TV Show," in *Washington State Farm Bureau News*, November 1963.

65. "Max Benitz Misquoted on Wheat," in *Prosser Record-Bulletin*, October 1963.

66. Benitz, Private Diary, September 1963.

67. Ibid.

68. "Berlin Wall," at History.com (A&E Television, New York)   at http://www.history.com/topics/berlin-wall

69. "Killing of Peter Fechter," at Berlin Wall Memorial Foundation (Stiftung Berliner Mauer) (Berlin, Germany) at http://www.berliner-mauer-gedenkstaette.de/en/1962-300,353,2.html

70. Personal Communication, E.M.B. Wagner to M.S. Gerber, July 13, 2013.

71. McBride, Alex, "Reynolds v. Sims, 1964," in Supreme Court History: Expanding Civil Rights: Landmark Cases (Public Broadcasting System: New York, WNET), at http://www.pbs.org/wnet/supremecourt/rights/landmark_reynolds.html

72. "Farmers' Voice Diminishing," in *Ritzville Adams County Journal-Tribune* (Ritzville, WA), November 11, 1964, citing Max Benitz.

73. Ibid.

74. Ibid.

75. Benitz, Max, "A Look at 1980s," Speech delivered at various venues in 8th and 16th Legislative Districts, February - May1979, in Personal Papers, Prosser, WA.

76. Ibid.

77. Benitz, Tape 2, p. 13.

78. Toth, Steven, Jr., "Federal Pesticide Laws and Regulations," U.S. Department of Agriculture Extension Service National Agricultural Pesticide Impact Assessment Program (Washington, DC), Special Project 93-EPIX-1-145, March 1996 at http://ipm.ncsu.edu/safety/factsheets/laws.pdf

79. "Chemicals Far More Helpful Than Dangerous, Group Told," in *Yakima Herald*, November 7, 1964.

80. Personal Communication, E.M.B Wagner to M.S. Gerber, July 13, 2013.

81. "Behind Scenes Labor Activity," in *The Packer* (Los Angeles, California), January 28, 1961; Personal Communication, E.M.B. Wagner to M.S. Gerber, September 2013.

82. "Food and Agriculture Act of 1965," Public Law 89-321, 89th Congress, (Washington, DC) November 3, 1965.

83. "Food and Agriculture Act of 1965" as amended, Public Law 90-559, 90th Congress, (Washington, DC), 1968 at http://law.justia.com/codes/us/1999/title7/chap35/subchapii/partd/sec1379e/

84. Jesse, Ed and Cropp, Bob, "Basic Milk Pricing Concepts for Dairy Farmers," Cooperative Extension Service of Wisconsin (Madison), Publication A3379, 2008 at http://www.midmd-dairyvets.com/docs/MilkPricingWisc.pdf

85. Benitz, Max, "The President Reports," in *Washington State Farm Bureau News*, December 1965.

86. Ibid.

87. Read, Leonard, "Featherbedding: A Way of Life," at Foundation for Economic Education (Irvington, NY), 1960 at http://www.fee.org/the_freeman/detail/featherbedding-a-way-of-life#axzz2cNNDPGmb

88. U.S. Directorate of Intelligence, "India's Food Situation a Continuing Crisis," (Declassified) (Washington, DC), December 23, 1966, in Chaudhry, Praveen, and Vanduzer-Snow, Marta, "The United States and India: A History Through Archives," p. 313, Sage Publications, Inc. (Thousand Oaks, CA and New Delhi, India), 2011 at http://books.google.com/books?id=6cf-n_8rJH-0C&pg=PA313&lpg=PA313&dq=india+food+rationing+1965&source=bl&ots=xZlB-VYVXZS&sig=99MSzPa09TEgkxf2RG5RbBn3Nz8&hl=en&sa=X&ei=7mfQUfKJF-fkiAKvxo-CACg&ved=0CD4Q6AEwAw#v=onepage&q=india%20food%20rationing%201965&f=false

89. Benitz, "The President Reports," December 1965.

90. "Benitz Candidate for Legislature," in *Prosser Record Bulletin*, May 1968, citing Max Benitz.

91. Benitz, "The President Reports," December 1965.

92. Benitz, Max, "Personal Profile," Transcript of Tape 3, Family Records, Prosser, WA, 1986.

93. "Agricultural Fair Practices Act of 1967," Public Law 90-288, 90th Congress, 1st Session, (Washington, DC), April 16, 1968 at http://www.louisianadigitallibrary.org/cdm/compoundobject/collection/p120701coll25/id/102228/rec/10

94. Benitz, Max, "A Real Peak Behind the Bamboo Curtain," Personal Diary, Family Papers. 1968.

95. Ibid.

96. Ibid.

97. Ibid.

98. Jones, James "Why LBJ Bowed Out," in *Los Angeles Times*, March 30, 2008 at http://articles.latimes.com/2008/mar/30/opinion/op-jones30

99. Benitz, "A Real Peak...".

100. Ibid.

101. Dikotter, Frank, <u>Mao's Great Famine: the History of China's Most Devastating Catastrophe (1958-62),</u> Walker Publishing Co. (New York), 2010; Jisheng, Yang, <u>Tombstone: The Great Chinese Famine, 1958-62</u>, Farrar, Straus and Giroux (New York), 2012.

102. Kraus, Richard Curt, <u>The Cultural Revolution: A Very Short Introduction</u>, Oxford University Press (New York), 2012; Benitz, "A Real Peak...".

103. "Challenge of China Outlined by Benitz," in *Tri-City Herald*, June 18, 1968, partially citing Max Benitz.

104. "Benitz Resigns Farm Bureau Post," in *Tri-City Herald*, May 22, 1968.

105. Jones, "Senator Max Benitz....," p. 24, citing Max Benitz.

106. "Benitz Candidate for State Legislature."

107. Wynne, Robert, "Drought a Lingering Benitz Foe," in *Tri-City Herald*, March 18, 1977, partially citing Max. Benitz.

108. "He Cares…Elect Max Benitz State Representative, District 8-B, G.O.P.," Campaign Flier, Prosser, WA, 1968.

109. Benitz, Max, Candidate Statement, in *Tri-City Herald*, September 8, 1968.

110. Briggs, Jack, "Hermiston Flier Tries to Cut Debt," in *Tri-City Herald*, September 22, 1968, partially citing Emery Tresham.

111. Benitz, Tape 2, p. 13; Office of the Secretary of State, "Elections and Voting: General Election, November 1968," Washington Secretary of State (Olympia), at http://www.sos.wa.gov/elections/results_report.aspx?e=27&c=&c2=&t=&t2=&p=&p2=&y=; Prosser Carries Benitz' Victory," in *Tri-City Herald*, November 6, 1968; "Election Campaign Publicity and Advertising Budget Form; Max E. Benitz," National Research Agency, Inc. (Washington, DC), May 10, 1968 (in Personal Family Records, Prosser, WA).

Chapter 2

112. Bureau of Transportation Statistics, "Historical Air Traffic Statistics, Annual 1954-1980," U.S. Department of Transportation, 2012 at http://www.rita.dot.gov/bts/sites/rita.dot.gov.bts/files/subject_areas/airline_information/air_carrier_traffic_statistics/airtraffic/annual/1954_1980. html; Boswell, Sharon, and McConaghy, Lorraine, "Lights Out, Seattle," in *Seattle Times*, citing Miner Baker, November 3, 1996 at http://seattletimes.com/special/centennial/november/lights_out.html; Port of Tacoma, "1961-1970: The Era of Containerization," Port of Tacoma, 2007 at http://www.portoftacoma.com/Page.aspx?cid=27

113. Boswell and McConaghy, "Lights Out, Seattle;" Lacitis, Erik, "Iconic "Will the Last Person" Seattle Billboard Bubbles up Again," in *Seattle Times*, February 2, 2009 at http://seattletimes.com/html/localnews/2008696819_lightsout02m.html

114. "State is on the Verge of Heavy Deficit Spending, Rep. Benitz says," in *Tri-City Herald* (Kennewick, WA), February 25, 1970.

115. Benitz, Max, "Balancing the State's Budget, 1979-1981," Report to the 8th District, Prosser, WA, June 8, 1982.

116. Brazier, Peter, "History of the Washington Legislature, 1965-1992," Washington State Senate (Olympia), 2007, pp. 10-14.

117. Benitz, Max, 43rd Legislative Wrap-Up Report, 43rd Session, Office of Senator Max Benitz, Olympia, WA, 1970.

118. Personal Papers, Family Records, Prosser, WA.

119. Burns, Adam, "The Burlington Northern, The West's First Mega-Railroad," American-Rails. com at http://www.american-rails.com/burlington-northern.html

120. Benitz Elected, in *Tri-City Herald*, January 19, 1970; "Rep. Benitz Appointed to Levy Unit," in *Tri-City Herald*, May 6, 1970.

121. Benitz, Max, "Personal Profile," Transcript of Tape 2, Prosser, WA, 1986, p. 12.

122. Miller Center, "American President: Lyndon Baines Johnson," University of Virginia (Charlottesville), 2013 at http://millercenter.org/president/lbjohnson/essays/biography/print

123. National Aeronautics and Space Administration (NASA), "Text of President John F. Kennedy's Moon Speech – Rice Stadium" September 12, 1962 at http://er.jsc.nasa.gov/seh/ricetalk.htm

124. NASA, "Orders of Magnitude: A History of the NACA and NASA, 1915-1990," NASA SP-4406, NASA (Washington, DC), 1989 at http://www.hq.nasa.gov/office/pao/History/SP-4406/cover.html

125. Ibid.

126. "Benitz Seeks Re-election," in *Tri-City Herald,* July 15, 1970; Benitz, Max, Candidate Statement, in *Tri-City Herald,* October 10, 1970.

127. "Northwest Harvest: History," at NorthwestHarvest.org (Seattle), at http://www.northwest-harvest.org/About_Us/About_Us/History.htm

128. Bushey, Pat, "Benitz, Shipman Collide on Issues," in *Tri-City Herald,* October 27, 1970, partially citing Max Benitz.

129. Office of the Secretary of State, "Elections and Voting; General Election, November 1970," Washington Secretary of State (Olympia), at http://www.sos.wa.gov/elections/results_report. aspx?e=27&c=&c2=&t=&t2=&p=&p2=&y=; "Reps. Jolly, Benitz Reelected," in *Tri-City Herald,* November 4, 1970.

130. Personal Communication, E.M.B. Wagner to M.S. Gerber, 7/16/2013.

131. "Benitz Given Committee Post," in *Tri-City Herald,* November 26, 1970; "Benitz Elected Council Head," in *Tri-City Herald,* June 20, 1971; "Benitz Appointed," in *Tri-City Herald,* March 15, 1972; "Benitz Re-Elected as Chairman," in *Tri-City Herald*, June 18, 1972..

132. Brazier, "History of the Washington Legislature," pp. 14-18.

133. Personal Communication, E.M.B. Wagner to M.S. Gerber, July 27, 2013.

134. Brazier, "History of the Washington State Legislature," pp. 18-20.

135. Office of the Secretary of State, "Elections and Voting: General Election, November 1972," Washington Secretary of State (Olympia), at http://www.sos.wa.gov/elections/results_report.aspx?e=27&c=&c2=&t=&t2=&p=&p2=&y=

136. Brazier, History of the Washington State Legislature," p. 24.

137. Benitz, Max, "Wrap-Up Report, 1973 Legislative Session," in Personal Papers, Family Records, Prosser, WA.

138. Brazier, History of the Washington State Legislature," pp. 20-26; Scott, George, <u>A Majority of One: Legislative Life</u>, Civitas Press (Seattle), 2002, pp. 36-63.

139. Wynne, Robert, "Drought a Lingering Benitz Foe," in *Tri-City Herald*, March 18, 1977.

140. Rose, Bob, "Washington's Open Space Taxation Act (Chapter 84.34 RCW): A Review from the Perspective of Farmland Protection," Washington Conservation Commission (Lacey, WA), July 25, 2008 at http://www.spokanecounty.org/data/assessor/OFP%20-%20Open%20 Space%20Taxation%20Act.pdf

141. Benitz, "Wrap-Up Report, 1973…".

142. Boswell and McConaghy, "Lights Out, Seattle."

143. Pope, Daniel, <u>Nuclear Implosions: The Rise and Fall of the Washington Public Power Supply System,</u> Cambridge University Press (New York), 2008.

144. Evans, Daniel, Letter to Max Benitz, Olympia, WA, June 14, 1974.

145. Lippert, Werner, *The Economic Diplomacy of Ostpolitik: Origins of NATA's Energy Dilema*, Berghanh Books (New York), 2011, pp. 143-147.

146. Moh, Caroline, Klaus, David, and Hughes, Kent, "The Jackson-Vanik Amendment and U.S.-Russian Relations," Woodrow Wilson International Center for Scholars (Washington, DC), 2010.

147. Personal Communication, E.M.B. Wagner to M.S. Gerber, September 7, 2013.

148. Howard, Midge, "Less Partisanship, Leadership Chance Prompts Benitz," in *Tri-City Herald*, February 3, 1974; Vander Houwen, Boyd, "Legislation to Limit Corporate Farming in Washington is not Dead," in *Tri-City Herald*, May 10, 1974..

149. Benitz, Max, Campaign Brochure, Prosser, WA, 1974.

150. "Food Production Expansion in Area Urged by Benitz," in *Tri-City Herald*, October 10, 1974, partially citing Max Benitz.

151. Office of the Secretary of State, "Elections and Voting: General Election, November 1974," Washington Secretary of State (Olympia), at http://www.sos.wa.gov/elections/results_report.aspx?e=27&c=&c2=&t=&t2=&p=&p2=&y=

152. "Benitz Beats Johnson for Canfield Senate Seat," in *Tri-City Herald*, November 6, 1974.

153. Benitz, Max, "A Look at 1980s," Speech delivered at various location in 8th and 16th Districts, February through May, 1979, in Personal Papers, Prosser, WA .

154. Hoemann, Thomas, and Baker, Barbara, "Members of the State Legislature by Districts Since 1889," State of Washington (Olympia), May 2012.

155. Scott, pp. 62-63; Brazier, "History of the Washington State Legislature," pp. 28-30.

156. Brazier, "History of the Washington State Legislature," pp. 26-30; Scott, pp. 36-37.

157. *Herbicide Use – Special Programs – Fees*, 44th Regular Session, Washington State Senate, S.B. 2147.

158. *Agriculture*, 44th Session, 1st Extraordinary Session, Washington State Senate, S.B. 2150.

159. *Irrigation Districts – Local Improvement Districts – Bonds*, 44th Session, 1st Extraordinary Session, Washington State Senate, S.B. 2619; *Hunting Licenses – Revocation*, 44th Session, 1st Extraordinary Session, Washington State Senate, S.B. 2201; *Gambling*, 44th Session, 2nd Extraordinary Session, Washington State Senate, Substitute House Bill (H.B.) 90; *University of Washington – Regionalized Medical Education – Tuition and Fees*; 44th Session, 1st Extraordinary Session, Washington State Senate, S.B. 2517; *Department of Veterans Affairs*, 44th Session, 2nd Extraordinary Session, Washington State Senate, Engrossed Substitute S.B. 2006.

160. National Park Service, *National Register of Historic Places, 1966-1994*, Preservation Press (Washington, DC), 1995, p. 871.

161. "Heart Surgery for Benitz," in *Tri-City Herald*, June 21, 1976; Personal Communication, E.M.B. Wagner to M.S. Gerber, July 27, 2013.

162. Benitz, Max, Personal Notes, "1978 Trip to Red China," in Family Records, Prosser, WA.

163. Benitz, Max, "First Hand Report to the 8th District," Prosser, WA, June 1978.

164. "Washington Governor Dixie Lee Ray," National Governor's Association (Washington, DC), 2011 at http://www.nga.org/cms/home/governors/past-governors-bios/page_washington/col2-content/main-content-list/title_ray_dixy.html

165. "State Opens Trade Office in Singapore," In *Ellensburg Daily Record*, September 24, 1977, p. 6.

166. Benitz, "First Hand Report...," June 1978.

167. Philip, Jim, "Gas Tax Approval Forecast by Hansen," in *Tri-City Herald*, June 16, 1977; "Benitz Plugs Local Gas Tax Use Option," in *Yakima Herald-Republic*, July 26, 1977; Office of the Secretary of State, "Elections and Voting: General Election, November 1977," Washington Secretary of State (Olympia), at http://www.sos.wa.gov/elections/results_report.aspx-?e=27&c=&c2=&t=&t2=&p=&p2=&y

168. *Energy Facility Sites*, 45th Session, 1st Extraordinary Session, Washington State Senate, Engrossed Substitute S.B. 2910.

169. *Cloud Seeding – Emergency*, 45th Session, Washington State Senate, Engrossed S.B. 2561.

170. *Washington State University Tree Fruit Research Center – Financing*, 45th Session, Washington State Senate, S.B. 2225; *Veterans – Estates and Burial Rights – State Homes – Arms to Sons of Veterans*, 45th Session, Washington State Senate, Engrossed S.B. 2190.

171. *Agriculture – Horticulture District Funds – Seed Labeling and Certification – Marketing Powers – Weights and Measures – Noxious Weed Control Boards*; 45th Session, 1st Extraordinary Session, Washington State Senate, S.B. 2208; *Emergency Water Withdrawal – Authority – Fiscal Support – Penalties*, 45th Session, 1st Extraordinary Session, Washington State Senate, Re-engrossed Second Substitute S.B. 2620; *Minimum Wages – Seasonal Employees at Agricultural Fairs*, 45th Session, 1st Extraordinary Session, Washington State Senate, S.B. 2251; *Irrigation Districts – Local Improvement Districts – Bonds*, 45th Session, 1st Extraordinary Session, Washington State Senate, Engrossed Substitute S.B. 2619.

172. Department of Social and Health Services (DSHS), "Summary of the State's Juvenile Justice Code," DSHS (Olympia), 2010 at http://www.dshs.wa.gov/pdf/ojj/AnnualReport2009/SummaryofJJC.pdf

173. Benitz, "First Hand Report...," June 1978.

174. Billings, Judith, "Organization and Financing of Washington Public Schools," Office of the Superintendent of Public Instruction (Olympia), p. 7, November 1996 at http://www.k12.wa.us/safs/PUB/ORG/96/org_fin96.pdf

175. Max. "First Hand Report..."

176. Wynne, "Drought a Lingering Benitz Foe," partially citing Max Benitz.

177. Benitz, Max, "Initiative 59- The Family Farm Water Act," Speech in Personal Papers, Prosser, WA, 1978.

178. Wynne, Robert, "U&I to Sell Farm," in *Tri-City Herald* (Kennewick, WA), March 8, 1977.

179. Office of the Secretary of State, "Elections and Voting: General Election, November 1977."

180.DepartmentofEcology,"JohnDay&McNaryPools,ColumbiaRiver,"Olympia,October1978athttps:// fortress.wa.gov/ecy/publications/publications/7811001.pdf; Revised Code of Washington 90.03.345, "Establishment of Reservations of Water for Certain Purposes and Minimum Flows or Levels as Constituting Appropriations with Priority Dates," at http://apps.leg.wa.gov/rcw/default. aspx?cite=90.03&full=true#90.03.345. See also Washington Administrative Code (WAC), 173-531A-40.

181. Wynne, "Drought a Lingering Benitz Foe."

182. Ibid.; "Benitz to Introduce Bills Aimed at Providing Adequate Water Supplies," News Release, Washington State Senate Republican Caucus (Olympia), December 11, 1978.

183. Schrick, Ray, "Water on State's Agenda," in *Wenatchee World,* January 8, 1979.

184. U.S. Bureau Of Reclamation, "Yakima River Basin Water Enhancement Project Authorization Documents, U.S. Department Of The Interior, Pacific Northwest Regional Office (Boise, Id), 2012 At Http://Www.Usbr.Gov/Pn/Programs/Yrbwep/Authorization/Index.Html

185. Browne, William and Dinse, John, "The Emergence of the American Agriculture Movement, 1977-1979," in *Great Plains Quarterly* (University of Nebraska: Lincoln), Fall 1985, pp. 220-235 at http://digitalcommons.unl.edu/cgi/viewcontent.cgi?article=2831&context=greatplainsquarterly

186. "American Agriculture Movement Records," MS 463, Iowa State University Library (Ames), 2011.

187. Benitz, Max, "First Hand Report" Newsletter to Constituents, Olympia WA, June 1978.

188. Personal Communication, G. Wirth to M.S. Gerber, Richland, WA, August 26, 2013.

189. Association of Washington Generals, 2010, at http://www.wagenerals.org

190. Benitz, "1978 Trip to Red China."

191. Benitz, Max, "A Look at 1980s."

192. Wirth, Gene, "Stories About Max Benitz," Personal Communication to E.M.B. Wagner, August 12, 2013.

193. Casey, Jim, "I Talked to a VP and it Wasn't Teng," in *Everett Herald* (Everett, WA), February 5, 1979, p. 2A.

194. Carter, Jimmy, "Taiwan Relations Act Statement on Signing H.R. 2479 Into Law," Referencing Public Law 96-8, 96th Congress (Washington, DC), April 10, 1979 at http://www.presidency. ucsb.edu/ws/?pid=32177

195. Benitz, Max, "A Look at 1980s."

196. Benitz, Max, Campaign Literature, Prosser, WA, 1978.

197. Moody, Dick, "Benitz Claims He's on Labor, Teacher 'Hit List,'" in *Tri-City Herald*, November 1, 1978.

198. Office of the Secretary of State, "Elections and Voting: General Election, November 1978," Washington Secretary of State (Olympia), at http://www.sos.wa.gov/elections/results_report.aspx?e=27&c=&c2=&t=&t2=&p=&p2=&y=

199. Benitz, Max, "A Look at 1980s."

200. Hastings Leads GOP Legislative Victory," in *Tri-City Herald,* November 8, 1978,.

201. Benitz, "First Hand Report," June 1978; "Sen. Benitz Opposes Continuing Same Timber Tax," News Release, Washington State Senate Republican Caucus, February 21, 1979.

202. *Taxation of Timber and Forest Land*, 46th Session, Washington State Senate, Engrossed S.B. 2111.

203. "Increased Tolls to Pave the Way for Access Road to North Richland Bridge," News Release, Washington State Senate Republican Caucus, April 10, 1979; "Ray OKs Bonds for North Richland Bridge," News Release, Washington State Senate Republican Caucus, June 14, 1979; *Columbia River Toll Bridge, Horn Rapids – Construction, Bonds Authorization – Appropriation,* 46th Session, 1st Extraordinary Session, Washington State Senate, Engrossed Substitute S.B. 3034.

204. *Agriculture Omnibus Regulations – Appropriation,* 46th Session, Washington State Senate, Engrossed Substitute S.B. 2254; *Pesticide Control – Registration – Board,* 46th Session, Washington State Senate, S.B. 2255; *Commercial Feed Distributors – Inspection Fees,* 46th Session, Washington State Senate, S.B. 2206; *Pesticide Applicators – Licensure,* 46th Session, Washington State Senate, Substitute S.B. 2265; *Agricultural Water Supply Facilities – Appropriation,* 46th Session, 1st Extraordinary Session, Washington State Senate, Substitute S.B. 2504; *Irrigation Districts – Hydroelectric Generation Development – Powers and Duties,* 46th Session, 1st Extraordinary Session, Washington State Senate, Engrossed Second Substitute S.B. 3033; *Agricultural Activities – Protection from Nuisance Lawsuits,* 46th Session, Washington State Senate, Engrossed S.B. 2180; *Food Donation Program – Legal Immunity,* 46th Session, Washington State Senate, Engrossed S.B. 2147.

205. *Institutions of Higher Education – Definition – State Student Financial Aid Program,* 46th Session, 1st Extraordinary Session, Washington State Senate, Substitute S.B. 2744; *College Scholarships – Performing Arts Students,* 46th Session, 1st Extraordinary Session, Washington State Senate, Substitute S.B. 2140; *Public Utility Services – Rate Reduction – Low Income Senior Citizens,* 46th Session, Washington State Senate, S.B. 2077; *Nursing Homes – Resident Care, Operating Standards,* 46th Session, 1st Extraordinary Session, Washington State Senate, Engrossed Substitute S.B. 2336; *Mental Illness – Commitment, Treatment Procedure,* 46th Session, 1st Extraordinary Session, Washington State Senate, Engrossed Substitute S.B. 2415; *Geothermal Resources – Ownership – Surface Landowner,* 46th Session, 1st Extraordinary Session, Washington State Senate, S.B. 2191; *Inheritance Taxes,* 46th Session, 1st Extraordinary Session, Washington State Senate, S.B. 2181.

206. "Benitz Named Vice-Chairman, in *Tri-City Herald*, Aril 30, 1979; "Benitz Elected to Regional Agricultural Post," News Release, Office of Senator Max E. Benitz, Olympia, April 25, 1979.

207. "GOP Senators Confer Over Budget Negotiations," News Release, Washington State Senate Republican Caucus, April 30, 1979; in *University Herald* (Seattle).

208. Office of the Secretary of State, "Washington State Legislative Sessions," Olympia, at http://www.sos.wa.gov/library/legsession.aspx

209. Benitz, Max, "A Look at 1980."

210. "Senator Max E. Benitz, Chairman Republican State Committee of Washington," in *Tri-City Herald*, June 1, 1980.

211. Ibid.

212. Scott, pp. 127-28.

213. Scates, Shelby, *Warren G. Magnuson and the Shaping of Twentieth-Century America*, University of Washington Press, Seattle, 1997.

214. Collard, Fabrice, and Dellas, Harris, "The Great Inflation of the 1970s," International Finance Discussion Paper #799, Board of Governors of Federal Reserve System (Washington, DC), April 2004 at http://www.federalreserve.gov/pubs/ifdp/2004/799/ifdp799.pdf

215. *Motor Vehicle Insurance – Minimum Mandatory Amounts – Uninsured Motorist Coverage*, 46th Session (1980), Washington State Senate, Substitute H.B. 1983; *Delinquency Prevention Services Program – Maintenance*, 46th Session (1980), Washington State Senate, S.B. 3574.

216. Bagley, Mark, "Mount St. Helens Eruption: Facts and Information," in *LiveScience* (TechMedia Network: Ogden, Utah), February 28, 2013 at http://www.livescience.com/27553-mount-st-helens-eruption.html

217. "God, I Want To Live," in Time Magazine (New York), June 2, 1980 at http://www.time.com/time/magazine/article/0,9171,924152,00.html

218. Personal Communication, E.M.B. Wagner to M.S. Gerber, July 27, 2013.

219. *North Richland Toll Bridge – Appropriation*, 47th Session, Washington State Senate, Engrossed Substitute S.B. 3871; *Emergency Cloud Seeding*, 47th Session, Washington State Senate, Substitute S.B. 4087.

220. Brazier, "History of the Washington Legislature," pp. 43-46; *Motor Vehicles – Fuel Tax Rate, Alcohol Tax Credit – License Fee – Ferry Tolls – State Patrol Funding*, 47th Session, Washington State Senate, Engrossed Substitute S.B. 4283.

221. Scott, pp. 102-103, 155, and 158-159.

222. Benitz, Max, "In Touch," Newsletter to Constituents, Prosser, WA, October 2, 1981.

223. Brazier, "History of the Washington Legislature," pp. 46-47; Scott, pp. 158-170.

224. Brazier, "History of the Washington Legislature," pp. 46-50; Scott, pp. 159-161.

225. Chesley, Frank, "Washington State Taxation," HistoryLink.org (Seattle), September 4, 2004 at http://www.historylink.org/index.cfm?DisplayPage=output.cfm&file_id=5735
226. Benitz, "Balancing the State's Budget, 1979-1981."

227. *Child Abuse – Admissibility of Child's Statement – Incest – Abuse Reports – Temporary Protective Custody*, 47th Session (1982), Washington State Senate, Substitute S.B. 4461.

228. *Plant Pests and Disease – Emergency Prevention Measures – Liability – Appropriation*, 47th Session (1982), Washington State Senate, Substitute S.B. 4684.

229. Benitz, "Balancing the State's Budget, 1979-1981."

230. Strieby, Matt, "Interstate 82, Washington," *AARoads.com*, September 29, 2011 at http://www.aaroads.com/guide.php?page=i0082wa

Chapter 3

231. Spirit Lake Memorial Highway, 47th Session (1982), Washington State Senate, S.B. 4706.

232. Benitz, Max, "1981 Trip Diary," Personal Papers, Prosser, WA.

233. Crowell, Todd, "Expo '83 Energy Fair Generating Interest," in *Spokesman-Review* (Spokane,

WA), February 29, 1980, p. 6.

234. Dodds, Gordon, *The American Northwest: A History of Oregon and Washington*, Forum Press (Arlington Heights, IL), 1986, p. 345.

235. "An Axe Murder Nearly Triggers War," in *Frontline World*, University of California (Berkeley), January 2003 at http://www.pbs.org/frontlineworld/stories/northkorea/1976.html

236. Kirk, Jeremy, "Eerie Calm Governs Village in Korea DMZ," in *Stars and Stripes*, (Washington, DC), January 17, 2003 at http://www.stripes.com/news/eerie-calm-governs-farming-village-in-korea-dmz-1.1055

237. Benitz, Max, "1981 Trip Diary," Personal Papers, Prosser, WA.

238. "Washington to Strengthen Relations with ROC," in *Central News Agency* (Taipei), June 24, 1981, partially citing John Spellman.

239. Benitz, Max, "Re-Elect Senator Max Benitz," Campaign Flier, prosser, WA, 1982.

240. Ganders, Larry, "Benitz, Seeking 2nd Term in Senate, Opposes Income Tax," in *Tri-City Herald* (Kennewick, WA), July 15, 1982.

241. Office of the Secretary of State, "Elections and Voting; General Election, November 1982," Washington Secretary of State (Olympia), at http://www.sos.wa.gov/elections/results_report.aspx?e=27&c=&c2=&t=&t2=&p=&p2=&y=

242. Benitz, Max, "Potential Funding Sources for the Prosser Grant Avenue Bridge Project, Memo to Oliver, Claude, Skeate, Dennis, Willard, Jim and Benitz, Max Jr., Washington State Senate (Olympia), January 27, 1983

243. Benitz, Max, "Benitz's Efforts Create Jobs," Campaign Flier, Prosser, WA, 1982.

244. *Hydroelectric Resource Development – Political Subdivisions*, 48th Session, Washington State Senate, Substitute S.B. 3511; *Tree Fruit Assessments – Horticultural Advisory Committee – Injunctions Against Nursery Dealers*, 48th Session, 1st Extraordinary Session, Washington State Senate, Engrossed Substitute S.B. 3864; *Property Tax Limitation – Levies – Determination*, 48th Session, Washington State Senate, Substitute S.B. 3522; *Higher Education – Tuition and Fee Refunds – Medical Withdrawals*, 48th Session, Washington State Senate, S.B. 3531; *Community College Board of Trustees – Removal for Misconduct or Malfeasance*, 48th Session, Washington State Senate, Engrossed S.B. 3532; *Joint Operating Agencies – Compensation – Open Public Meetings Act Compliance*, 48th Session, 1st Extraordinary Session, Washington State Senate, Engrossed Substitute S.B. 3266; *Legal Proceedings – Non-English-Speaking Persons – Interpreters Provided*, 48th Session, Washington State Senate, Engrossed S.B. 3501; *High Technology Education and Training Act*, 48th Session, 1st Extraordinary Session, Washington State Senate, Second Substitute S.B. 3155.

245. Benitz, Max, Letter to Constituents, in Personal Papers, Prosser, WA, June 1983.

246. Benitz, Max, "Benitz Appointed to Senate Committees," Press Release, Office of Senator Max Benitz, Olympia, June 6, 1983.

247. "Exports Key to Survival of Washington Agriculture," in *Capitol Press* (Salem, OR), June 17, 1983, citing Max Benitz.

248. Ibid.

249. Tate, Cassandra, "Daniel J. Evans," at *HistoryLink.org* (Seattle), December 15, 2004 at http://

www.historylink.org/index.cfm?DisplayPage=output.cfm&file_id=7167

250. Benitz, Max, "Benitz to Continue on Key Senate Committees," Press Release, Washington State Senate, January 8, 1984

251. Ganders, Larry, "Sen. Benitz Doing Well, Staff Says," in *Tri-City Herald* (Kennewick, WA), February 7, 1984; "Prosser Senator on the Mend," News Release, Republican Caucus, Washington State Senate, Olympia, February 15, 1984; Personal Communication, E.M.B. Wagner to M.S. Gerber, July 27, 2013.

252. Ganders, Larry, "Sen. Benitz Promises to Be Careful," in *Tri-City Herald*, February 25, 1984.

253. *Milk and Milk Products – Standards – Testing*, 48th Session (1984), Washington State Senate, Substitute S.B. 4419; *Regional Planning Council – One Eastern Washington Representative and One Western Washington Representative*, 48th Session (1984), Washington State Senate, Substitute S.B. 3827.

254. Scott, George W., *A Majority of One: Legislative Life*, Civitas Press (Seattle), 2002, pp. 108-109.

255. Benitz, Max, "In Touch," Newsletter to Constituents, 8th Legislative District, Prosser, WA, March 14, 1985.

256. Benitz, Max, "In Touch," Newsletter to Constituents, 8th Legislative District, Prosser, WA, April 4, 1985.

257. Benitz, Max, Tax increase Unnecessary and Unwise Benitz Says," Press Release, Office of Senator Max Benitz (Olympia), April 9, 1985

258. *Public Employees – Voluntary Payroll Deductions for Political Committees*, 49th Session, Washington State Senate, Engrossed S.B. 3189.

259. "Benitz Blasts Union Payroll Deduction Bill," in *Prosser Record Bulletin*, March 7, 1985.

260. *Aquatic Farming*, 49th Session, Washington State Senate, Engrossed S.B. 3067; *Salmon Enhancement*, 49th Session, Washington State Senate, Substitute S.B. 3384; *Irrigation District Voting Rights*, 49th Session, Washington State Senate, Substitute S.B. 3594; *Streams, Lakes or Public Water Sources – Minimum Flow – Notice Requirements*, 49th Session, Washington State Senate, S.B. 3298.

261. *Higher Education Tuition and Fees – Installment Payments*, 49th Session, Washington State Senate, Reengrossed S.B. 3134; *Victims of Sexual Assault Act – Termination Repealed – State-Wide Plan to be Developed Biennially – Financial Assistance Authorized*, 49th Session, Washington State Senate, Substitute S.B. 3198; *Child Abuse – Restraining Orders or Injunctions*, 49th Session, Washington State Senate, Substitute S.B. 3240; *Washington State Honors Awards Program for High School Students*, 49th Session, Washington State Senate, Engrossed S.B. 3782; *Refueling Services for Disabled Drivers*, 49th Session, Washington State Senate, Engrossed Substitute S.B. 3027; *Spanish or Japanese Language Instruction in Selected School Districts*, 49th Session, Washington State Senate, Engrossed Substitute S.B. 3156.

262. *Polychlorinated Biphenyls – Department of Ecology to Regulate*, 49th Session, Washington State Senate, Substitute S.B. 3201.

263. Benitz, Max, "In Touch," Newsletter to Constituents, 8th Legislative District, Prosser, WA, April 25, 1985.

264. Benitz, Max, "In Touch," Newsletter to Constituents, 8th Legislative District, Prosser, WA, May 2, 1985.

265. Benitz, Max, "In Touch," Newsletter to Constituents, 8th Legislative District, Prosser, WA, May 9, 1985.

266. Ibid., Partially citing Booth Gardner.

267. Benitz, Max, "In Touch," Newsletter to Constituents, 8th Legislative District, Prosser, WA, May 30, 1985.

268. Benitz, Max, "What's the Matter with Washington?" Press Release, Office of Senator Max Benitz, Olympia, WA, April 25, 1985.

269. Benitz, Max, "In Touch," Newsletters to Constituents, 8th Legislative District, Prosser, WA, March 21, June 6, June 13, and June 28, 1985.

270. Benitz, Max, "In Touch," Newsletter to Constituents, 8th Legislative District, Prosser, WA, July 3, 1985.

271. Benitz, Max, "In Touch," Newsletter to Constituents, 8th Legislative District, Prosser, WA, June 19, 1985.

272. Benitz, Max, "In Touch," Newsletter to Constituents, 8th Legislative District, Prosser, WA, May 23, 1985.

273. Benitz, Max, "Remarks," Speech at American Legion Post 34, Pasco-Kennewick, WA, May 27, 1985.

274. Benitz, Max, "In Touch," Newsletter to Constituents, 8th Legislative District, Prosser, WA, March 14, 1986

275. Ibid.

276. *Beef Commission – Additional Assessment for National Beef Promotion and Research*, 49th Session, Washington State Senate, Substitute S.B. 4553; *Irrigation Districts – Defense of Officers, Agents, Employees,* 49th Session, Washington State Senate, S.B. 4770; *Crop Liens*, 49th Session, Washington State Senate, Substitute S.B. 4547; *Deadly Force*, 49th Session, Washington State Senate, Engrossed Substitute S.B. 4465; *Health Care Claims – Fraud*, 49th Session, Washington State Senate, Engrossed S.B. 4582.

277. *Park Passes – Veterans*, 49th Session, Washington State Senate, S.B. 4456; *Pornography – Promotion – Criminal Profiteering,* 49th Session, Washington State Senate, S.B. 4959; *Indecent Liberties – Child Victims of Sexual Abuse,* 49th Session, Washington State Senate, S.B. 4982; *Gambling Commission – Lottery Commission – Members of Employees – Conflict of Interest,* 49th Session, Washington State Senate, Substitute S.B. 3590.

278. Ganders, Larry, "Benitz to Seek Re-Election; Wants to Cahir Energy Panel," in *Tri-City Herald,* May 3, 1986.

279. Benitz, Max, "Senator Max Benitz – Experience and Leadership Working for Us," Campaign Fliers, Prosser, WA, 1986

280. Ganders, "Benitz to Seek…".

281. Office of the Secretary of State, "Elections and Voting; General Election, November 1986," Washington Secretary of State (Olympia), at http://www.sos.wa.gov/elections/results_report.aspx?e=27&c=&c2=&t=&t2=&p=&p2=&y=

282. Ibid.

283. Ganders, Larry "Full-Time Farmers Lose Spots on Ag Committee," in *Tri-City Herald*, December 13, 1986.

284. Benitz, Max, "In Touch," Newsletter to Constituents, 8th Legislative District, Prosser, WA, February 4, 1987.

285. Benitz, Max, "In Touch," Newsletter to Constituents, 8th Legislative District, Prosser, WA, March 18, 1987.

286. Benitz, Max, "In Touch," Newsletter to Constituents, 8th Legislative District, Prosser, WA, 1987.

287. Eskenazi, Stuart, and Ganders, Larry, "Benitz Won't Seek Vacant Commission Seat." in *Tri-City Herald,* February 6, 1987.

288. Hoover, Dave, "Hanford Faring Well in Session: Benitz," in *Tri-City Herald*, March 29, 1987, partially citing Max Benitz.

289. Benitz, Max, "In Touch," Newsletter to Constituents, 8th Legislative District, Prosser, WA, April 23, 1987.

290. Benitz, Max, "In Touch," Newsletter to Constituents, 8th Legislative District, Prosser, WA, February 1987.

291. *Homicide by Abuse*, 50th Session, Washington State Senate, Substitute S.B. 5089; Youth Employment – Washington Conservation Corps – Program Goals Prioritized – Contract Revisions, 50th Session, Washington State House, H.B. 707.

292. *Custodial Assault – Assault at State Correctional Facilities*, 50th Session, Washington State Senate, Substitute S.B. 5824; *Highway Advertising Control*, 50th Session, Washington State House, Substitute S.B.5123; *Fraternal Benefit Societies,* 50th Session, Washington State Senate, Engrossed H.B. 432.

293. Benitz, Max, "In Touch: Don't Raise the Electric Rates," Newsletter to Constituents, 8th Legislative District, Prosser, WA, February 1987.

294. Benitz, "In Touch," Letter to Constituents, 1987.

295. *Nursery Dealer Licenses and Fees – Rootstock Annual Assessment – Funds*, 50th Session, Washington State Senate, Engrossed Substitute S.B. 5170; *Custom Slaughtering Establishments or Custom Meat Facilities – License Revisions – Inspections,* 50th Session, Washington State Senate, S.B. 5381; *Hops – Tax Exemption*, 50th Session, Washington State Senate, Substitute S.B. 6033; *Seed Conditioning*, 50th Session, Washington State House, H.B. 67.

296. Lehr, Jay, "Alar: The Great Apple Scare," in *Heartlander* (The Heartland Institute: Chicago, Illinois), March 1, 2007 at http://news.heartland.org/newspaper-article/2007/03/01/alar-great-apple-scare

297. Polman, Dick, "Supermarkets Ban Alar-Treated Apples," in *Philadelphia Inquirer*, January 6, 1987 at http://articles.philly.com/1987-01-06/news/26190511_1_alar-apple-products-apple-in-dustry-officials;Bollier, David, *Citizen Action and Other Big Ideas: A History of Ralph Nader and the Modern Consumer Movement*, Center for Responsive Law (Washington, DC), 1991, Chapter 7.

298. Benitz, Max, "In Touch," Newsletter to Constituents, 8th Legislative District, Prosser, WA, April 23, 1987.

299. "Benitz Heads Committee," in Prosser Record-Bulletin, November 11, 1987, p. 7.

300. Benitz, Max, "In Touch," Newsletter to Constituents, 8th Legislative District, Prosser, WA, February 22, 1988.

301. Ibid.; "1988- A Landmark Year for State AIDS Legislation," in *American Journal of Public Health*, American Public Health Association (Washington, DC), August 1989, Vol. 79, #8, p. 1005; "HIV and Sexual Health Education," Office of Superintendent of Public Instruction (Olympia, WA) at http://www.k12.wa.us/hivsexualhealth/PreventionEdRequirements.aspx

302. *Washington Scholars Program – Recipients May Attend Private Colleges or Universities*, 50th Session (1988), Washington State Senate, Substitute S.B. 5558; *Physical Therapy*, 50th Session (1988), Washington State Senate, Engrossed Substitute S.B. 6218; *Concealed Pistol Licenses – Application Requirements*, 50th Session (1988), Washington State Senate, Engrossed Substitute S.B. 6148.

303. *Hydraulic Projects – Streambank Stabilization to Protect Farm and Agricultural Land*, 50th Session (1988), Washington State Senate, Substitute S.B. 6024; *Bridge Replacement in Rural Areas*, 50th Session (1988), Washington State Senate, S.B. 6516; *Prosser Well*, 50th Session (1988), Washington State Senate, Substitute S.B. 6217.

304. Sancton, Thomas, "Planet of the Year: What on Earth Are we Doing?" in *Time* Magazine, January 2, 1989.

305. Lehr, "Alar: The Great Apple Scare."

306. McGregor, Mike, "Letter to the Editor," in *Seattle Times*, December 28, 1988.

307. Dodds, The American Northwest, p. 340.

308. Benitz, Max, "Food Safety," Speech to Western Washington Horticultural Association, 79th Annual Meeting, January 5, 1989.

309. *Branch Campuses*, 51st Session, Washington State Senate, S.B. 6095.

310. Benitz, Max, "Letter to 8th Legislative District," Senate Office (Olympia), March 28, 1989.

311. *Livestock Liens*, 51st Session, Washington State Senate, Substitute S.B. 5838; *Livestock Theft – Mandatory Fine*, 51st Session, Washington State Senate, Substitute S.B. 5488; *Equine Activities – Limitations on Civil Liability for Injuries Resulting From*, 51st Session, Washington State Senate, Substitute S.B. 5305; *Water Conservation and Waste Reduction Programs*, 51st Session, Washington State Senate, Substitute S.B. 5889; *Drought Relief – Department of Ecology – Emergency Powers*, 51st Session, Washington State Senate, Substitute S.B. 5196.

312. *Salmon Smolt – Production – Private Contracting Of*, 51st Session, Washington State Senate, Substitute S.B. 5288; *Regional Fisheries Enhancement Groups*, 51st Session, Washington State Sen-

ate, Substitute S.B. 5289, *Upland Fin Fish Rearing Facilities – Waste Disposal and Pollution Discharge Permits,* 51ˢᵗ Session, Washington State Senate, Substitute S.B. 5561; *Forest Management – Research and Policy Development,* 51ˢᵗ Session, Washington State Senate, Substitute S.B. 5911.

313. *Vocational Education – Certification of Instructors,* 51ˢᵗ Session, Washington State Senate, Substitute S.B. 5266; *School Employees – Revocation of Certificates and Termination of Employment for Crimes Against Children,* 51ˢᵗ Session, Washington State Senate, Substitute S.B. 5314; *Immigration Assistants – Practice and Conduct Rules,* 51ˢᵗ Session, Washington State Senate, S.B. 5715; *Allocation of Assets Between Institutionalized and Community Spouse,* 51ˢᵗ Session, Washington State Senate, Substitute S.B. 5011; *Commercial Telephone Solicitation Regulation,* 51ˢᵗ Session, Washington State Senate, Substitute S.B. 5088; *Telecommunications Companies – Rate Setting Procedures,* 51ˢᵗ Session, Washington State Senate, Substitute S.B. 5098.

314. *DNA Identification Program,* 51ˢᵗ Session, Washington State Senate, Second Substitute S.B. 5375; *Unranked Felonies – Seriousness Levels,* 51ˢᵗ Session, Washington State Senate, S.B. 5090; *Public Utility – Defrauding,* 51ˢᵗ Session, Washington State Senate, Substitute S.B. 5782; *Incorporation of Nonprofit Cooperatives,* 51ˢᵗ Session, Washington State Senate, Substitute S.B. 5018; *Public Works Board – Recommended Projects – Appropriations,* 51ˢᵗ Session, Washington State Senate, Substitute S.B. 5506; *Excursion Buses – Regulation by Utilities and Transportation Commission as Charter Buses,* 51ˢᵗ Session, Washington State Senate, Substitute S.B. 5553.

315. Gaidar, Yigor, "The Soviet Collapse," American Enterprise Institute (Washington, DC), partially citing Mikhail Gorbachev, at http://www.aei.org/issue/foreign-and-defense-policy/regional/europe/the-soviet-collapse/

316. Associated Press, "Collective Farms Will be Leased to Individuals, Gorbachev Says," in *Deseret News* (Salt Lake City, Utah), October 14, 1988.

317. "Biography: Mikhail Gorbachev," in *American Experience,* Public Broadcasting System (Arlington, Virginia) at http://www.pbs.org/wgbh/americanexperience/features/biography/reagan-gorbachev/

318. Benitz, Max, "Highlights of USSR Visit," Personal Notes, Prosser, WA, September 1989; Benitz, Max, "Great Change Likely in Soviet Future," in Personal Notes, October 30, 1989.

319. Benitz, Max, "In Touch," Letter to Constituents, Prosser, WA, January 1990.

320. *Act Relating to State Appropriations for Local Government Assistance,"* 51ˢᵗ Session (1990), Washington State Senate, Substitute S.B. 6547.

321. *An Act Relating to Fiscal Matters,* 51ˢᵗ Session (1990), Washington State Senate, Substitute S.B. 6407.

322. Smith, Erik, "Drugs Facts Foggy in Benitz Brochure," in *Tri-City Herald,* November 16, 1989, partially citing Max Benitz; Benitz, Max, "Proposed Budget Benefits Counties, WSU Tri-Cities, Public Schools," Press Release, Washington State Senate (Olympia), January 1990.

323. Benitz, "Proposed Budget Benefits Counties...;" *Community Colleges – Faculty Tenure,* 51ˢᵗ Session (1990), Washington State Senate, Substitute S.B. 6306; *Placebound Students – Educational Opportunity,* 51ˢᵗ Session (1990), Washington State Senate, Substitute S.B. 6626.

324. Benitz, "Proposed Budget Benefits Counties...;" *Utility Rates – Reduction for Low Income Disabled Citizens,* 51ˢᵗ Session (1990), Washington State Senate, S.B. 6802; *Telecommunications*

Devices for the Hearing and Speech Impaired, 51ˢᵗ Session (1990), Washington State Senate, Substitute S.B. 6290; *Telecommunications Fraud,* 51ˢᵗ Session (1990), Washington State Senate, Substitute S.B. 6572; *Public Water Systems,* 51ˢᵗ Session (1990), Washington State Senate, Substitute S.B. 6446; *Failing Public Water Systems,* 51ˢᵗ Session (1990), Washington State Senate, Substitute S.B. 6447; *Consumer Protection Civil Investigative Demands,* 51ˢᵗ Session (1990), Washington State Senate, Substitute S.B. 6330.

325. Benitz, "Proposed Budget Benefits Counties…;" *State-Wide 911 System Study;* 51ˢᵗ Session (1990), Washington State Senate, Substitute S.B. 6827; *Air Pollution Control Authorities,* 51ˢᵗ Session (1990), Washington State Senate, S.B. 6583; *Solid Fuel Burning – Limits on Use,* 51ˢᵗ Session (1990), Washington State Senate, Substitute S.B. 6698; *Food Products Transportation,* 51ˢᵗ Session (1990), Washington State Senate, Substitute S.B. 6164; *Motor Freight Carriers of Recovered Materials,* 51ˢᵗ Session (1990), Washington State Senate, Substitute S.B. 6700.

326. *Motor Vehicle Window Tinting,* 51ˢᵗ Session (1990), Washington State Senate, S.B. 6606; Smith, Erik, "Benitz's High Profile Surprises Some," in *Tri-City Herald,* March 4, 1990.

327. Benitz, Max, "New Cooperation on Water Policy Pledged, Benitz Says," Press Release, Washington State Senate, May 10, 1990.

328. Smith, "Benitz's High Profile…;" Smith, Erik, "Costly Campaign Seen Between Benitz, Jesernig," in *Tri-City Herald,* May 31, 1990, partially citing Max Benitz.

329. "No Win Battle for the Senate," Editorial Opinion, *Tri-City Herald,* March 21, 1990.

330. "New Tax Dollars Keep Mid-Columbia Road Projects on Course," in *Tri-City Herald,* July 12, 1990.

331. Benitz, Max, West, James, Nelson, Gary, Morris, Betty Sue and Braddock, Dennis, "Stopping to Violence: The Community Approach," Letter, Washington State Legislature (Olympia), August 21, 1990.

332. Benitz, Max, "Education," Speech written but not delivered, August 1990, in Personal and Family Papers, Prosser, WA.

333. Smith, Erik, "Benitz in Hospital with Pneumonia," in *Tri-City Herald,* August 29, 1990; Robinette, Gail and Smith, Erik, "Sen. Benitz Dies After Heart Attack," in *Tri-City Herald,* August 30, 1990.

Chapter 4

334. Gerber, Michele, <u>On the Home Front: The Cold War Legacy of the Hanford Nuclear Site</u>, University of Nebraska Press (Lincoln), 1992, 1997, 2002 and 2007.

335. Ibid.

336. Willard, Helen, "Members of Hanford Staff Tour Benton County Farms," in *Prosser Record-Bulletin* (Prosser, WA), September 14, 1963.

337. Lemon, John, "A-Project is Lauded," in *Spokane Daily Chronicle,* September 27, 1963, p. 13.

338. Bushey, Pat, "Benitz, Shipman Collide on Issues," in *Tri-City Herald* (Kennewick, WA), October 27, 1970.

339. "Reps. Jolly, Benitz Reelected," in *Tri-City Herald,* November 4, 1970.

340. Prochnau, William, Big Hanford Cut in Store," in *Seattle Times,* January 28, 1971; "Power

Picture Brightened by N-Reactor OK," in *Northwest Public Power Bulletin* (Northwest Public Power Association: Vancouver, WA), #25, May 1971.

341. Gerber, *On the Home Front...*

342. Pope, Daniel, *Nuclear Implosions, The Rise and Fall of the Washington Public Power Supply System*, Cambridge University Press (New York), 2008, p. 1, partially citing Glenn Seaborg.

343. Ibid., pp. 64-72.

344. Lee, Glenn, and Phillip, R.F., "Fast Shuffle in the Legislature," in *Tri-City Herald*, February 26, 1973.

345. Pope, *Nuclear Implosions . . .* p. 80.

346. "Fuel Crisis Real," in *Tri-City Herald*, January 22, 1975, citing Max Benitz.

347. Pope, *Nuclear Implosions . . .* pp. 85-108.

348. Ibid., p. 112.

349. *Energy Facility Sites*, 45th Session, Washington State Senate, Engrossed Substitute S.B. 2910.

350. Philip, Jim, "House Passes Hanford Insurance Bill," in *Tri-City Herald*, April 29, 1977

351. "Benitz Invites Nuclear Regulatory Commission to Meet in Tri-Cities," News Release, Republican Caucus, Washington State Senate, October 16, 1978.

352. Philip, John, "Hanford Tax Plan Passed," in *Tri-City Herald*, June 30, 1977.

353. "Area Legislators Looking to Plants for Future Petroleum Source," News Release, Republican Caucus, Washington State Senate Olympia), February 21, 1977, partially citing Max Benitz and Claude Oliver.

354. "Nuclear Still the Cheaper Source of Alternative Power," News Release, Republican Caucus, Washington State Senate, October 25, 1978, citing Max Benitz.

355. Andrews, Anthony, "Nuclear Fuel Reprocessing: U.S. Policy Development," Congressional Research Service (Washington, DC), Report RS22542, March 27, 2008.

356. News Release, Republican Caucus, Washington State Senate, September 20, 1978.

357. "Benitz Invites Nuclear Regulatory Commission...".

358. Coughlin, Con, <u>Khomeini's Ghost: The Iranian Revolution and the Rise of Militant Islam</u>, ECCO Books (Harper Collins Publishers: New York), 2010.

359. Nuclear Regulatory Commission (NRC), Backgrounder on the Three Mile Island Accident, U.S. NRC (Washington, DC), February 2013 at http://www.nrc.gov/reading-rm/doc-collections/fact-sheets/3mile-isle.html

360. Pope, <u>Nuclear Implosions...</u>", pp. 149-163.

361. Godfrey, Dennis, "WPPSS Bills Among Legislative Session's Toughest, Says Benitz," in *Tri-City Herald*, May 3, 1981; "WPPSS More Accountable," in *Re-Elect Senator Max Benitz*, Campaign Flier, Prosser, WA, 1982; Benitz, Max, "Balancing the State's Budget, 1979-1981: WPPSS," 8th District Report to Constituents, Prosser, WA, June 1982.

362. *Mill Tailings Licensing and Perpetual Care Act of 1979*, 46th Session, Washington State Senate, Engrossed Substitute S.B. 2197; *Alcohol Fuels – Tax Exemptions*, 46th Session (1980), Washington

State Senate, Engrossed Substitute S.B. 3551; *Hazardous Materials Transportation, Bills of Lading Color – Common Carrier Violations, Penalties, Enforcement*, 46th Session (1980), Washington State House, H.B. 1870;.

363. "8th District Senate: Democratic Attorney Challenges Republican Farmer," in *Tri-City Herald*, October 31, 1982.

364. Office of the Secretary of State, "Elections and Voting; General Election, November 1982," Washington Secretary of State (Olympia), at http://www.sos.wa.gov/elections/results_report.aspx?e=27&c=&c2=&t=&t2=&p=&p2=&y

365. *Nuclear Waste Policy Act, ,* 42 U.S.C. 10101: Public Law (P.L.) 97-425; 96 Stat.2201 Jan. 7, 1983.

366. Reagan, Ronald, "Remarks on Signing the Nuclear Waste Policy Act of 1982," January 7, 1983, *The American Presidency Project*, University of California at Santa Barbara at http://www.presidency.ucsb.edu/ws/?pid=40954

367. "Facts About Hanford: Basalt Waste Isolation Project," Westinghouse Hanford Co. (Richland, WA), September 1987.

368. Wilma, David, "Washington Public Power Supply System," at HistoryLink.org (Seattle), July 10, 2003 at http://www.historylink.org/index.cfm?DisplayPage=output.cfm&File_Id=5482\

369. Dr. Michelle Gerber, *On The Home Front* . . .

370. Benitz, Max, "Benitz to Continue on Key Senate Committees," Press Release, Office of Senator Max Benitz, Prosser, WA, January 8, 1984.

371. "State Legislators, Officials Assess DOE Studies of High-Level Waste," News Release, National Conference of State Legislatures (NCSL) (Denver), February 15, 1984.

372. "Possible High-Level Nuclear Waste Site: Benitz and Hankins 'Welcome Opportunity' At Hanford," News Release, Offices of Senator Max Benitz and Representative Shirley Hankins, Tri-Cities, WA, December 21, 1984.

373. "History of the NWIC," Northwest Interstate Compact on Low-Level Radioactive Waste Management (Olympia, WA), at http://www.ecy.wa.gov/nwic/history.htm

374. Thurmond, Strom, Letter to Sam Guess, Committee of the Judiciary, U.S. Senate (Washington, DC), May 1983; Low-level Waste Policy Amendments Act, Public Law 99-240, 99th Congress, 2nd Session (Washington, DC), January 15, 1986.

375. Benitz, Max, "Hazardous Waste Disposal," Memo, in Personal Papers, Prosser, WA, January 1983; Waste Management, "Chemical Waste Management of the Northwest," Waste Management (Portland, Oregon) at http://wmnorthwest.com/landfill/chemicalwaste.htm

376. *Oil and Gas Conservation – Exploration – Development – Production – Reclamation,* 48th Session, Washington State Senate, Substitute S.B. 3483; *Hydroelectric Resources Development – Political Subdivisions,* 48th Session, Washington State Senate, Substitute S.B. 3511.

377. Benitz, Max, "Hanford Lease Study Wastes Taxpayers' Money, Says Benitz," News Release, Office of Senator Max Benitz, Olympia, WA, January 16, 1984.

378. Associated Press, "Grandson Helps Benitz Put Stress in Perspective," in *Tri-City Herald*,

March 5, 1984, citing Max Benitz.

379. Benitz, Max, "High-Level Nuclear Waste Meeting Denver, NCSL," Personal Notes, February 15-16, 1985, in Personal Papers, Prosser, WA; "Legislators, Officials Assess DOE Studies of High-Level Radioactive Waste Sites," News Release, NCSL, February 15, 1984.

380. Alley, William and Rosemary, *Too Hot to Touch: The Problem of High-level Nuclear Waste*, Cambridge University Press (New York), 2013, pp. 160-161.

381. Benitz, Max, "In Touch," Letter to Constituents, Olympia, WA, 1985.

382. Benitz, Max, "In Touch: Radioactive Waste," Letter to Constituents, Olympia, WA, May 2, 1985.

383. Benitz, Max, "In Touch," Letter to Constituents, Olympia, WA, May 2, 1985.

384. Benitz, Max, "In Touch," Letter to Constituents, Kansas City, Missouri, May 16, 1985.

385. Benitz, Max, "In Touch," Letter to Constituents, Olympia, WA, June 6, 1985.

386. Benitz, Max, "Larry Bradley," News Release, Office of Senator Max Benitz, January 8, 1986.

387. Radioactive Operations – Liability Requirements, 49th Session, Washington State Senate, Substitute S.B. 4664.

388. "Benitz Authors Comprehensive Hazardous Material safety Plan," News Release, Office of Senator Max Benitz, Olympia, February 4, 1986.

389. Benitz, Max, "Transporting Hazardous Substances," News Release, Office of Senator Max Benitz, Olympia, WA, February 4, 1986; Benitz, Max, "In Touch," Letter to Constituents, Olympia, WA, February 20, 1986; Benitz, Max, Letter to Al Williams, Washington State Senate (Olympia),Jjanuary 14, 1986.

390. Benitz, Max, "Dear Friends," Letter to Constituents, Olympia, WA, March 7, 1986.

391. Benitz, Max, "Dear Friend," Letter to Constituents, Olympia, WA, 1986.

392. World Nuclear Association, "Chernobyl Accident 1986," World Nuclear Association (London), 2013 at http://www.world-nuclear.org/info/Safety-and-Security/Safety-of-Plants/Chernobyl-Accident/#.UkYNcjrn-Uk

393. Ganders, Larry, "56 Democrats Petition for N Reactor shutdown," in *Tri-City Herald*, June 7, 1986.

394. Benitz, Max, Letter to the Editor, *Daily Olympian* (Olympia, WA), Office of Max Benitz, Washington State Senate (Olympia), July 11, 1986.

395. Ganders, Larry, "Benitz to Seek Re-Election; Wants to Chair Energy Panel," in *Tri-City Herald*, May 3, 1986.

396. Alley, Too Hot to Touch...," pp. 196-201.

397. Gay, R.W., "Special Legislative Session Unwarranted," Editorial, *Prosser Record-Bulletin*, July 3, 1986.

398. Benitz, Max, Letter to Fellow Legislators," Prosser, WA, July 7, 1986.

399. Gardner, Booth, "USDOE's Site Selection Process for a High Level Nuclear Waste Repository," Press Release, Office of the Governor, State of Washington (Olympia), October 29, 1986.

400. Office of the Secretary of State, "Elections and Voting; General Election, November 1986," Washington Secretary of State (Olympia), at http://www.sos.wa.gov/elections/results_report.aspx?e=27&c=&c2=&t=&t2=&p=&p2=&y=

401. Office of the Secretary of State, "Elections and Voting; General Election, November 1986," Washington Secretary of State (Olympia), at http://www.sos.wa.gov/elections/results_report.aspx?e=27&c=&c2=&t=&t2=&p=&p2=&y

402. Ibid.

403. NCSL, "Postponement of Meeting in Amarillo, Texas," Memorandum, NCSL, October 20, 1986.

404. Walters, Robert, "Hanford's Health Probe Stymied," Newspaper Enterprise Association (New York), reprinted in *Yakima Herald-Republic,* July 24, 1986; Benitz, Max, "Letter to the Editor, *Yakima Herald-Republic,*" Office of Senator Max Benitz, Prosser, WA, July 25, 1986.

405. Mooney, Robert, "Special Report: Preliminary Dose Assessment of Historical Hanford Releases, 1944-1956," Office of Radiation Protection, Department of Social and Health Services (Olympia, WA), September 22, 1986; Ganders, Larry, "Tri-City Lawmakers Bite Hand of Compromise, Energy Advisor Says," in *Tri-City Herald,* June 20, 1987.

406. Steele, Karen, "No Warning After Hanford Contamination," in *Spokesman Review-Spokane Chronicle,* April 6, 1986; Monroe, Linda, and Heinz, Spencer, "Milk, Vegetation Prime Sources of Potential Exposure," in *Oregonian* (Portland), May 11, 1986; "Citizens Debate and Defend Hanford Amid Political Fallout," in *Seattle Post-Intelligencer,* May 13, 1986; Houff, Bill, "The Way We Have Traveled," in Hanford Education Action League (HEAL) Newsletter (Spokane), July/August 1986.

407. Benitz, Max, "In Touch: The Budget and Dollars Needed to Achieve Orderly Government," Letter to Constituents, Olympia, WA, February 4, 1987.

408. Moeller, Phil, "Bills Pending with Impacts on Hanford," Memorandum to Senator Hayner and Senator Benitz, Republican Caucus, Washington State Senate , February 10, 1987.

409. Benitz, Max, "In Touch: Hanford Family," Letter to Constituents, Olympia, WA, February 26, 1987

410. Benitz, Max, "In Touch," Letter to Constituents, Olympia, WA, March 4, 1987.

411. Benitz, Max, "In Touch," Letter to Constituents, Olympia, WA, April 23, 1987.

412. Ganders, Larry, "Radioactive Shipment Fees Sail Through Senate," in *Tri-City Herald,* March 11, 1987, partially citing Max Benitz.

413. Benitz, Max, "In Touch," Letter to Constituents, Olympia, WA, March 4, 1987.

414. Benitz, Max, "In Touch," Letter to Constituents, Olympia, WA, April 15, 1987.

415. American Nuclear Society, "Radioactive materials Transport," ANS Document PPS-18, American Nuclear Society (LaGrange Park, IL), 1986.

416. Hoover, Dave, "Hanford Faring Well in Session: Benitz," in *Tri-City Herald,* March 29, 1987, partially citing Max Benitz.

417. Benitz, Max, "In Touch: The Nuclear Industry," Letter to Constituents, Olympia, WA, 1987.

418. Benitz, Max, et al., "Nuclear Waste Policy Act," letter to Senator Brock Adams, Washington State Legislature, May 11, 1987.

419. Ganders, Larry, "Travels Take Mid-Columbia Lawmakers Far and Wide," in *Tri-City Herald,* September 22, 1987; Benitz, Max, Letter to Christine Gregoire, Director, Washington State Department of Ecology, Olympia, WA, May 4, 1988.

420. Office of the Secretary of State, "Elections and Voting; General Election, November 1987," Washington Secretary of State (Olympia), at http://www.sos.wa.gov/elections/results_report.aspx?e=26&c=&c2=&t=&t2=&p=&p2=&y=

421. Ganders, Larry, "Hayner Named Majority Leader," in *Tri-City Herald,* November 8, 1987; and reprinted in *Prosser Record-Bulletin,* November 11, 1987. p. 7.

422. Ganders, Larry, "Lawmakers Assail Agency for Not Seeking Radiation Funds, in *Tri-City Herald,* Nov. 8, 1987.

423. Arms Control Association, "Intermediate-Range Nuclear Forces Treaty," at aca.org (Arms Control Association: Washington, DC) at http://www.armscontrol.org/documents/inf

424. *Nuclear Waste Policy Act,* as Amended, Public Law 100-203, 100th Cong., 1st Session, December 22, 1987.

425. Majority Staff, U.S. Senate Committee on Environment and Public Works
"Yucca Mountain, the Most Studied Real Estate on the Planet," Report to the Chairman James Imhofe, March 2006 at http://www.epw.senate.gov/repwhitepapers/YuccaMountainEPWReport.pdf

426. Woehler, Bob, "Hundreds Attend Vigil for N," in *Tri-City Herald,* January 31, 1988; Lange, Larry, and Glover, Darrell, "N Reactor to Stay Closed – a Big Blow to Tri-Cities," in *Seattle Post-Intelligencer,* February 17, 1988.

427. Sivula, Chris, "Impact Stretches Into Mid-'90s," in *Tri-City Herald,* February 17, 1988; Sivula, Chris, "Hanford to Cut $809 Million," in *Tri-City Herald,* February 20, 1988;

428. Ganders, Larry, "N News Spurs Support for Tri-City Aid Bill," in *Tri-City Herald,* February 17, 1988.

429. Lange, "N Reactor To Stay Closed," partially citing Mike Lawrence.

430. Sivula, Chris, and Whitney, David, "Talks Aim to Cut Closure Impact," in *Tri-City Herald,* February 4, 1988; Benitz, Max, "In Touch," Letter to Constituents, Olympia, WA, February 1988.

431. Benitz, Max, Testimony at U.S. DOE Hearing Regarding Environmental Impacts of New Production Reactor," March 7, 1988.

432. Benitz, Letter to Christine Gregoire..., May 4, 1988.

433. Till, John, "Keynote Address," Delivered at Health of the Hanford Site Conference, Richland, WA, December 3, 1997; Technical Steering Panel, "Initial Hanford Radiation Dose Estimates," Hanford Environmental Dose Reconstruction Project, published by Washington State Department of Ecology, 1990.

434. Benitz, Max, Letter to Donald Gartman, District Manager, Houston Lighting and Power Company, Galveston, Texas, March 1988.

435. Benitz, Max, Letter to Governor Booth Gardner, Senate Energy and Utilities Committee, Olympia, WA, September 14, 1988.

436. "Benitz Named Vice-Chair of Nationwide Energy Committee," in *Tri-City Herald*, November 23, 1988.

437. Benitz, Max, "National Conference of State Legislatures," News Release, Office of Senator Max Benitz, Prosser, WA, November 21, 1989.

438. *Energy Code*, 50th Session, Washington State Senate, S.B. 6408.

439. Benitz, Max, "Benitz Calls Energy Code Agreement 'Critical Step' for WNP 1," Press Release, Office of Senator Max Benitz, Olympia, WA, January 8, 1989.

440. Benitz, Max, "Food Safety," Remarks to the Western Washington Horticulture Association," 79th Annual Meeting, January 5, 1989.

441. Ibid.

442. Benitz, Max, "Benitz Cautiously Optimistic About Clean-Up Pact," Press Release, Office of Senator Max Benitz, Olympia, WA, February 28, 1989.

443. Benitz, Max, "Bill to Promote 1,000 acres at Hanford Clears Senate,"
Press Release, Office of Senator Max Benitz, Olympia, WA, March 9, 1989; Benitz, Max, "Senate Approves Energy Education Bill," Press Release, Office of Senator Max Benitz, Olympia, WA, March 9, 1989; Benitz, Max, "Bill Setting CO2 Requirement for Power Plants Clears Senate," Press Release, Office of Senator Max Benitz, Olympia, WA, March 8, 1989.

444. *Hydropower* – Comprehensive State Plan, 51st Session, Washington State Senate, Second Substitute S.B. 5174; *Low-Level Radioactive Waste Disposal Surveillance Fees*, 51st Session, Washington State Senate, Substitute S.B. 5126; *Energy Conservation – Utilities – Assistance to Owners of Equipment*, 51st Session, Washington State Senate, S.B. 5172; *Nuclear and Radioactive Waste Management – Department of Ecology – Duties*, 51st Session, Washington State Senate, Substitute S.B. 603; *Hazardous Materials Transport – Clean-Up Liability*, 51st Session, Washington State Senate, Substitute S.B. 5810.

445. Rader, L. "Cost and Schedule," Memo to Jan Sass, copy to Max Benitz, Battelle Pacific Northwest Laboratories, March 24, 1989.

446. Benitz, Max, "Energy Supply and Sources," Memo to Mike Bey, Benton Rural Electric Association (West Richland, WA), October 30, 1989.

447. Lawrence, Mike, and Jura, James, Letter to Max Benitz, Offices of the Bonneville Power Administration (Portland, OR), May 23, 1989.

448. U.S. DOE, Washington Department of Ecology, and U.S. EPA, Hanford Federal Facility Agreement and Consent Order, published by Washington Department of Ecology, Olympia, May 1989.

449. Lakis, Stephen, "Energy Strategies for the 21st Century," Letter to Max Benitz, State Legislative Leaders Foundation (Centerville, Massachusetts) May 22, 1989.

450. Benitz, Max, Testimony Before Energy Secretary Admiral James Watkins, Hearing on National Energy Strategy," Seattle, WA, August 28, 1989.

451. Ibid.

452. Benitz, Max, "Highlights of European Visit," Personal Notes, Prosser, WA, September 1989; Miller, Louise, Telecommunication with Eileen Wagner, February 11, 2011.

453. Benitz, Max, "B.C. Leaders Say 'Don't Rely on Us for Your Power," Press Release, Office of Senator Max Benitz, Olympia, WA, October 31, 1989.

454. Benitz, Max, "Dear Tri-Citizens Embarking on Washington's Third Century," Energy and Utilities Committee, Washington State Senate, November 11, 1989.

455. Daniels, Lee, Letter to Max Benitz, NCSL, November 13, 1989; Benitz, "National Conference...", November 21, 1989.

456. Energy Committee, NCSL, "Policy: National Energy Plan," NCSL, December 15, 1989.

457. Ibid.

458. Ibid.

459. Ibid.

460. Ibid.

461. Smith, Erik, "Benitz's High Profile Surprises Some," in *Tri-City Herald*, March 4, 1990.

462. Benitz, Max, "Energy Issues for 1990," Personal Notes, in Personal Papers, Prosser, WA.

463. Ibid.

464. Benitz, Max, "HB 2198, State Energy Code," Press Release, Office of Senator Max Benitz, Olympia, February 7, 1990.

465. Benitz, Max, "Senate Votes to Lower Tax on Low-Level Waste Site," Press Release, Office of Senator Max Benitz, Olympia, February 27, 1990.

466. Benitz, Max, "Tri-City Bills in Good Shape as Session Winds Down," Press Release, Office of Senator Max Benitz, Olympia, March 2, 1990; Benitz, Max, "Tri-City Bills One Step From Law," Press Release, Office of Senator Max Benitz, Olympia, March 3, 1990; *Energy Education*, 51st Session, Washington State Senate, Second Substitute S.B. 5835; *Waste Management Education and Training Program Feasibility Study*, 51st Session, Washington State Senate, Second Substitute S.B. 5996; *Hanford Reservation Lease Promotion*, 51st Session, Washington State Senate, Second Substitute S.B. 5993; *Nuclear Operations – Liability Coverage Requirements*, 51st Session, Washington State Senate, Substitute S.B. 6575; *Air Pollution Control Authorities*, 51st Session, Washington State Senate, S.B. 6583; Benitz, Max, "Energy Report," Report to Constituents, Olympia, WA, Spring 1990.

467. Smith, Benitz's High Profile...", citing Max Benitz.

468. Benitz, "Energy Report," Spring 1990.

469. Daniels, Lee, Letter to Max Benitz, NCSL, April 25, 1990; "Benitz Named to High Level Waste Transportation Task Force," Press Release, Office of Senator Max Benitz, Olympia, WA, May 2, 1990.

470. Benitz, Max, "Benitz and Other Energy Leaders Take Necessary First Step Toward National Energy Policy," Office of Senator Max Benitz, Prosser, WA, May 22, 1990.

471. Bush, George H.W., Press Release, The White House (Washington, DC), June 26, 1990; U.S. Department of the Interior (USDI), "Statement by Secretary of the Interior Manual Lujan," Press Release, USDI (Washington, DC), June 26, 1990; Vann, Adam, "Offshore Oil and gas Development: Legal Framework," Congressional Research Service (Washington, DC), Report RL33404, June 25, 2013 at http://www.fas.org/sgp/crs/misc/RL33404.pdf

472. Jones, Aaron. "Senator Max Benitz - "Mr. Energy" - Still Going Strong, in Washington Rural Electric Cooperative Association News (Olympia), July 1990.

473. Runyon, L. Cheryl, Letter to Senator Max Benitz, National Conference of State Legislatures, August 13, 1990.

Chapter 5

474. Benitz, Max, Remarks at National Conference of State Legislatures, (Nashville, Tennessee), August 6-10, 1990.

475. Brazier, Don, "History of the Washington Legislature, 1965-1982," Washington State Senate (Olympia), 2007, p. 11.

476. *Family Wine*, 47th Session (1981), Washington State Senate, S.B. 3722.

477. "Research History," Washington Association of Wine Grape Growers (Cashmere, Washington), 2013 at http://www.wawgg.org/index.php?page_id=122

478. *Class C, H Licensed Premises - Unconsumed Wine Removal*, 47th Session (1981), Washington State Senate, Engrossed S.B. 3057; *Wine and Beer Licenses - Free Samples,* 47th Session (1981), Washington State Senate, Substitute S.B. 3060.

479. *Beer and Wine Instruction*, 47th Session (1982), Washington State Senate, Engrossed S.B. 4748.

480. Benitz, Max, "Balancing the State's Budget, 1979-1981," State Senate Re-Election Campaign Flier, 8th District, in Family Papers, Prosser, WA, 1982.

481. Benitz, Max and Newhouse, Irv, "Legislative Report to Washington Brewers Enological Society Members and Washington Wine Society Members," Washington State Senate (Olympia), 1982.

482. "Prosser Wine and Food Fair," Prosser Chamber of Commerce, 2013 at http://www.prosserchamber.org/index.php?option=com_events&task=view_detail&agid=18&-year=2012&month=08&day=11&Itemid=113

483. "State Sen. Max Benitz says Exports Key to Survival of Washington Agriculture," in *Capitol Press* (Salem, Oregon), June 17, 1983, partially citing Max Benitz.

484. "Exports Key to Survival of Washington Agriculture, in Wine Grower newsletter, 1983, citing Max Benitz.

485. "Trade Mission, June 13, 1983, citing Max Benitz.

486. "Crop Switch Key to Avoiding Cash Crunch, in *Tri-City Herald* (Kennewick, WA), February 11, 1984, citing Max Benitz.

487. *Wine and Beer Product Information - Retail Premises*, 48th Session, Washington State Senate, S.B. 4445.

488. *Wine Warehouses*, 48th Session, Washington State Senate, Substitute S.B. 4503.

489. *Liquor Licenses – Class H and Class* I, 49th Session (1985), Washington State Senate, S.B. 3326.

490. *Class H License – Hotels – Liquor by the Bottle*, 49th Session (1986), Washington State Senate, S.B. 3336; *Liquor Establishments – Minors May Stock or Handle Beer or Wine*, 49th Session (1986), Washington State Senate, Substitute S.B. 3532; *Wine – Grower's License – Licensed Premises, Content of Spoken Language*, 49th Session (1986), Washington State Senate, S.B. 4538.
491. Benitz, Max. "Benitz Applauds Committee Approval of Wine Commission," Radio Release Speech, Olympia, WA, February 17, 1987.

492. Benitz, Max, Text of Radio Speech, June 1987, in Family Papers, Prosser WA.

493. *Washington Wine Commission*, 50th Session (1987), Washington State Senate, S.B. 5503; *Washington Wine Commission*, 50th Session, Washington State House, Second Substitute HB 569.

494. Ibid.

495. Benitz, Radio Speech, June 1987.

496. *Beer – Retailers May Offer Samples*, 50th Session (1987), Washington State Senate, Substitute S.B. 5581.

497. *Wine Retailers Class P License – Gift Sales Businesses – Eligibility*, 51sth Session (1989), Washington State Senate, S.B. 5871.

498. Mitchell, M. Carter, Letter to Senator Max Benitz, Washington State Liquor Control Board (Olympia), March 3, 1989.

499. Siegal, Simon, Letter to Senator Max Benitz, Washington Wine Institute (Seattle), February 21, 1989.

500. Jones, Aaron, "Senator Max Benitz – Mr. Energy – Still Going Strong," in *Washington Rural Electric Cooperative News*, Washington Rural Electric Cooperative Association (Olympia), July 1990, p. 25, citing Max Benitz.

501. Smith, Erik and Robinette, Gale, "Sen Benitz Dies After Heart Attack," in *Tri-City Herald*, August 30, 1990, citing Mike Kreidler, Booth Gardner, Sam Volpentest, Ray Isaacson, Sandy Strawn, Craig Buchanan and Leslie Donovan.

502. "Max Benitz: He was Really Special," Editorial, *Tri-City Herald*, August 30, 1990.

503. Smith, Erik, "State Leaders Remember Benitz," in Tri-City Herald, September 2, 1990, citing Jeannette Hayner.

504. Slater, Frederick, "Max, Who Never Forgot His Roots," Editorial from *St. Joseph, Missouri News Press/Gazette*, reprinted in *Tri-City Herald*, September 26, 1990, citing Jim Jesernig.

505. Senator Irving Newhouse, Statement, in Personal Papers, Prosser, WA.

506. Senator Al Bluechel, Statement, in Personal Papers, Prosser, WA.

507. Clore, Walter, "In Memory of Senator Max Benitz," September 30, 1999, in Personal Papers, Prosser, WA.

508. Walter Clore Wine and Culinary Center, at http://www.theclorecenter.org/dr-walter-clore

509. Personal Communication, E.M.B. Wagner to M.S. Gerber, June 2013.

510. "WSU Branch Library Named After Benitz," in *Tri-City Herald*, April 5, 1991.

511. Gorton, Slade. Letter to Marie Benitz, U.S. Senate (Washington, DC), January 10, 1992.

512. "Governor Lauds Partnership; Looks to Economic Growth as Construction Starts on Wine Science Center at WSU-Tri-Cities," in WSU Tri-Cities News (WSU: Richland, WA), September 30, 2013 at http://news.wsu.edu/2013/09/30/governor-lauds-partnership-looks-to-economic-growth-as-construction-starts-on-wine-science-center-at-wsu-tri-cities/#.Unv9GzrTmUk

Additional Testimonials

513. Personal Communication, George W. Scott to E.M.B. Wagner, October 18, 2010.

514. Personal Communication, Sidney Morrison to E.M.B. Wagner, January 25, 2011.

515. Personal Communication, Philip Moeller to E.M.B. Wagner, August 24, 2011.

516. Personal Communication, Jim Boldt to E.M.B. Wagner, January 11, 2011.

517. Personal Communication, Leo Kocher to E.M.B. Wagner, November 27, 2013.

518. Personal Communication, Wanda Munn to E.M.B. Wagner, 2011.

Index

Colorado Springs, Colorado 177
Columbia Basin 136, 159, 160
Columbia Basin College 199
Columbia Basin Irrigation Project 6
Columbia River 5, 75, 85, 93, 155, 159, 160
Committee on Agriculture 58
Concord, Massachusetts 1
Congressional Record 221-222
Cooperative Extension Club 2
Coordinating Council for
      Occupation Education 55
Coordination Council for North American
      Affairs 82
Copeland, Tom 55
Cronkite, Walter 27
Cuba 19
Cuban Missile Crisis 19, 22
Cultural Revolution 70

D

Deaf Smith, Texas 169, 176
Deck, Erret 60
Defense Nuclear Agency 191
DeKalb Corp. 9
DeKalb, Illinois 10
Denver, Colorado 11
Deoxyribonucleic acid 139
Dexter, Dorian 114
Diamond, Neil 82
Dietrich, Fred 27
Ding, Mou-shih 111
District of Columbia 8, 82
Dobrynin, Anatoly 19
Dole, Bob 3
Doniphan County, Kansas 2, 3
Donovan, Leslie 219
Doo-hwan, Chun 106
Doran, Judge Robert 73
Draft Environmental Assessments 168

E

Ecumenical Metropolitan Ministry 58
Edmonds, Washington 185
Edsel 68
Education Commission of the States 59
Egypt 62, 163
Eikenberry, Ken 220
Eisenhower, Dwight 8, 22, 39, 55
Ellensburg Washington 4, 75, 160

Emergency Feed Grains Program 14
Emergency Water Advisory Committee 75
Endrin 136
Energy and Utilities Committee 71, 127, 183,
      186
Energy Fair 103
England 22, 24, 160
Environmental Impacts Statements 63
Environmental Policy Act 63
Environmental Protection Agency 33, 34
Equal Rights Amendment 60
Estes, Billie Sol 15
Evans, Dan 38, 47-48, 52-53, 59-60, 63, 68,
      79, 116, 153, 162, 205
Everett Herald 81
Everett, Washington 51, 81
Evergreen State College 69

F

Family Farm Water Act 74
Family Independence Program 132
Family Wine Act 206
Farm Bureau 11, 44, 78
Farmers' Home Administration 38
Federal Emergency Management Agency 92
Fernald Site, Ohio 178
Florida 203
Foley, Tom 191
Ford, Gerald R. 65-67, 115
Ford Motor Company 67
Forrest, General Nathan Bedford 1
Fortner, Norma June Benitz 222
France 105, 141, 182, 193, 218
Franklin County, Washington 179
Freedom of Information Act 20
Freeman, Orval 17, 23
Ft. Columbia, Washington 2
Fungicide and Rodenticide Act 33
Future Farmers of America 9, 38

G

Gardner, Booth 78, 117, 121-122, 125, 128,
      153, 172, 177, 183, 188, 191, 219
Gaspard, Marcus 138
General Fund Budget 122
General Motors 67
Gentry, Wayne 44
George, Gilder 101
German Democratic Republic 64

National Aeronautics and Space
 Administration 56
National Communist Party 142
National Conference of State Legislatures 169
National Council of Governors 64
National Energy Plan 196
National Energy Strategy 192
National Labor Relations Board 13
National Marine Sanctuary 201
National Register of Historic Places 70
National Resources Defense Council 133
National Security Council 19
Nebraska Farm Bureau 14
Neighbors in Need 58
Nevada 168, 171, 193
Nevada Test Site 178
Newhouse, Irving 135, 193, 208, 220
New Mexico 159, 165
New York New York 93, 133, 137
New Zealand 44
Nixon, Richard 34, 48, 56, 58-59, 61, 64, 66
North Atlantic 203
Northern Pacific Railway 54
North Korea 107, 108
North Richland Bridge 100
North Vietnam 42
Northwest Farm Forum 17
Northwest Harvest 58
Northwest Low-Level Radioactive Waste
 Compact 170
N Reactor 160, 161, 179, 180, 181
Nuclear Regulatory Commission 165
Nuclear Waste Board 199
Nuclear Waste Policy Act 167, 168, 182

O

Odessa, Russia 141, 145
Oklahoma 64
Oliver, Claude 164
Olympia, Washington 12, 36, 53, 59-62, 68,
 85, 116, 128, 131, 155-156, 173, 180-
 181, 184, 188
Open Space Taxation Act 61
Oregon 106, 170, 182, 194, 203
Organization of Petroleum Exporting
 Countries 62, 163
Osaka Bay 102
Osaka Japan 44, 46
Outer Continental Shelf 196, 201

P

Pacific Fleet 69
Pacific Northwest Legislative Leadership
 Forum 194
Pacific Rim 121
Packwood, Bob 191
Pasco Chamber of Commerce 18, 46
Pasco Washington 46, 199
Passionada 218
Patterson, Tom 138
Peking, China 79
Pennsylvania 171
People's Republic of China 24, 78, 82, 106,
 107
Perrigo, Lyle 47
Peterson, T.C. 18
Pierce County, Washington 117
Pittsdorff, Russia 28
Plutonium Uranium Extraction (PUREX)
 Plant 169
Poland 1, 24, 160
polychlorinated biphenyls 120
Pomerania, Prussia 1
Portland, Oregon 165
Portland Oregonian 179
Port of Tacoma 51
Portopia, Japan 102
Potsdamer Platz 149
Pribaltiyskaya Hotel 146
Price-Anderson Act 171
Prosser Chamber of Commerce 14, 47, 53, 83
Prosser, Colonel William 5
Prosser Land Development Company 214
Prosser Washington 5, 6, 10, 18, 46, 48, 70,
 113, 114, 134, 160, 179, 206, 210, 214,
 220-221
Prosser Wine and Food Fair 210
Puget Sound 51, 69, 72, 123
Puget Sound Cleanup Act 124
Puget Sound Naval Shipyard 70
Puget Sound Naval Station 51
Pullman, Washington 92

R

Ray, Dixie Lee 71, 75, 85, 78, 88, 164
Reagan 148
Reaganomics 89
Reagan, Ronald 88-89, 94, 117, 148, 157, 167-
 169, 169, 176-177, 183

Red China 30, 45, 46, 79, 82, 106, 107
Red Square 29, 144
Reese, Walt 47
Regan, Donald 177
Reichbauer, Peter von 93, 138
Republic of China 44, 45, 111, 112
Research Triangle Park, North Carolina 136-137
Reynolds v. Sims 31
Rice University 55
Richland Washington 46, 59, 61, 110, 158, 218
Ritzville, Washington 92
Rocky Flats Plant, Colorado 178
Rocky Mountain Compact 172
Roosevelt, Franklin D. 5, 92
Rossellini, Albert 12, 78
Roza Dam 6
Roza Irrigation District 6, 7
Russia 1, 175

S

Sacramento, California 86
Sadie Louise 219
Safeway 12
Salem, Oregon 210
Saling, Jerry 138
San Francisco, California 46
San Juan Islands 4
San Luis Obispo, California 21
Santa Ana River 76
Satsop, Washington 162, 168
Savannah River Site, South Carolina 161, 185
Schakne, Robert 27
Scott, George W. 86
Seaborg, Glenn 162
Sea-Tac Airport 216
Seattle City Light 163
Seattle-First National Bank 51
Seattle Post-Intelligencer 179
Seattle Times 134
Seattle Washington 51-52, 58, 93, 157, 169, 183, 192, 194, 214
Sebero, Bill 129
Seoul, South Korea 106
Shah of Iran 166
Shanghai, China 79
Shipman, Walter Joe 58, 161
Shuman, Charles 21

Siegal, Simon 214
Silent Spring 33
Singapore, China 79
Sinker, Sarah 1
Skanska Construction Company 146
Skeenland, A.P. 9
Small Business Administration 92
Smitherman, Bill 138
Smith, Linda 139, 183
Smith, Shelby 3, 57
Snake River 75
Snipes, Ben 6
Snipes Canyon 6
Solna, Sweden 148
Sony Corporation 40
South Carolina 162
South Korea 41, 101, 107, 108, 210
South Vietnam 42
Soviet Union 19, 22, 25, 63, 106, 141, 148, 150, 160
Spellman, Governor 79, 87-88, 93-94, 102-103, 105, 107, 109, 111, 113, 116-117, 210
Spellman, Lois 88
Spirit Lake Memorial Highway 100
Spokane Hospital 70
Spokane Portland & Seattle Railroad 54
Spokane, Washington 17, 70, 170, 179, 181, 183, 191
Spokesman-Review-Spokane Chronicle 178
Sputnik 55, 160
Stalin, Josef 24
Star Wars 169
Statuary Hall 3
St. George Bank 203
St. Peter Hospital 116
Stratton, Lois 138, 181, 183, 193
Strawn, Sandy 219
Streep, Meryl 134
Suharto, President 41
Sumitomo Shoji Kaisha 105
Sunnyside, Washington 65
Superconducting Magnetic Energy Storage Engineering Test Model 191
Supreme Court 31
Sweden 141, 182, 193
Swift Foods Company 20
Switzerland 141, 182, 193
Syria 62, 163

About the Authors

Eileen M. Benitz Wagner

Eileen M Benitz Wagner has devoted her business career to product design, manufacturing, and national sales for the wholesale floral, nursery and mass merchant markets throughout the United States. As an owner of a small business, each category demands unlimited attention.

The late 1990s took her to the agricultural field and the growing of newly planted wine grapes. During this period she traveled to the wine grape regions of France, Canada, Chile, Argentina and Australia seeking additional information to improve her product.

A founding member of the International Pirates, (a charity entertainment group from across America) that began in the middle 1980s, she sang and danced to warm the hearts of elderly, special needs children, Shrine Burn Hospital patients and all she met as a Lady Pirate. "It is giving something back. We say it is putting a little color in black and white worlds when nothing but pain is in sight."

Her love of history and growing up very close to her father, she learned his values. His integrity, honesty, but most of all he taught what freedom meant. Reading thousands of news articles, hand written speeches and notes, as well as legislative documents, she assembled the information to share his role in the history of Washington state history. Dr. Michele Gerber wove that information into this wonderful story of his life.

She lives in The Woodlands, Texas near her family. One daughter lives in Dallas and the other lives in Spring, Texas.

Dr. Michele S. Gerber

Dr. Michele S. Gerber has had a long and distinguished career in World War II and Cold War History. She has become an authority on operations, environmental and waste management practices throughout the nuclear facilities that are the legacy of World War II and the Cold War. She has contributed to major proposals for Department of Energy procurements, and consulted to multi-national corporations, the National Park Service, the General Accounting Office, and many other government agencies and private entities.

Dr. Gerber served on the National Academy of Sciences Committee on the Declassification of Department of Energy Documents, and on multiple Federal Advisory Committees. She has traveled across the nation and world as an invited guest speaker about the Hanford Site. She also developed and taught a university class on Hanford History under a grant from Nuclear Regulatory Commission

She led the effort involving the National Park Service, the Department of Energy, non-profit and community organizations and Congressional and other sponsors to achieve designation of Hanford's B Reactor as a National Historic Landmark. Dr. Gerber has appeared in more than 66 television programs and interviews about nuclear history, including feature-length films televised nationally. She has presented to, toured and instructed many of the Hanford Site's most distinguished visitors, including cabinet Secretaries, Senators, Congressional Representatives, Governors and their staffs, and others.

Dr. Gerber is the author of *On the Home Front: The Cold War Legacy of the Hanford Nuclear Site*, the first and only comprehensive history of America's largest nuclear defense site. The book has been published in four editions. She has published more documents about Hanford's operations and facilities than any other author, and has won numerous awards, honors and commendations. She lives with her family in Richland, Washington.

www.ingramcontent.com/pod-product-compliance
Lightning Source LLC
Chambersburg PA
CBHW060745100426
42813CB00032B/3403/J